8th Workshop on Natural Language Processing for Computer Assisted Language Learning (NLP4CALL 2019)

NEALT Proceedings Series Volume 39

Turku, Finland
30 September 2019

Editors:

David Alfter **Ildikó Pilán**
Elena Volodina **Herbert Lange**
Lars Borin

ISBN: 978-1-5108-9442-6

NEALT Proceedings Series Vol. 39

Proceedings of the 8th Workshop on

Natural Language Processing for Computer Assisted Language Learning

(NLP4CALL 2019)

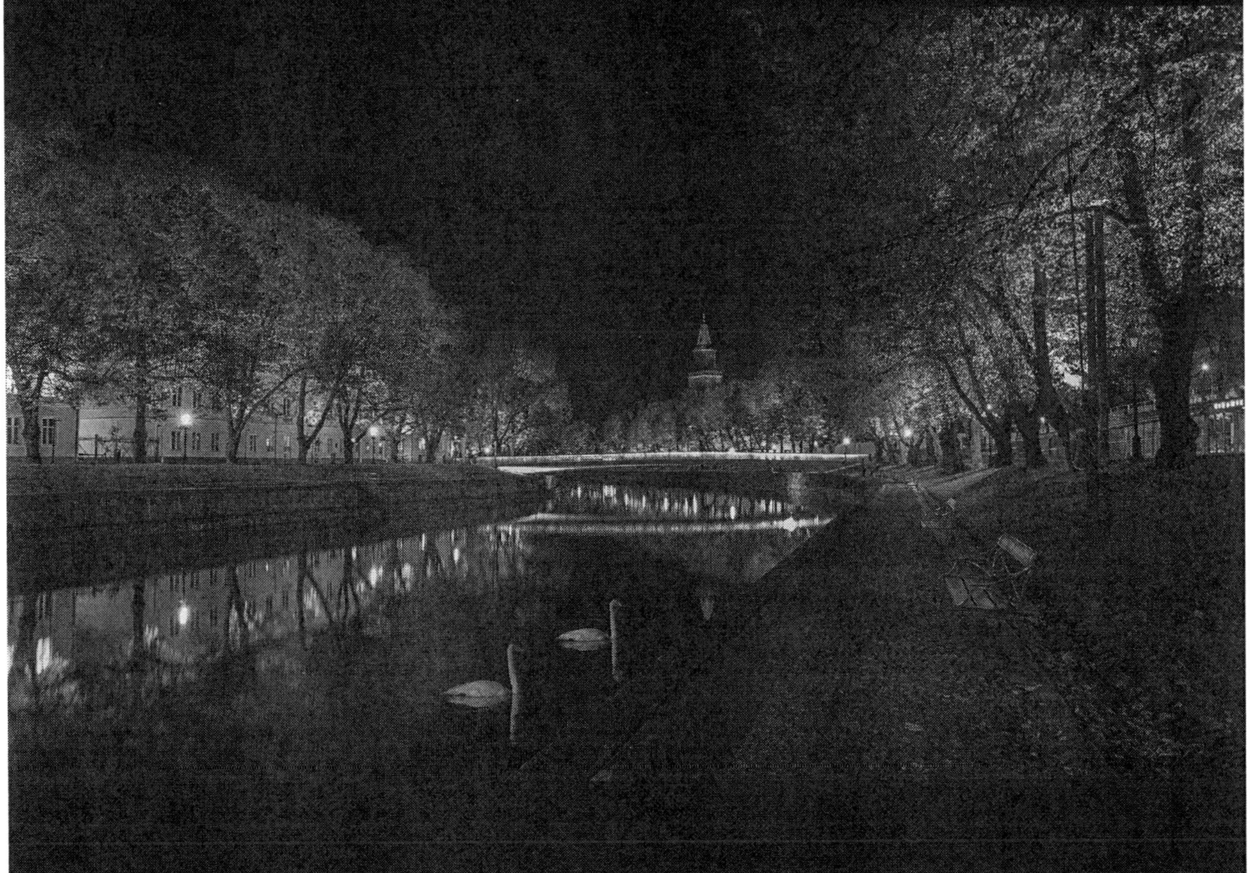

Proceedings of the

8th Workshop on
Natural Language Processing
for Computer Assisted Language Learning
(NLP4CALL 2019)

edited by

David Alfter, Elena Volodina, Lars Borin, Ildikó Pilán and
Herbert Lange

Preface

The workshop series on Natural Language Processing (NLP) for Computer-Assisted Language Learning (NLP4CALL) is a meeting place for researchers working on the integration of Natural Language Processing and Speech Technologies in CALL systems and exploring the theoretical and methodological issues arising in this connection. The latter includes, among others, insights from Second Language Acquisition (SLA) research, on the one hand, and promote development of "Computational SLA" through setting up Second Language research infrastructure(s), on the other.

The intersection of Natural Language Processing (or Language Technology / Computational Linguistics) and Speech Technology with Computer-Assisted Language Learning (CALL) brings "understanding" of language to CALL tools, thus making CALL intelligent. This fact has given the name for this area of research – Intelligent CALL, ICALL. As the definition suggests, apart from having excellent knowledge of Natural Language Processing and/or Speech Technology, ICALL researchers need good insights into second language acquisition theories and practices, as well as knowledge of second language pedagogy and didactics. This workshop invites therefore a wide range of ICALL-relevant research, including studies where NLP-enriched tools are used for testing SLA and pedagogical theories, and vice versa, where SLA theories, pedagogical practices or empirical data are modeled in ICALL tools. The NLP4CALL workshop series is aimed at bringing together competences from these areas for sharing experiences and brainstorming around the future of the field.

We invited papers:

- that describe research directly aimed at ICALL;
- that demonstrate actual or discuss the potential use of existing Language and Speech Technologies or resources for language learning;
- that describe the ongoing development of resources and tools with potential usage in ICALL, either directly in interactive applications, or indirectly in materials, application or curriculum development, e.g. learning material generation, assessment of learner texts/responses, individualized learning solutions, provision of feedback;
- that discuss challenges and/or research agenda for ICALL;
- that describe empirical studies on language learner data

As in the previous edition of the workshop, a special focus was given to the established and upcoming infrastructures aimed at SLA and learner corpus research, covering questions such as data collection, legal issues, reliability of annotation, annotation tool development, search environments for SLA-relevant data, etc. We encouraged paper presentations and software demonstrations describing the above-mentioned themes primarily, but not exclusively, for the Nordic languages.

This year, we had the pleasure to welcome two invited speakers: Thomas François (Université catholique de Louvain) and Egon Stemle (Eurac Research).

David Alfter, Elena Volodina, Lars Borin, Ildikó Pilán and Herbert Lange 2019. Preface. *Proceedings of the 8th Workshop on Natural Language Processing for Computer Assisted Language Learning (NLP4CALL 2019).* Linköping Electronic Conference Proceedings 164: i–v.

Thomas François is Assistant Professor in Applied Linguistics and Natural Language Processing at UCLouvain (Cental). His work focuses on automatic assessment of text readability, automatic text simplification, complex word identification, efficient communication in business, and the use of French as a professional language. He has been an invited researcher at IRCS (University of Pennsylvania) as a Fulbright and BAEF fellow and, later, has been a FNRS post-doctoral researcher. He has led research projects such as CEFRLex[1], a CEFR-graded lexicon for foreign language learning or AMesure[2], a platform to support simple writing. His work on readability for French as a foreign language has been awarded the best thesis Award by the ATALA in 2012 and the best paper in the TALN2016 conference.

In this talk entitled *Assessing language complexity for L2 readers with NLP techniques and corpora*, he summarized the main trends regarding the automatic assessment of language complexity for L2 readers and focus on three research projects. To illustrate the readability approach, the DMesure project was presented. It is the first computational readability formula specialized for readers of French as a foreign language. Secondly, the talk discussed the use of corpora to assess language complexity through CEFRLex, an international project providing, for some of the main European languages, lexical resources describing the frequency distributions of words across the six levels of competence of the Common European Framework of Reference for Languages (CEFR). These distributions have been estimated on corpora of pedagogical materials intended for L2 purposes such as textbooks and simplified readers. The resulting resources have been manually checked and are machine-readable and open-licensed. The project also offers an interface allowing to automatically assess difficult words in a text in accordance with CEFRLex knowledge. Thirdly, the Predicomplex project illustrated the use of learner data. It consists in a personalized approach of vocabulary knowledge prediction using machine learning algorithms. He concluded his talk by highlighting some of the current challenges and research opportunities relative to language difficulty assessment for L2 learners.

Egon Stemle is a researcher in the Institute for Applied Linguistics at Eurac Research, Bolzano, Italy. He is a cognitive scientist with a focus in the area where computational linguistics and artificial intelligence converge. He works on the creation, standardisation, and interoperability of tools for editing, processing, and annotating linguistic data and enjoys working together with other scientists on their data but also collects or helps to collect new data from the Web, from computer-mediated communication and social media, and from language learners. He is an advocate of open science to make research and data available for others to consult or reuse in new research.

In recent years, the reproducibility of scientific research has become increasingly important, both for external stakeholders and for the research communities themselves. They all demand that empirical data collected and used for scientific research is managed and preserved in a way that research results are reproducible. In order to account for this, the FAIR guiding principles for data stewardship have been established as a framework for good data management aiming at the findability, accessibility, interoperability, and reusability of research data. A special role is played by natural language processing and its methods, which are an integral part of many other disciplines working with language data: Language corpora are often living objects – they are

---

[1] http://cental.uclouvain.be/cefrlex/
[2] http://cental.uclouvain.be/amesure/

constantly being improved and revised, and at the same time the processing tools are also regularly updated, which can lead to different results for the same processing steps.

In his talk entitled *Towards an infrastructure for FAIR language learner corpora*, he first investigated CMC corpora, which resemble language learner corpora in some core aspects, with regard to their compliance with the FAIR principles and discuss to what extent the deposit of research data in repositories of data preservation initiatives such as CLARIN, Zenodo or META-SHARE can assist in the provision of FAIR corpora. Second, he showed some modern software technologies and how they make the process of software packaging, installation, and execution and, more importantly, the tracking of corpora throughout their life cycle reproducible. This in turn makes changes to raw data reproducible for many subsequent analyses.

Previous workshops

This workshop follows a series of workshops on NLP4CALL organized by the NEALT Special Interest Group on Intelligent Computer-Assisted Language Learning (SIG-ICALL[3]). The workshop series has previously been financed by the Center for Language Technology[4] at the University of Gothenburg, and the Swedish Research Council's conference grant.

Submissions to the eight workshop editions have targeted a wide range of languages, ranging from well-resources languages (Chinese, German, English, French, Portuguese, Russian, Spanish) to lesser-resourced languages (Erzya, Arabic, Estonian, Irish, Komi-Zyrian, Meadow Mari, Saami, Udmurt, Võro). Among these, several Nordic languages have been targeted, namely Danish, Estonian, Finnish, Icelandic, Norwegian, Saami, Swedish and Võro. The wide scope of the workshop is also evident in the affiliations of the participating authors as illustrated in Table 1.

COUNTRY	NUMBER OF AUTHORS
Australia	2
Belgium	4
Canada	4
Denmark	2
Estonia	3
Finland	9
France	6
Germany	77
Iceland	3
Ireland	2
Japan	2
Netherlands	1
Norway	12
Portugal	5
Russia	10
Slovakia	1
Spain	3
Sweden	62

---

[3] https://spraakbanken.gu.se/swe/forskning/ICALL/SIG-ICALL
[4] http://clt.gu.se

Switzerland	10
UK	1
US	5

Table 1: Authors by affiliation country, 2012-2019

The acceptance rate has varied between 50% and 77%, the average being 64% (see Table 2). Although the acceptance rate is rather high, the reviewing process has always been very rigorous with two to three double-blind reviews per submission. This indicates that submissions to the workshop have usually been of high quality.

WORKSHOP YEAR	SUBMITTED	ACCEPTED	ACCEPTANCE RATE
2012	12	8	67%
2013	8	4	50%
2014	13	10	77%
2015	9	6	67%
2016	14	10	72%
2017	13	7	54%
2018	16	11	69%
2019	16	10	63%

Table 2: Submissions and acceptance raters, 2012-2019

We would like to thank our Program Committee for providing detailed feedback on the reviewed papers.

- Lars Ahrenberg, Linköping University, Sweden
- David Alfter, University of Gothenburg, Sweden
- Lisa Beinborn, University of Amsterdam, Netherlands
- Eckhard Bick, University of Southern Denmark, Denmark
- Lars Borin, University of Gothenburg, Sweden
- António Branco, University of Lisbon, Portugal
- Jill Burstein, Educational Testing Service, USA
- Andrew Caines, University of Cambridge, UK
- Simon Dobnik, University of Gothenburg, Sweden
- Thomas François, UCLouvain, Belgium
- Johannes Graën, University of Gothenburg, Sweden
- Andrea Horbach, University of Duisburg-Essen, Germany
- Herbert Lange, University of Gothenburg and Chalmers University of Technology, Sweden
- John Lee, City University of Hong Kong, China
- Peter Ljunglöf, University of Gothenburg and Chalmers University of Technology, Sweden
- Montse Maritxalar, University of the Basque Country, Spain
- Beata Megyesi, Uppsala University, Sweden
- Detmar Meurers, University of Tübingen, Germany
- Ildikó Pilán, City University of Hong Kong, China and University of Oslo, Norway
- Martí Quixal, Universitat Oberta de Catalunya, Spain
- Robert Reynolds, Brigham Young University, USA

- Gerold Schneider, University of Zurich, Switzerland
- Irina Temnikova, Sofia University, Bulgaria
- Cornelia Tschichold, Swansea University, UK
- Francis M. Tyers, Indiana University Bloomington, USA
- Sowmya Vajjala, National Research Council Canada, Canada
- Elena Volodina, University of Gothenburg, Sweden
- Mats Wirén, Stockholm University, Sweden
- Victoria Yaneva, University of Wolverhampton, UK
- Torsten Zesch, University of Duisburg-Essen, Germany
- Robert Östling, Stockholm University, Sweden

We intend to continue this workshop series, which so far has been the only ICALL-relevant recurring event based in the Nordic countries. Our intention is to co-locate the workshop series with the two major LT events in Scandinavia, namely SLTC (the Swedish Language Technology Conference) and NoDaLiDa (Nordic Conference on Computational Linguistics), thus making this workshop an annual event. Through this workshop, we intend to profile ICALL research in Nordic countries as well as beyond, and we aim at providing a dissemination venue for researchers active in this area.

Workshop website:

https://spraakbanken.gu.se/eng/research-icall/8th-nlp4call

Workshop organizers

David Alfter[1], Elena Volodina[1], Ildikó Pilán[2], Herbert Lange[3], Lars Borin[1]

[1] Språkbanken, University of Gothenburg
[2] City University of Hong Kong and University of Oslo
[3] Department of Computer Science and Engineering, University of Gothenburg and Chalmers University of Technology

Acknowledgements

We gratefully acknowledge Riksbankens Jubileumsfond for the financial support for the two invited speakers: from the project on Development of lexical and grammatical competences in immigrant Swedish[5] (through a grant P17-0716:1) that provided funding for the invited speaker Thomas François, and from the SweLL research infrastructure project on Swedish Second language[6] (through a grant IN16-0464:1) regarding the invited speaker Egon Stemle.

---

[5] https://rj.se/en/anslag/2017/utveckling-av-lexikala-och-grammatiska-kompetenser-i-invandrarsvenska/
[6] https://rj.se/en/anslag/2016/swell---electronic-research-infrastructure-on-swedish-learner-language/

Contents

Predicting learner knowledge of individual words using machine learning

Drilon Avdiu, Vanessa Bui
Department of Informatics
Technical University of Munich
{drilon.avdiu,vanessa.bui}@tum.de

Klára Ptačinová Klimčíková
Class of Language Education
LMU Munich
k.klimcikova@lmu.de

Abstract

Predicting the knowledge of language learners is crucial for personalized interactions in any intelligent tutoring system for language learning. This study adopts a machine learning approach to the task of predicting the knowledge of single words for individual learners of English. We experiment with two machine learning models, neural networks and random forest, and with a set of learner-specific and word-specific features. Both the models are trained for all the learners together. However, since learner-specific features are used, the prediction is personalized for every learner. Both of the models achieve state-of-the-art results for the task of vocabulary prediction for English learners.

1 Introduction

This study is part of a larger project which attempts to develop an intelligent personal assistant for English learning called *Elia*. This assistant aims to support English learners in their informal contexts by reading or writing in English online through a browser plugin. The browser plugin also allows the collection of data about the learner's interests, knowledge and learning patterns which are used to create additional opportunities for practice in a mobile app to enhance their vocabulary acquisition. For the creation of personalized materials and personalized interaction, it is crucial to be able to automatically identify the learner's English knowledge.

Focusing on vocabulary knowledge first, the aim of this study is to create a model that would be able to predict the knowledge of single words for each learner individually. This task was firstly formulated by Ehara et al. (2014) as the *vocabulary prediction task* of which the goal is "to predict whether a learner knows a given word based on only a relatively small portion of his/her vocabulary" (p. 1374).

To tackle this problem, we adopt a machine learning approach where we engineer two sets of features, i.e., word-specific and learner-specific features, using three data sources: COCA wordlist (Davies, 2008), MRC Psycholinguistic Database: Machine Usable Dictionary. Version 2.00 (Wilson, 1988) and the English Vocabulary Knowledge Dataset (Ehara et al., 2012, 2013), the last which is also used for evaluation. We experiment with two models, i.e., Random Forest model which uses learner-specific as an input to differentiate between learners, and Neural Network model which learns the learner-specific features from the word-specific features.

The rest of the paper is structured as follows. The next section provides an overview of recent studies which are most relevant to this work (section 2). In section 3, the dataset used to evaluate the model is introduced. The features used for training and testing the models are described in section 4 and the two machine-learning models are described in section 5. Section 6 presents results and discussion. The last section summarizes the findings and suggest future directions (section 7).

2 Related Work

The knowledge prediction task is closely related to other tasks that go by different names, e.g., complex word identification (Yimam et al., 2018), automatic text simplification (Shardlow, 2014), and vocabulary size estimation (Meara and Alcoy, 2010). The studies addressing these tasks differ in their focus on a) the type of the object to be predicted, i.e., vocabulary, single words or the whole

Drilon Avdiu, Vanessa Bui and Klára Ptačinová Klimčíková 2019. Predicting learner knowledge of individual words using machine learning. *Proceedings of the 8th Workshop on Natural Language Processing for Computer Assisted Language Learning (NLP4CALL 2019)*. Linköping Electronic Conference Proceedings 164: 1–9.

text; b) the specific aspect of the object, i.e. size, knowledge, difficulty or complexity; and c) the process name, i.e. identification, prediction, estimation. Moreover, they differ in a) the target group, i.e., native vs. non-native speakers of different languages, and b) application, i.e., reading support, vocabulary testing, text simplification. Our study focuses on the prediction of knowledge (known/unknown) of single words similar to the following studies.

Tack et al. (2016) developed an expert model which predicts known and unknown words to a learner of a given Common European Framework of Reference (CEFR) level. They annotated words and multi-word expressions in 51 texts with their level of difficulty based on a French graded vocabulary list FLELex. The same texts were then annotated by four Dutch learners of French of certain proficiency level. They used the FLELex resource, not a machine learning model, as a predictive model of the learner's lexical knowledge. They compared the predictions to learner's annotation reaching the accuracy of 87.4% to 92.3%. However, the recall of unknown words did not even reach 50%.

Alfter and Volodina (2018) is another recent study which used CEFR-annotated wordlists SVALex (François et al., 2016) and SweLLex (Volodina et al., 2016) to predict the lexical complexity (i.e. appropriate CEFR level) of single words for learners of Swedish as a second language. In addition, they used a corpus-based vocabulary list, namely the Kelly list, to extract features grouped into count-based, morphological, semantic and context-based sets. They trained several machine learning models reaching the accuracy of 59% for seen words. Features including topic distributions were found to significantly improve the accuracy.

Lee and Yeung (2018) presented a personalized complex word identification model for Chinese learners. They trained models which predict whether the learner knows a word or not for each learner separately. Graph-based active learning was used to select the most informative words which were annotated by six learners as known or unknown. They extracted several features, e.g., difficulty level, the number of characters, the word frequency in a standard and learner corpus. Trained on a set of 50 words, they obtained the best accuracy of 78% with SVM classifier with features based on word difficulty levels from pedagogical vocabulary lists.

Ehara et al. (2018) also used a personalized model trained for each learner separately. He used the dataset created by Ehara et al. (2012, 2013) where sixteen English learners annotated 12,000 words on a five-point knowledge scale making it the most exhaustive dataset for this task. For features, he used the negative log of the 1-gram probabilities of each word in several corpora. He did not use a typical machine-learning classifier because it does not have an interpretable weight vector which was the criterion of the research. Instead, he used a modified mathematical function based on the Rasch model reaching 77.8% accuracy which outperformed the other two models which were not learner-specific, namely the Rasch model and the Shared Difficulty model.

Similarly to Ehara, Yancey and Lepage (2018) learned the learners' proficiency levels and word complexities simultaneously. However, in contrast, they learned the general CEFR-level proficiency, not the learner-specific. The dataset consisted of 2,385 passages annotated by 357 learners of Korean as known or not known. For feature selection, they used Pearson's correlation and Recursive Feature Elimination with Cross Validation. With their probabilistic results, they reached the accuracy of 84.3% for unseen words at threshold 0.5.

3   Dataset

We used the dataset provided by Ehara et al. (2012, 2013) as it is the largest freely available dataset for vocabulary knowledge prediction. It contains 11,999 English single words annotated by 16 learners of English accounting for 191,984 data points in total. Most of the learners were native speakers of Japanese and attended the University of Tokyo. The sampled words were taken from the SVL 12000 wordlist (ALC, 1998). The learners were asked to indicate how well they knew the given words on a scale from 1 (I have never seen the word before) to 5 (I know the word's meaning). Similarly, as in Ehara et al. (2018) and Lee and Yeung (2018), we assigned the words marked with 5 to "known" and the rest of the words marked with 1-4 to "unknown".

4   Features

Since there can be a high variation between the knowledge of learners even of the same CEFR level (Tack et al., 2016), the goal is to make the knowledge prediction for each learner individually. As Ehara et al. (2018) rightly pointed out, "For example, a learner interested in music may know music-related words that even high-level learners may not be familiar with" (p. 801). Knowledge prediction which is learner-specific can be achieved by training an independent classifier for each learner separately (Ehara et al., 2018; Lee and Yeung, 2018). However, we train the model for all the learners together while keeping the prediction individualized. This can be achieved by adding learner-specific features which would differentiate one learner from another.

4.1   Word-specific Features

Word knowledge has often been associated with word difficulty which, in turn, has often been associated with word frequency. This was also empirically supported in the 2016 SemEval shared task for complex word identification: "word frequencies remain the most reliable predictor of word complexity" (Paetzold and Specia, 2016, p. 560). However, Tack et al. (2016) warn against word frequencies as they "approximate the use of native speakers, but do not provide any information about the frequency of words within the different stages of the L2 curriculum" (p. 230). This is, however, not the problem of frequencies but rather of the resource from which the frequencies were calculated. If the resources reflected a representative sample of the learner's experience, whether in the classroom or beyond the classroom, word frequencies could be a reliable predictor of the knowledge of second language learners. The logic behind this is as follows: the word frequency conceptualized as the repeated opportunity to learn the word is the main predictor of the learner having learned the word. We follow this logic and create features representing different frequencies of the words taken from the Corpus of Contemporary American English (COCA) wordlist[1] (Davies, 2008) which contains word frequencies on 20,000 words from dozens of subcorpora of different genres (from academic to spoken conversations) and domains (from sports to biol-

ogy). Topic distribution was also found to be the most important feature in the study by Alfter and Volodina (2018). In order to ensure comparability, the frequencies were normalized per million words across all genres.

Apart from word frequencies, we also encode the psycholinguistic properties of words into features. For this, we use the data from the MRC database[2], e.g., the number of letters, the degree of meaningfulness, the age of acquisition or the degree of abstractness. The psycholinguistic properties of words have been found to be associated with learning difficulty (Laufer, 1997), even though not directly with vocabulary knowledge. The degree of their importance in the prediction task together with the degree of importance of all the other features will be tested and described in section 4.3.

Since graded vocabulary lists have also been found to be useful in predicting the vocabulary knowledge of second language learners (Tack et al., 2016; Lee and Yeung, 2018; Alfter and Volodina, 2018), we add a feature representing CEFR difficulty level obtained from the English Vocabulary Profile (EVP)[3] resource. If one word is assigned to multiple CEFR levels, we use the lowest level of the word. If a word is not found in the database, it is automatically assigned the highest level which is the C2 level.

4.2   Learner-specific Features

For learner-specific features, we identify the number of known words in every keyword list which were created from COCA subcorpora. The proportion of known words in each keyword list should represent the knowledge of the learner across different genres and domains. The idea behind this is that if the learner knows a lot of frequent words occurring in the domain of, for example, sports, it is very probable that he/she knows another high-frequency word from this domain. However, if the learner does not know a lot of low-frequency words from the domain, it is not probable that he/she knows another low-frequency word from this domain. To operationalize this idea, we need to use a combined measure which would not

---

[1]Available online at https://www.wordfrequency.info/purchase.asp

[2]For further details, see the MRC documentation on http://websites.psychology.uwa.edu.au/school/MRCDatabase/mrc2.html

[3]The EVP contains information about the known words for learners of each CEFR level and is available on https://www.englishprofile.org/wordlists

only reflect the amount of known words but also the frequencies of the known words in a particular domain. The calculation of the learner-specific features is carried out in the following steps:

1. For each subcorpus, we extract keywords[4], that is, words which occur significantly more frequently in the specific subcorpus than in the general corpus. This results in a keyword list for each subcorpus.

2. For each keyword list, $k = \lceil \sqrt{n/2} \rceil$ of frequency bands[5] is created using the k-means algorithm[6] where n denotes the number of words in the keyword list. We use the Elkan variant of the k-means algorithm for better efficiency with a maximum number of iterations set to 300.[7]

3. In order to mitigate the effect of outliers with high frequencies, for each subcorpus, we calculate an average of the top 10 words[8] with the highest frequencies denoted as s_{max}. For the keyword lists where k is less than 10, we take k words to calculate s_{max}.

4. For each band B, we calculate the "power of band" ϕ_i by taking the difference between the subcorpus high frequency representative s_{max} and the average of all the word frequencies in the band as follows:

$$\phi_i = \frac{s_{max} - \text{avg}(B_i)}{\sum_{j=1}^{k} \left(s_{max} - \text{avg}(B_j) \right)},$$

for $i = \{1, 2, ..., k\}$.

5. For each learner, each word labeled as known from the dataset used for training/testing is looked up in the keyword lists to identify the subcorpus of the word and consequently the respective frequency band.

6. The subcorpus-specific knowledge φ_s for each learner is calculated by adding up the respective power of bands as many times as the number of words identified in those bands as follows:

$$\varphi_s = \sum_{j=1}^{k} \frac{\phi_j \cdot |\hat{B}_j|}{|B_j|},$$

where $\hat{B}_j$ denotes the set of words which the learner knows and which belong to the band B_j, and $|\cdot|$ denotes set cardinality.

4.3 Selection of Features

The combination of the two above-mentioned types of features resulted in an exhaustive list of 105 features. Having in mind that it is very probable that the list included redundant features, a feature selection procedure was needed. To remove irrelevant and less important features, we used a Tree Classifier, a method for determining feature importance. This method gives a score for each feature where the higher the score, the more important or relevant the feature is. Not surprisingly, the word-specific features with a lot of missing values and the learner-specific features containing a limited number of keywords were ranked very low in the feature importances list and thus were discarded. Furthermore, we estimated the Pearson Correlation between the remaining features. We created groups of features with a correlation of higher than 0.99 and picked only one feature from the group with the highest rank in the feature importances list. These two procedures reduced the initial list to a final set of 39 features (see table 1 and table 2). It is worth noting that these procedures decreased the final scores slightly due to the occasional losses in information caused by the reduced word-representation.

5 Models

The objective is to train a machine learning model which would predict whether a given learner knows a given word in English or not. The problem can be formulated as follows: Let p denote the number of learners, and q the number of words in our training dataset $\mathcal{D} = \{X, Y\}$, where X denotes the set of datapoints and Y their respective labels. Let $\mathbf{u_i} = (u_{i_1}, u_{i_2}, ..., u_{i_m})^t$ and $\mathbf{w_j} = (w_{j_1}, w_{j_2}, ..., w_{j_n})^t$ denote the learner-specific features, and word-specific features, for

---

[4] As in Gardner and Davies (2013), we use a ratio of 1.5, i.e., all words which occur 1.5 times more often in a specific corpus compared to the general corpus are considered keywords in the specific domain.

[5] We take this number as a rule of thumb. Other heuristics can apply as well.

[6] https://scikit-learn.org/stable/modules/generated/sklearn.cluster.KMeans.html

[7] We do not use a fixed number for frequency bands due to the Zipfian nature of the frequency distribution.

[8] We take this number after a manual inspection of the top frequencies in each keyword list.

Feature	
Number of letters in the word	✓
Number of syllables in the word	✓
Familiarity	✓
Concreteness	✓
Imagery	✓
Mean Colerado Meaningfulness	✓
Mean Pavio Meaningfulness	
Age of Acquisition	✓
Type	
Alphasyllable	
Status	✓
Written Capitalized	

Table 1: Initial list of features from the MRC database. Selected features for the final list are marked with a check mark.

$i = \{1, 2, ..., p\}$ and $j = \{1, 2, ..., q\}$, respectively. The goal is to learn the function $f : X \rightarrow Y$, or $y = f(\mathbf{w}; \mathbf{u}; \mathcal{D})$ that fits the dataset $\mathcal{D}$ to the extent of not overfitting it.

We experiment with two kinds of settings: one where both the learner-specific and word-specific features are used as input (the Complete Feature Space Dependent Model described in section 5.1) and another one where only the word-specific features are used as input and the learner-specific features are learned by the model (the Neural Network based model described in section 5.2).

5.1 The Complete Feature Space Dependent Model

For the Complete Feature Space Dependent model (CFSD), both word-specific and learner-specific features are included in the input. We tried out the following well-known machine-learning algorithms using scikit-learn (Pedregosa et al., 2011): Support Vector Machine (SVM) with various kernels, k Nearest Neighbors, Logistic Regression, and Random Forest. Random Forest (Breiman, 2001) provided the highest scores. Moreover, we have seen that training a Random Forest model, that achieved a respectable score, required way less efforts in comparison to other models. This lies to better prospects for constructing an automatic online-training pipeline in the Elia software. Consequently, Random Forest was chosen for further experimentation with the hyperparameter search.

	w	l
COCA total frequency	✓	✓
dispersion	✓	
score		
SPOKEN		
CBS (Columbia Broadcasting Company)		✓
MSNBC (Microsoft/National Brcst. Comp.)		✓
PBS (Public Broadcasting Service)		✓
NPR (National Public Radio)	✓	✓
independent	✓	✓
ABC (American Broadcasting Company)		
NBC (National Broadcasting Company)		
CNN (Cable News Network)		
FOX (Fox Broadcasting Company)		
NEWSPAPER		✓
international newspaper		✓
national newspaper		✓
local newspaper		✓
money; life		✓
miscellaneous		✓
sports; editorial		
ACADEMIC	✓	✓
education	✓	
geographical/social science		✓
law/political science; humanities		
science/technology; medicine; history		
philosophy/religion; miscellaneous		
FICTION		✓
journals	✓	✓
movies	✓	
science fiction/fantasy		
juvenile; books		
POPULAR MAGAZINES		
news/opinion		✓
religion		✓
sports; entertainment		✓
women/men	✓	
financial; science/technology		
home/health; African American		
social/arts; children		

Table 2: Initial list of features from the COCA wordlist. For word-specific features (w), the frequency of the word in the particular subcorpus was used, and for learner-specific features (l), the proportion of known words in the subcorpus was used. Selected features for the final list are marked with a check mark. Individual subcorpora are separated by a semicolon.

Proceedings of the 8th Workshop on Natural Language Processing for Computer Assisted Language Learning (NLP4CALL 2019)

The Random Forest model learns the function $f : \mathbb{R}^{m+n} \to \{0, 1\}$ by using Decision Trees. The process of predicting the label for a specific input $\mathbf{x} = (\mathbf{u}, \mathbf{w})^t$ consists of all Decision Trees assigning a label. The label assigned by most of the trees is taken as the final prediction.

To come up with the best values for the parameters, we used 3-fold cross validation on 80% of the data.[9] First, we applied a random search of parameters in 100 configurations comprised of the most crucial hyperparameters of Random Forest. The selected values by random search are marked in italics in the list below. Second, we ran a grid search in a close neighborhood of the values of the parameters provided by the random search to come up with the final parameter setting. The values in the close neighborhood were chosen arbitrarily. The parameter setting that performed the best as to F1 score are marked bold:

- the use of bootstrap sampling (True, ***False***)

- the number of estimators (**55**, *75*, 95)

- the maximum depth of the trees (91, ***101***, 111)

- the minimum number of samples an internal node should contain for a split (13, *17*, 21)

- the minimum number of samples a leaf node should contain for a split (**1**, *8*, 15)

Other preassigned parameters include the number of features to be picked randomly for a node split, which we set to the square root of the number of features, and the entropy measure which we set to Gini.

5.2 The Neural Network Based Model

In contrast to the former model, in the Neural Network based model (NN), only the word-specific features were used as input. The discrimination between the learners is achieved by constructing a unique set of parameters for each learner by the model. We learn the function $f : \mathbb{R}^n \to \{0, 1\}^p$ by a plain Fully Connected Neural Network using PyTorch (Paszke et al., 2017).

The architecture of the model is comprised of the input layer of n dimensions, 5 hidden layers with a number of nodes that changes geometrically using a factor f set to 4 (i.e., $\mathrm{f} \cdot \mathrm{n}$, $\mathrm{f} \cdot \mathrm{n} \cdot \mathrm{f}/2$, $\mathrm{f} \cdot \mathrm{n} \cdot (\mathrm{f} - 1)$, $\mathrm{f} \cdot \mathrm{n} \cdot \mathrm{f}/2$, $\mathrm{f} \cdot \mathrm{n}$) and an output layer of dimension p which is linear. For numerical stability, we use a modified binary cross-entropy loss that transforms the linear output using a Sigmoid function and afterwards employs the log-sum-exp trick.

Each of the hidden layers contains nodes with $\mathrm{ReLu}(x) = \max(0, \mathrm{x})$ activation functions.

We optimize the loss by making use of the Adam optimizer which is a more sophisticated version of the plain gradient. The hyperparameters are set upon manual analysis of the loss change. The learning rate is initially set to 0.0001, and we use mini-batches of size 15. After each layer, except layer 5, we employ a dropout regularization of 0.2 and a weight decay equal to 0.003.

We use 80% of the data for training, 3% for validation, and 17% for testing which is the same ratio as in Ehara et al. (2018). The training runs for a total of 40 epochs. For the first 20 epochs, we use the same learning rate whereas for the remaining 20 epochs we re-set the learning rate to be the $7/8$ of the previous value. We noticed that in this training setting, the accuracy in the validation set saturates after the 40th epoch.

6 Evaluation

6.1 Isolated Testing

We call this the isolated testing as we prevent any kind of data leakage from the training set to the testing set; the testing set is separated in the beginning before any tuning with the model is undertaken; the learner-specific features in the CFSD model are computed using information only from the words used for training. We use roughly the same ratio between the training and testing sets as Ehara et al. (2018) for comparability purposes, i.e., 80% for training in both of the models, and 20% and 17% for testing for the CFSD and the NNet model, respectively. As the classes are imbalanced—67351 labeled as 0 and 96073 as 1— we report scores other than accuracy as well (see table 3). Precision, recall, and F1 scores are calculated as a weighted average for both labels. Thus, the values of the scores are similar. The scores for both models are shown in table 3. The evaluation, including the training of our models, can be reproduced using the code accompanying this paper.[10]

---

[9]3 folds were used due to limitations in time and computing capacities.

[10]The link to the code: `drive.google.com/drive/folders/1ukdm3ekkfIV_86PyGRhijC_tf07SVFxe`

	CFSD	Neural Network
Precision	**79.90%**	79.19%
Recall	**79.89%**	79.18%
F1	**79.89%**	79.18%
Cohen's Kappa	**58.26%**	56.93%
Accuracy	**79.89%**	79.18%

Table 3: The results of our models.

6.2 Discussion

The CFSD model trained on two sets of hand-crafted features, one representing the words and another representing the learners, achieved the highest accuracy, i.e., 80%. The overall results of the CFSD model support the fact that frequencies from different genres and domains—which reflect the different opportunities for learning the learner might have had—can be used as a valid representation of word-specific features. Moreover, the learner-specific features—calculated as the amount of knowledge of the keywords of specific frequencies in various genres and domains—can lead to a personalized prediction of unseen words, even in one-time training for all the learners. However, a complete feature pre-calculation, as it is the case with this model, comes with the burden of limiting the feature space to a human-defined set of features, which can not be seen as exhaustive and universal in encoding learner-specificity.

The NN model led to a slightly lower accuracy and F1 scores. This model comes with the downside of not being able to predict for learners for whom we did not train the model in the dataset as the output is fixed to the number of learners. On the other hand, it circumvents the limitation of having hand-crafted learner-specific features by learning such weight vectors from the data. In addition, we can increase the capacity of the model to encode as many learner-specific aspects as required upon data availability. Those aspects can go beyond the use of word frequencies on encoding learner-specificity as given in the CFSD model.

Comparing it to related work, both the models performed similarly to Ehara et al. (2018) who used the same dataset but different model. Their proposed model builds on top of the Rasch Model by introducing a feature map function which enriches the model with the out-of-sample

setting and learner-specific learnable weight vectors. Their approach seems to be more similar to our NN model than the CFSD model in that it learns the learner representations and uses frequencies as features to represent words. However, despite the obvious similarities, there are also considerable differences, e.g., our feature map takes frequencies along dozens of different specialized corpora as opposed to few general corpora and on top adds additional non-frequency features.

Furthermore, they limit the learner-specific word difficulty vectors to the number of features constructed by their feature map which can be understood as of dimension the number of corpora they take frequencies from. On the other hand, the nature of our feature map which takes different aspects of the word into account, makes it sensical to up-project the initial feature map to higher dimensions, and thus encode learner-specificity into higher dimension weight vectors, whose size can change accordingly upon data availability.

Another difference lies in the fact that our NN approach does not model the likelihood using a single sigmoid transformation on the difference between learner's ability (a_u) and learner-specific word difficulty (w_d) and learning the parameters using a MAP estimation, but, instead, models the likelihood as a chain of ReLu transformations on standard weights. Put differently, the NN model encodes learner-specificity only on standard weights as given by the architecture. Those weights can be taken as the weights of the last hidden layer (made of f · n nodes).

7 Conclusion and Future Work

This study presented an evaluation of two supervised machine learning models which perform the task of learner's knowledge prediction of single words in the context of an intelligent tutoring system. The main challenge in this task, and thus the main goal of this study, was to make the prediction specific for every learner. We compared two approaches, one which implemented an explicit set of manually constructed learner-specific features, and another one which implemented an implicit set of learner-specific features which were learned by the model from the data.

The Random Forest model which used a complete set of hand-crafted features, both learner-specific and word-specific, led to the state-of-the-art results (accuracy of 80%) for English as a foreign language. This supports the idea of using various frequencies from different genres and domains to represent words and calculating the knowledge of keywords from those very same genre and topics to represent learners in predicting which words a given learner knows or does not know.

The Neural Network based model, using word-specific features as input and learning learner representations, led to the accuracy of 79% which sends positive signals for future work as this model does not require the construction of learner-specific features, and thus not limit the learner representation to a human-defined set of features and their calculation.

This model was initiated with the idea of building an end-to-end architecture, which firstly would encode learner specificity in the sense of dense-vector representations, and then use such encoding to create an intermediate input in concatenation with word specific features, to come up with the final prediction at the end. The idea of using the intermediate input is similar to the CFSD model, in the sense of training a one-time model which will serve our platform in long term. This way we would circumvent the limitation of our actual Neural Network based model, which does not allow the usage of a pre-trained model to generate predictions for learners whose data did not participate in the initial training. It is inferable that for such learners, we will need to run a learner-representation encoder, similar to the encoding step given in the envisioned end-to-end architecture. This is a subject of our future work.

Despite having used a large dataset of words for training and testing, the learner base was limited to 16 learners of the same language background and thus might not generalize well to heterogeneous learners which will be the case in the intelligent tutoring system Elia. However, it gives a good starting point. In future work, we plan to collect data on more learners of different background and proficiency which can be then used for further training and testing.

In conclusion, picking one model over the other introduces trade-offs, as discussed above. Thus, it is up to the designers of similar tutoring systems to decide what goes on par with their goals. For the intelligent tutoring system *Elia*, we are inclined to the idea of using a cross-learner model that exploits inter-learner similarities, such as the CFSD model, instead of using a model that does not allow for transfer of information between learners in a collaborative fashion, as the NN model. However, as stated above, our future work goes in the direction of taking the best aspects of two models. Thus, it is more likely that our platform will utilize such a model on its production state.

References

SPACE ALC. 1998. Inc. standard vocabulary list 12,000.

David Alfter and Elena Volodina. 2018. Towards single word lexical complexity prediction. In *Proceedings of the Thirteenth Workshop on Innovative Use of NLP for Building Educational Applications*, pages 79–88.

Leo Breiman. 2001. Random forests. *Machine learning*, 45(1):5–32.

Mark Davies. 2008. The corpus of contemporary american english (coca): 560 million words, 1990–present. bye, brigham young university.

Yo Ehara, Yusuke Miyao, Hidekazu Oiwa, Issei Sato, and Hiroshi Nakagawa. 2014. Formalizing word sampling for vocabulary prediction as graph-based active learning. In *Proceedings of the 2014 Conference on Empirical Methods in Natural Language Processing (EMNLP)*, pages 1374–1384.

Yo Ehara, Issei Sato, Hidekazu Oiwa, and Hiroshi Nakagawa. 2012. Mining words in the minds of second language learners: Learner-specific word difficulty. In *Proceedings of COLING 2012*, page 799–814, Mumbai, India. The COLING 2012 Organizing Committee.

Yo Ehara, Issei Sato, Hidekazu Oiwa, and Hiroshi Nakagawa. 2018. Mining words in the minds of second language learners for learner-specific word difficulty. *Journal of Information Processing*, 26:267–275.

Yo Ehara, Nobuyuki Shimizu, Takashi Ninomiya, and Hiroshi Nakagawa. 2013. Personalized reading support for second-language web documents. *ACM Transactions on Intelligent Systems and Technology (TIST)*, 4(2):31.

Thomas François, Elena Volodina, Ildikó Pilán, and Anaïs Tack. 2016. Svalex: a cefr-graded lexical resource for swedish foreign and second language learners. In *Proceedings of the Tenth International Conference on Language Resources and Evaluation (LREC 2016)*, pages 213–219.

Dee Gardner and Mark Davies. 2013. A new academic vocabulary list. *Applied linguistics*, 35(3):305–327.

Batia Laufer. 1997. What's in a word that makes it hard or easy? intralexical factors affecting the difficulty of vocabulary acquisition. *Vocabulary: Description, acquisition and pedagogy*, pages 140–155.

John Lee and Chak Yan Yeung. 2018. Automatic prediction of vocabulary knowledge for learners of chinese as a foreign language. In *2018 2nd International Conference on Natural Language and Speech Processing (ICNLSP)*, pages 1–4. IEEE.

Paul M Meara and Juan Carlos Olmos Alcoy. 2010. Words as species: An alternative approach to estimating productive vocabulary size. *Reading in a foreign Language*, 22(1):222–236.

Gustavo Paetzold and Lucia Specia. 2016. Semeval 2016 task 11: Complex word identification. In *Proceedings of the 10th International Workshop on Semantic Evaluation (SemEval-2016)*, pages 560–569.

Adam Paszke, Sam Gross, Soumith Chintala, Gregory Chanan, Edward Yang, Zachary DeVito, Zeming Lin, Alban Desmaison, Luca Antiga, and Adam Lerer. 2017. Automatic differentiation in pytorch.

F. Pedregosa, G. Varoquaux, A. Gramfort, V. Michel, B. Thirion, O. Grisel, M. Blondel, P. Prettenhofer, R. Weiss, V. Dubourg, J. Vanderplas, A. Passos, D. Cournapeau, M. Brucher, M. Perrot, and E. Duchesnay. 2011. Scikit-learn: Machine learning in Python. *Journal of Machine Learning Research*, 12:2825–2830.

Matthew Shardlow. 2014. A survey of automated text simplification. *International Journal of Advanced Computer Science and Applications*, 4(1):58–70.

Anaïs Tack, Thomas François, Anne-Laure Ligozat, and Cédrick Fairon. 2016. Evaluating lexical simplification and vocabulary knowledge for learners of french: Possibilities of using the flelex resource. In *LREC*.

Elena Volodina, Ildikó Pilán, Lorena Llozhi, Baptiste Degryse, and Thomas François. 2016. Swellex: second language learners' productive vocabulary. In *Proceedings of the joint workshop on NLP for Computer Assisted Language Learning and NLP for Language Acquisition at SLTC, Umeå, 16th November 2016*, 130, pages 76–84. Linköping University Electronic Press.

Michael Wilson. 1988. Mrc psycholinguistic database: Machine-usable dictionary, version 2.00. *Behavior research methods, instruments, & computers*, 20(1):6–10.

Kevin Yancey and Yves Lepage. 2018. Korean l2 vocabulary prediction: Can a large annotated corpus be used to train better models for predicting unknown words? In *Proceedings of the Eleventh International Conference on Language Resources and Evaluation (LREC-2018)*.

Seid Muhie Yimam, Chris Biemann, Shervin Malmasi, Gustavo Paetzold, Lucia Specia, Sanja Štajner, Anaïs Tack, and Marcos Zampieri. 2018. A report on the complex word identification shared task 2018. In *Proceedings of the Thirteenth Workshop on Innovative Use of NLP for Building Educational Applications*, pages 66–78.

Automatic Generation and Semantic Grading of Esperanto Sentences in a Teaching Context

Eckhard Bick
University of Southern Denmark
`eckhard.bick@mail.dk`

Abstract

This paper presents a method for the automatic generation and semantic evaluation of exercise sentences for Esperanto teaching. Our sentence grader exploits both corpus data and lexical resources (verb frames and noun/adjective ontologies) to either generate meaningful sentences from scratch, or to determine the acceptability of a given input sentence. Individual words receive scores for how well they match the semantic conditions projected onto their place in the syntactic tree. In a CALL context, the system works with a lesson-/level-constrained vocabulary and can be integrated into e.g. substitution table or slot filler exercises. While the method as such is language-independent, we also discuss how morphological clues (affixes) can be exploited for semantic purposes. When evaluated on out-of-corpus course materials and short stories, the system achieved a rejection precision, in terms of false positives, of 98-99% at the sentence level, and 93-97% at the word level.

1 Introduction

Automated writing evaluation (AWE) can be a cost-efficient and consistent, albeit controversial, alternative to human grading of L2 student production. One possible approach is to focus on learner error detection in terms of spelling and grammar at the sentence level (e.g. Lee et al. 2011), a task for which a wide range of tools and methods is available, covering both rule-based, machine learning (ML) and hybrid approaches (e.g. Ng et al. 2014). Semantic assessment is usually seen as having a wider scope than the individual sentence, and is mainly used to address properties of a text as a whole. In Yannakoudakis (2013), for instance, machine learning (ML) techniques based on word embeddings are employed to assess textual coherence through the semantic similarity of adjacent sentences. By contrast, the semantic correctness of the individual sentence is less important in AWE, since human-produced sentences generally do have a coherent meaning, and by and large sentence understanding is quite robust even in the face of multiple spelling and grammatical errors. Therefore, semantic oddities are usually not independent errors, but either a byproduct of lower-level errors or word pair confusion errors that are recognizable as such in context. Even beginner-level L2 students know what they *want* to say.

In the research presented here, however, we focus on the semantics of the individual sentence, and we are interested not only in human-generated sentences, but also in automatically generated random sentences. In the latter - unlike in AWE - meaning coherence at the sentence level is not governed by an underlying intellect, but has to be controlled and evaluated.

While sentence generatio in our own project is intended for use in language learning exercises with a controlled vocabulary and controlled syntactic complexity, adding a semantic component to random sentence generation is also useful for other tasks, such as creating training data for text-to-speech (TTS) or voice recognition systems. Thus, Lilley et al. (2012) describe an HPSG-based generator with a 20-category noun ontology, a lexicon of 2181 wordforms (1100 lemmas) and 39 production rules that achieved a human meaningfulness

Eckhard Bick 2019. Automatic generation and semantic grading of Esperanto sentences in a teaching context.
Proceedings of the 8th Workshop on Natural Language Processing for Computer Assisted Language Learning (NLP4CALL 2019). Linköping Electronic Conference Proceedings 164: 10–19.

rating of 3.09 on a 0-6 scale, as opposed to 0.66 for a semantics-free system and 4.52 for human text.

We here adopt a similar approach, matching head words with semantically and categorically constrained slot fillers for valency and modifier slots. However, we go beyond this framework on several important accounts:

- We apply the method to both sentence generation and the evaluation of existing sentences

- For evaluation, lexical frames and valency patterns are combined with combinatorial corpus statistics

- Vocabulary size and content are parameters controlled by the user, lesson or text book, and has no upper boundary - in principle, free input sentences can be evaluated, and the semantic ontology has a high coverage even on unabridged text

2   The project

Though it can be used for different purposes, the sentence generator/evaluator was developed primarily with a pedagogical framework in mind. Specifically, the idea was to allow the creation of CALL exercises, where a pre-defined vocabulary would yield a maximum number of meaningful sentences for substitution table exercises and their more constrained variants, such as slot filler exercises, one word substitution exercises, question-answering sentence pairs etc. The currently funded international project aims at teaching Esperanto to children in the first grades of primary school, as propedeutic foreign language with a transparent, modular and highly regular linguistic system supposed to facilitate general linguistic awareness and subsequent learning of other foreign languages. All course materials (lessons, songs, dialogues, exercises) were lexicographically analyzed with the EspGram parser (Bick 2009, 2016) in order to determine the introduced morpheme vocabulary of root words, affixes and inflection categories. Our tool is then used to generate sentences from the accumulated vocabulary at a given stage of the course, to evaluate and semantically filter combinatorial sentences from teacher-defined substitution tables or to suggest wrong, but not absurd, semantic alternatives for word substitution exercises, the idea being that

substitution with a semantically close word (e.g. an animal for a human agent subject in an activity sentence) would create fun effects that substitution with something completely unrelated would not (e.g. an abstract feature or activity noun for a food object in an eating sentence).

3   Sentence generation

3.1   Vocabulary base

In preparation for sentence generation, a morpheme and word lexicon is established for the current teaching level, analyzing all words up to and including the current lesson block, in our case 6 lesson levels with 5 blocks each. Fig 1 plots vocabulary growth per lesson for the four inflection-marked content word classes (POS). Esperanto marks word class systematically with an endings vowel (nouns -o, verbs -i, adjectives -a, adverbs -e). Where semantically feasible, Esperanto word roots can change word class by changing this vowel, e.g. *amiko (friend), amika/amike (friendly), amiki (be friends)*. Thus, in our course material, the number of words was about 10-13% higher than the number of roots (table 1). The language also allows compounding (e.g *amletero 'love letter'*) and uses a number of semantically transparent agglutinative affixes e.g. *-ej* for places (*vendejo 'shop'*) and *mal-* for antonyms (*malvarma 'cold'*). Therefore, the number of N/V/A-roots exhibits a steeper per-lesson increase than the number of morphemes (table 1).

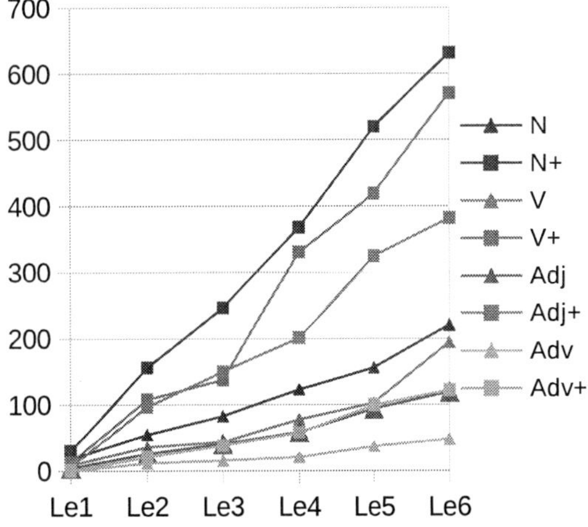

Fig. 1: Vocabulary size by POS for Lesson 1-6, as-is and extended (POS+)

In order to provide more lexical variation, the sentence generator can optionally expand its lexicon with compounds and affix-derivations that do not themselves occur in the course material, but can be formed using known morphemes. For this, EspGram's parser lexicon (58,000 lemmas) is morphologically analyzed. All words that do not contain unknown morphemes, and are not marked as "rare" or "archaic", will then be added to the respective POS lexica in the generator. As can be seen in table 1, this extended lexicon is about three times the size of the original course material at all levels.

L	mor-phemes	N/V/A roots	N/V/A words	N/V/A extended	affixes
1	45	32	32	51	-in,-ist
2	139	118	129	382	-ebl,-ej, ge-,mal-
3	177	165	184	572	-ul
4	246	252	281	958	-iĝ,re-
5	335	341	390	1364	-et,-ind
6	392	516	581	1707	-eg,-er

Table 1: Overall vocabulary size for content POS, roots vs. words

3.2 Valency frames for verbs

As a sentence skeleton for generation we use valency frames based on framenet entries for verbs. The Esperanto frames follow the system described in (Bick 2012) and contain, besides the semantic category of the verb, a list of arguments with semantic and morphosyntactic slot filler information.

(a) manĝi <FN:eat/S§AG'H|A/O§PAT'food>

(b) instrui <FN:instrui/S§AG'H/O§BEN'H/P-pri§TP'all><FN:teach/S§AG'H/O§TP'domain| ling|fcl/P-al§BEN'H>

(c) diri <FN:say/S§SP'H/O§MES'sem-s|fcl/P-al§REC'H>

The word for 'eat' (a), for instance, has two frame arguments, an agent (§AG) and a patient (§PAT), the former as subject (S), the latter as object (O). Semantic types are added with an apostrophe - 'human' (H) and 'food', respectively. Sometimes, more than one frame construction is possible. Thus, the word for 'teach' (instrui), can have either the human beneficiary (§BEN) or the teaching topic (§TP) as object, with the other argument as a prepositional complement ('P-' plus the preposition, *pri 'about'* or *al 'to')*. The second construction, and example (c) can also

vary in syntactic form, allowing a finite clause object (fcl) rather than a noun phrase. All in all, we created frame entries for 6235 verb lemmas, providing 100% coverage for the course material. In a 1.3 million word newspaper corpus[1] coverage for verb tokens was 96%. There are similar frames for 157 nouns and 50 adjectives, but they are not used by the sentence generator.

3.3 Semantic ontologies for nouns and adjectives

When the generator expands a verb frame into a sentence, it randomly picks slot-filler nouns from the lesson-constrained vocabulary, making sure the noun in question is semantically compatible with the head verb. For this we use Esp Gram's existing ontology of semantic prototypes for nouns. The ontology has about 200 categories, organized in a shallow hierarchy. For instance, the human <H> category has sub-types like <Hprof> (profession), <Hideo> (follower of an ideology), <Hfam> (family relation term) etc., and the <tool> class is subdivided into <tool-cut>, <tool-mus> (musical instruments), <tool-light> etc. Since the majority of Esperanto affixes allows a safe prediction of semantic class (e.g. *-ej* for <L> 'place' or *-uj* for <con> 'container'), it is possible to increase coverage through morphological analysis, creating semantic entries for the productive, unlisted part of the lexicon, too. Thus, 99.3% of the nouns in the test corpus received a semantic entry. For the course material, all entries were manually checked.

For adjectives, we used a scheme with about 110 categories, suggested for Danish in (Bick, 2019). The categories can be seen as semantic prototypes (e.g. *<jcol> colour* or *<jpsych> psychological state*), but are at the same time intended for distributional restriction, i.e. to purvey information on which (semantic) type of head noun they can combine with. Thus, *<jcol>* will combine with physical objects, and *<jpsych>* with human and semiotic nouns. The adjective ontology can be ordered into 14 primary and 25 secondary umbrella categories. For Esperanto, we tagged about 4140 adjective lemmas in the dictionary, amounting to a token coverage of 100% for the course material and 71% for the news corpus. Inspection indicates

---

[1] The corpus is based on *Monato,* a monthly news magazine published in Esperanto by *Flandra Esperanto-Ligo.*

that coverage could probably be increased considerably for the latter by systematic class transfer, because 2/3 of untagged cases were derivations from nouns or verbs, either by direct conversion or by affixation.

3.4 Syntactic and morphological generation

The sentence generator builds and joins phrases for a list of main syntactic constituents (subject, object, subject complement, object complement, adverbial arguments and adjuncts) around a governing verb frame. Therefore, as a first step, a random verb is chosen and assigned a random tense, expanding into a VP in the case of auxiliaries. Second, the list of arguments is culled depending on the frame's valency, and for each argument, an phrase-generating subroutine is called. In most cases, this will be an NP, but if the frame demands a subclause, step 1 will be iterated and a conjunction added.

In the NP subroutine, a random head noun is chosen, looping until the frame's semantic slot filler condition is matched. In most cases, frames only ask for a supercategory such as 'human' or 'food', and here we allow all subcategories to match on the noun side. The chosen noun is then inflected depending on syntactic function (-*n* for direct objects). Number (singular/plural) is in principle assigned randomly, but has to observe the fact that some verbs take only plural subjects or plural objects, and that the semantics of the noun may make a plural meaningless (e.g. domain and mass words). If no semantically matching noun is found in the lesson vocabulary, a matching pronoun is used instead, e.g. *li (he), io 'something'*) or *ĝi (it).*

With a likelihood of 0.25% for subjects and objects, and 0.20% for other constituents, NP's will be expanded with a definite article, possessive or demonstrative pronoun. The same likelihood threshold holds for expansion with an adjective phrase (ADJP), and both types of modifiers will be inflected in agreement with the head noun. Like for nouns, there are semantic restrictions on the choice of adjective, depending on the semantic category of the phrase head. In the absence of explicit selection information on the noun, we constructed a table of many-to-many matches for groups of semantic noun prototypes on the one side and groups of adjective prototypes on the other, roughly mirroring the granularity of the secondary

umbrella terms in the adjective ontology, e.g. a list of concrete object types (containers, clothes, furniture, tools, machines, vehicles ...) matching a list of physical property adjectives (colour, size, shape, weight, state, texture ...). In some cases, there was some isomorphism in the ontologies, allowing one-on-one matches, e.g. <cloH> (clothing) - <jclo> (clothing adjective), <f-q> (quantifiable feature) - <jchange> (change adjective).

On average, the generator produces sentences with 4-5 words, with no clear correlation to the size of the accumulated lesson vocabulary. Word length increased slightly, from 6.8 letters/word in the first lesson to 7.4 for the last lesson. Using the extended vocabulary increases both word and sentence length for the first lesson. At later stages, there is a tendency towards longer but fewer words, probably due to a higher percentage of words that are morphologically complex, but at the same time rarer and simpler in terms of valency.

4 Semantic Sentence Grading

While vocabulary-constrained semantic sentence generation is useful for creating random training sentences, other course-related tasks call for semantic grading of student-produced sentences rather than the generation of completely new sentences. Such sentences can, for instance, be prompted online in a question-answering scenario, or they can be the result of substitution table or slot filler exercise in a graphical user interface (GUI). Here, a backend program has to decide, if a certain combination of words from the substitution table, or a suggested slot filler word creates a semantically acceptable sentence or not. Impossible or odd sentences indicate that the student has not understood the sentence context and is unsure of one or more words. An automatic tutoring program can use this information to flag words or structures as "probably known" or "problematic", even in a monolingual L2 setting.

Our sentence grader implements a two-thronged co-occurrence approach based on annotated corpus data. First bigrams and trigrams (combinations of two or three consecutive words, respectively)[2] are checked against a corpus-

---

[2] BOS (beginning-of-sentence) and EOS (end-of-sentence) dummies are used to create ngrams for the first and last words in a sentence.

derived frequency table of such co-occurrences. Second, we apply a similar check to what we call *depgrams* (word pairs with a syntactic dependency link such as verb-object or noun-attribute), in a fashion similar to the method used in (Sidorov et al. 2013) to detect and correct grammatical errors. While the former (ngrams) is a surface fluency check of what is "normal", the latter (depgrams) evaluates deeper, word order-independent, syntactic relations.

4.1 Corpus-based statistics

For the ngram and depgram frequency data, mixed corpora were used, amounting to a total of 50 million tokens (words and punctuation):

Corpus	Size
	(million tokens)
Classical literature[3]	9.76
Eventoj[4] (news magazine)	1.80
Monato[5] (news magazine)	1.44
Wikipedia	16.48
Internet (mixed)[6]	19.78
All	**49.26**

Table 2: Corpus sources

After morphosyntactic analysis with EspGram, we counted word bigrams and trigrams, as well as depgrams. For the former, only word form was used, for the latter we also stored - where applicable - syntactic function (func), semantic type (semtype) and a possible preposition header (prp), in the following combinations of dependent (left) and head (right), cf. table 3:

(prp) dependent (func)	head word_2	semtype_2
lemma_1	word-word	word-sem
semtype_1	sem-word	sem-sem

Table 3: Depgram types

Part-of-speech (POS) is a (vowel-coded) morpheme category in Esperanto, and hence need not be stored separately. For PP's (b2, d2), we stored both the preposition and its - semantically more important - head. The

syntactic function field (also called edge label) was added for clause level dependents (subjects, objects, adverbials etc., cf. a2, c, d1-2), but not for phrases (a1, a3, b1), since function here is already almost unambiguously implied by POS and head type. Subject and object complement relations were treated like in-NP attributes (a4).

(a1) *tute -> same* ('completely equal')
(a2) *PHUM@SU -> organizis* ('Peter organized')
(a3) *NUM -> mm/m2* (e.g. 37 mm/m2)
(a4) *NUM -> aĝo* (e.g. 'her age was 23')

(b1) *aŭtomata -> <act>* ('automatic action')
(b2) *al/EWORD -> <FN:send>*
    (e.g. 'send [email] to xxx@gmail.com')

(c) *<f-right>@AC -> havis* ('have the right')

(d1) *<Hprof>@SU -> <FN:create>*
    (e.g. 'the carpenter built ...')
(d2) *per/<Vground>@AD -> <FN:run>*
    (e.g. 'he went by train)

As semantic types we used semantic prototypes for nouns (e.g. <act>, <f-right>) and adjectives (e.g. <jshape>), and framenet categories for verbs (<FN:....>). In order to avoid sparse data problems and to keep the database manageable, certain highly productive word types were replaced with a letter dummy: PHUM (human proper noun), PTIT (work-of-art title), PORG (organization name) POTH (other proper nouns), PTWIT (twitter name), EWORD (emails, URLs), YEAR, DATE and NUM (non-letter cardinal numbers).

In the database, ngram counts are stored as *relative* frequencies (i.e. divided by unigram/lower order frequencies), so they can be used to predict the likelihood of a given ngram given its left part. For depgrams, mutual information is used:

- bigrams: f(ab) / f(a)

- trigrams: f(abd) / f(ab)

- depgrams: f(a->b) * n / f(a)*f(b)

where a, b and c are adjacent words (or, for depgrams, lemmas), and n is the number of tokens in the corpus.

---

[3] A mixed corpus of internet-available Esperanto books

[4] An Esperanto biweekly published 1992-2002

[5] http://www.monato.be/

[6] A 2012 crawl downloaded from: http://wortschatz.uni-leipzig.de/en/download/

4.2 Sentence grading

We compute the acceptability score of a sentence as the sum of its bigram, trigram and depgram scores, which again are the sums of the corresponding scores for the individual words in context, divided by the number of bigrams, trigrams and depgrams that contributed to the score.

$$\frac{\sum_{i=1}^{n} bg_i}{n-1} + \frac{\sum_{i=1}^{n} tg_i}{n-2} + \frac{\sum_{j=1}^{d} dg_j}{d}$$

Since bigrams (bg) and trigrams (tg) are used to measure cohesion at the surface level, they only are computed for words, and their number therefore depends directly on the number of words in the sentence (n).

The depgram score, on the other hand, is designed to measure the semantic acceptability of word relations, and is computed in a more complex and more semantic fashion. First, inflected forms are lemmatized, function labels added for clause level dependents and relations copied from preposition dependents to their arguments, regarding the preposition as a kind of case marker. Second, for all content words, corpus depgram frequencies are checked for all 4 combinations of lemma and semantic type (cf. table 3).

By using different weights for the different types[7] of ngrams and depgrams, their respective impact on the sum count can be controlled. For instance, since trigrams contain more information (are more constrained) than bigrams, we use higher weights for the former. Depgrams are scored with the square root of their likelihood, and in addition assigned the following weight factors:

depgram type	weighting
clause level dependent (with function label)	* 3
sem -> sem relation	log 2
coarse/simpli ed sem categories	* 0.2

Table 4: Weights

When no depgram corpus match is found for any of the 4 word/sem combinations[8], a second round of look-ups is performed, where a more coarse-grained semantic ontology is used for nouns, collapsing all subcategories for the types of 'human', 'animal', 'plant', 'things', 'place', 'vehicle', 'tool', 'food', 'domain', 'semantical' and 'substance', and by allowing internal cross-matching for all action/event categories and for all unit categories. A few ambiguous categories are tested twice, for different umbrella categories. For instance, <sem-r> ('readable', e.g. *book*) can be used as either a 'thing' (combining with verbs like *throw*, *put* and *borrow*) or 'semantical', being *read*, *written* or *translated*.

In addition, zero frequencies are punished by negative weights, i.e. when there is no example of a given depgram relation in the corpus:

depgram type	clause level	other
sem -> sem	-12	-8
word -> sem sem -> word	-6	-3
word -> word	-2	-0.1

Table 5: Punishments

Finally, there is a grammatically motivated punishment (-5) for NP agreement mismatches, and a frame-based punishment (-20), if neither the ordinary or coarse-grained semantic type of a verb argument matches the semantic condition of the corresponding argument slot in the verb frame.

4.3 Word grading

In addtion to grading whole sentences, it is pedagogically useful to be able to identify "outlier" words, that do not fit the rest of the sentence. Possible applications are slot filler exercises, but also as a kind of "fuzzy" proofing tool, that goes beyond simple spell- and grammar checking and is able to flag odd lexical choices in written L2 production.

Every time, an ngram or depgram combination is evaluated, the sum score of the participating words is adjusted correspondingly. Implementing

---

[7] Multiple occurrence of the same ngram in the sentence is weighted down by using the square root.

[8] Obviously, words can be semantically ambiguous and carry more than one semantic tag, with the parser being unable to choose. In these cases, the matching check is performed twice, before progressing to the fallback option of more coarse-grained umbrella tags.

a left-to-right prediction approach, the affected word is the last one in bigrams and trigrams. For depgrams it is intuitively more likely that the head is seen as the primary part, and the dependent as either matching or offending, assuming that the brain thinks *idea* first, and then is more likely to expand the concept into a *good idea* than a *blue idea*, rather than coming up with a colour and then finding a head noun for it. Therefore, when inheriting depgram scores, dependents are weighted twice as heavily as heads, and heads cannot inherit negative (punishing) scores. Still, heads should get some depgram scoring, too, because learners may make lexical errors and wrong synonym choices for heads, too, and in these cases it is useful to know if a given head is supported by a matching choice of attributes (for nouns) or arguments (for verbs).

After a long row of experiments and improvements, weights and punishments were ultimately chosen in a mostly empirical fashion, designed to yield positive scores for acceptable word choices and negative scores for conflicting words, balancing the positive values from corpus data matches on the one hand with negative values for lexical punishments on the other.

However, while both sentence and word scores represent a cline of acceptability without discrete breaks, we also introduced three types of unary flags for specific dependent mismatches:

'?'   frame mismatch at the clause level

'*'   missing corpus evidence for a sem/sem match or a clause-level word/sem match[9]

'%'   agreement mismatch in noun phrases

These markers can either be used for specific error flagging, or as a secondary filter (3) after eliminating sentences with (1) negative overall scores or (2) one or more negative word scores.

(a) 12.4 *patrino* (33.5 *bakis* (62.2) *bongustan* (18.3) *kukon* (98) . 'mother baked a delicious cake'

(b) 5.25 *viro* (8.0) *vendis* (25) *bluan* (4.67) auxton (41.41) . 'a man sold a blue car'

(c) 2.04 *patrino* (11.9) *vendis* (11) *bluan* (-4.29) *kukon** (5.15) . 'mother sold a blue cake'

(d) 0.24 *patrino* (11.9) *vendis* (11) *bluajn*% (-12.7) *kukon** (5.91) . 'mother sold blue cakes'

(e) -0.09 *viro* (2.8) *mangxis* (3.35) *bluan* (4.67) *auxton*?* (-21.7) . 'a man ate a blue car'

(f) -3.51 *oro*?* (-40) *bakis* (1.1) *bluan* (4.67) *auxton*?* (-24). 'a ower baked a blue car'

(g) -4.05 *oro*? *(-27) *bakis* (0) *bluan* (-5.36) *sonĝon*?* (-32.14). 'a ower baked a blue dream'

In the graded example sentences, (a-d) have positive scores and would be semantically acceptable, but (d) could be filtered out for grammatical reasons - it exhibits an agreement error, because the object (-n) NP *'blue cakes'* has the adjective in the plural (-j), and its head in the singular. Furthermore, both (c) and (d) contain a negative word score, due to the lack of corpus evidence for blue cakes. At the clause level, the selling of cakes has lexical frame support, but an asterisk is added, because the corpus does not have an example of a selling verb with 'cake' as object. At the top end, a *mother baking* and a *cake* being *delicious* (a) are both more typical (i.e. have higher mutual information in statistical terms) than a *man selling* and a *car* being *blue* (b). The negatively scored sentences all contain one or more words that not only fail the corpus test, but also violate generalized frame conditions ('?'-mark). Thus, cars can't be eaten (e), plants can't bake (f). *Dream* (g) mismatches both at the clause level (with *bake*) and at the phrase level (with *blue*).

5   Language-specific adaptations

In principle, the sentence-grading system presented here is largely language independent, as long as a corpus of sufficient size, a dependency parser of sufficient quality and - not least - a framenet and semantic ontology are available for the language in question. However, two areas of language-specific adaptation should be born in mind, both concerning morphology.

First, we used words rather than lemmas, and treated prepositions as a kind of noun-prefix. While this is an easy way to capture surface clues for co-occurrence, and would work for e.g. Germanic languages in general, it is problematic for morphologically rich languages, where inflectional variation would create a sparse data problem. For such languages, lemmas should be

[9] There can be more than one asterisk, because they are assigned for each level separately. The worst case (***) means a mismatch even at the coarse-grained semantic level.

used instead of words. In the absence of prepositions, case categories should be used instead.

The second language-specific adaptation was the exploitation of the regular affixation system of Esperanto for semantic purposes. We already discussed the use of semantic class-conveying affixes in section 3.3. A different method is to strip semantically transparent affixes off roots in order to classify otherwise unlisted, productive forms:

verb affixes: *ek-* (inchoative), *-ad* (durative), *re-* (iterative), *fin-* (resultative)

general affixes: *-eg* (big, intensely), *-et* (small, moderately)

The suffixes *-ig* (turn into) and *-iĝ* (become) are not transparent when added to a noun root. With verbs, however, they are used to increase *(-ig)* or decrease *(-iĝ)* transitivity. Thus, *-ig* means 'make (object) do', and the frame of the root verb can be used for semantic matching, with the original object becoming the subject of the recovered root verb. Conversely, *-iĝ* has a passivization effect on a transitive verb, and the original subject can be matched against the object slot of the root verb.

Finally, two verb-adjectivizing affixes, *-ebl* (x-able) and *-ind* (worth x-ing) can be used to match an NP head against the object slot of the adjectivized verb. For instance, in *manĝ-ebla planto* (eat-able/edible plant) the NP head 'plant' can be matched against the object slot of 'eat'. Similarly, in *manĝ-inda kuko*, 'cake' becomes the object worth eating.

6 Evaluation

Obviously, sentence generation (section 3) is more robust than sentence grading (section 4), because the former will only produce what is sanctioned by the input vocabulary and dictionary-based frames. Sentence grading, however, has to work on unknown sentences, and its performance may suffer from lexical coverage problems, sparse data in the corpus database and, not least, missing or too-constrained frames. Especially the latter is a problem in the face of free, creative input from ordinary language users. Thus, in the controlled environment of course-based substitution table sentences, and with the course itself as part of its

database, the tool performed very well, and accepted very few sentences that should have been discarded. In order to test for false positives (falsely discarded) sentences in a less constrained environment, we removed the course texts from the database, and submitted the entire teaching material[10] (7,363 words) to the sentence grader. In this run, only 1.4% of the (supposedly correct) sentences received negative scores. At the word level, there were 3.3% negative scores. Flags for missing frame support (?-flag) and missing dependency corpus support (*-flag) appeared in 5.3% and 2.4% of cases. However, neither negative score nor flags are a safe marker for unacceptability. For instance, negative scores can be caused by bad ngram scores even in the face of a frame match, and conversely, corpus "proof" can compensate for a missing frame, preventing a negative score. Therefore, to increase precision and limit the number of false positives, flags and scores should be combined for automatic use. Thus, at the clause-level, a combined frame failure (?) and corpus evidence failure (*) only occurred in 0.1% of words, and with a double condition for negative score AND a '?' or '*' flag, false positives were down to 0.64% and 1.6%, respectively.

Without a corpus of L2 learner texts, and in the absence of funding for extensive manual evaluation, it is difficult to evaluate the risk of false negatives (i.e. accepted sentences that should have been discarded) in external texts, but it is still possible to use the above method and estimate the prevalence of false positives, even on a larger scale, by simply running the evaluator on text that is not produced by learners, and is supposed to be correct. For our experiments we used a collection of short stories[11] (61,676 words), that are part of the advanced-learner material on the Esperanto teaching site lernu.net.

As expected, the short stories, with almost 4 times as many morphemes and lemmas, and sentences that were on average 75% longer, were more difficult for the evaluator program, with considerably more false positives, i.e. words with negative scores in supposedly normal sentences.

---

[10] after removing non-sentence parts such as word lists.

[11] 46 texts, written by Claude Piron, accessed at https://lernu.net/eo/biblioteko/106 (June 2019). Together, the texts contain approximately 5000 non-name lemmas, built from about 1200 morphemes.

	Course materials	Lernu.net short stories
sentences	*1,233*	*5,921*
with neg. score	1.4 %	0.86 %
words	*7,363*	*61,676*
per sentence	*5.97*	*10.4*
with neg. score	2.6%	7.3 %

	%	neg.	%	neg.
frame failure (?)	5.3	0.64	3.5	1.5
corpus failure (*)	2.4	1.6	5.9	3.7
both ? and *	0.1	0.1	0.5	0.5

Table 6: Evaluation - False positives

However, at the sentence level there were fewer false positives, indicating that the individual negative scores were milder, or that there was more corpus support from ngrams. One reason for the former could be the lower incidence of frame failures[12], which are punished harder than corpus failures and therefore contribute more to a negative word score than corpus failures. In any case the unclear balance between ? and * flags is another reason for a 'in dubio pro reo' approach, where words are regarded as problematic only, if they fail on all accounts (both frames and corpus). With this condition, the rate of false positives is very low even for the more complex short story corpus (0.5%).

7   Conclusions and outlook

We have shown how a combination of syntactic-analytic (dependency parsing) and semantic-lexical resources (verb frames and noun/adjective ontologies) on the one hand, and corpus data on the other can be used to build a semantically constrained sentence generator and grader for Esperanto. While intended for teaching use with a restricted vocabulary, the method is also applicable to unrestricted input. However, performance is dependent on corpus size and variety, as well as on lexical coverage for frames. Inspection of scoring errors suggested that future work should focus not just on the number of frames, but - maybe more importantly - on the the coverage of the semantic

slot filler information for frame arguments. Still, with a limited vocabulary, this is a tractable task and can be addressed for a given course or textbook individually (as was done for our own course materials), not least by simply making the annotated materials part of the corpus[13]. In practical terms, words with a negative score in our evaluation (i.e. false positives) could be used as a point of departure for this work.

Apart from improving linguistic resources for a CALL-prioritized lexicon, future work should include evaluation with human annotators grading both automatic test sentences and learner sentences for (semantic) acceptability. This would make it possible to evaluate recall (false negatives) rather than just precision (false positives), and also to examine if machine scores can emulate a human scale of *degree* of sentence acceptability from least to most acceptable.

Acknowledgments

This research was carried out at the University of Southern Denmark, in the framework of an international 2-year CALL project co-funded by the European Union's Erasmus+ programme.

References

Bick, Eckhard. 2009. A Dependency Constraint Grammar for Esperanto. Constraint Grammar Workshop at NODALIDA 2009, Odense. NEALT Proceedings Series, Vol 8, pp. 8-12. Tartu: Tartu University Library. ISSN 1736-6305

Bick, Eckhard. 2012. Towards a Semantic Annotation of English Television News - Building and Evaluating a Constraint Grammar FrameNet, In: Proceedings of the 26th Pacific Asia Conference on Language, Information and Computation (Bali, 7-10 November, 2012). pp. 60-69. Faculty of Computer Science, Universitas Indonesia. ISBN 78-979-1421-17-1

Bick, Eckhard. 2016. A Morphological Lexicon of Esperanto with Morpheme Frequencies, In: Calzolari, Nicoletta et al. (eds.), Proceedings of the 10th International Conference on Language Resources and Evaluation, LREC2016 (Portorož, May 23-28, 2016). pp. 1075-1078. ISBN 978-2-9517408-9-1

Bick, Eckhard. 2019. A Semantic Anthology of Danish Adjectives. In: Simon Dobnik, Stergios Chatzikyriakidis, Vera Demberg (editors):

---

[12] With correct input, frame failures are basically lexical coverage errors. Since frequent verbs usually have the most complex grammar, the larger lemma spread in the short stories possibly leads to a higher percentage of less frequent, but easier verbs, while the teaching corpus exploits its relative few verbs to the full in combinatorial terms.

---

[13] It should be born in mind that for our evaluation on course materials, these were intentionally removed from the corpus first.

Proceedings of IWCS 2019 - 13th International Conference on Computational Semantics (Gothenburg, 23-27 May 2019). ACL Anthology W19-04. pp. 71-78. URL: http://aclweb.org/anthology/W19-04

Lee, K.J.; Y. Choi and J.E.Kim. 2011. Building an Automated English Sentence Evaluation System for Students Learning English as a Second Language. Computer Speech and Language, 25. pp. 246-60

Lilley, Jason; Amanda Stent; Ilija Zeljkovic. 2012. A Random, Semantically Appropriate Sentence Generator for Speaker Verification. In: Proceedings of ICSLP (INTERSPEECH-2012). pp. 739-742.

Ng, Hwee Tou; Siew Mei Wu; Ted Briscoe; Christian Hadiwinoto; Raymond Hendy Susanto; Christopher Bryant. 2014. The CoNLL-2014 Shared Task on Grammatical Error Correction. In: Proceedings of the Eighteenth Conference on Computational Natural Language Learning (2014, Baltimore): Shared Task, pp. 1-14. ACL

Sidorov, Grigori; Anubhav Gupta; Martin Tozer; Dolors Catala; Angels Catena; Sandrine Fuentes. 2013. Rule-based System for Automatic Grammar Correction Using Syntactic N-grams for English Language Learning (L2). In: Proceedings of the Seventeenth Conference on Computational Natural Language Learning (CoNLL2013, Sofia): Shared Task, pp. 96-101

Yannakoudakis, Helen. 2013. Automated Assessment of English-learner Writing. Technical Report Number 842. University of Cambridge Computer Laboratory. UCAM-CL-TR-842. ISSN 1476-2986

Toward automatic improvement of language produced by non-native language learners

Mathias Creutz   **Eetu Sjöblom**

Department of Digital Humanities

Faculty of Arts

University of Helsinki

Unioninkatu 40, FI-00014 University of Helsinki, Finland

{mathias.creutz, eetu.sjoblom}@helsinki.fi

Abstract

It is important for language learners to practice speaking and writing in realistic scenarios. The learners also need feedback on how to express themselves better in the new language. In this paper, we perform automatic paraphrase generation on language-learner texts. Our goal is to devise tools that can help language learners write more correct and natural sounding sentences. We use a pivoting method with a character-based neural machine translation system trained on subtitle data to paraphrase and improve learner texts that contain grammatical errors and other types of noise. We perform experiments in three languages: Finnish, Swedish and English. We experiment with monolingual data as well as error-augmented monolingual and bilingual data in addition to parallel subtitle data during training. Our results show that our baseline model trained only on parallel bilingual data sets is surprisingly robust to different types of noise in the source sentence, but introducing artificial errors can improve performance. In addition to error correction, the results show promise for using the models to improve fluency and make language-learner texts more idiomatic.

1 Introduction

It is difficult to express oneself well in a new language. Language students can learn grammar and vocabulary by filling in blanks in carefully prepared exercise sentences, but the students also need to practice speaking and writing in realistic scenarios. When students write their own texts, they need corrective feedback. We are interested in finding out to what extent computers can provide the necessary corrections, a task traditionally performed by human teachers. However, human teachers are not always available and the students will want to carry on using the language outside the language class. A tool helping language learners to produce more correct and more natural sounding expressions can enhance the learning process and encourage the students to use the new language in real situations. In addition, findings since the 1980s suggest that language students that receive corrective feedback from computers rather than human teachers learn better and perceive the feedback as more neutral and encouraging (Behjat, 2011).

In this paper, we study automatic paraphrasing methods on sentences produced by learners of three languages: Finnish, Swedish and English. A paraphrase is an alternate way of expressing a meaning using other words than in the original utterance, such as the sentence pair: *"Why don't you watch your mouth?"* ↔ *"Take care what you say."*

Our goal is to discover to what extent we can improve the spelling, grammar and naturalness of text written by non-native language users. We are not primarily interested in creating spell or grammar checkers, but we are interested in seeing whether it is possible to make "noisy" non-standard sentences sound more natural. Non-native users may be struggling to find fluent, natural sounding idiomatic expressions. Paraphrase generation may be a way to "translate" sentences produced by language learners to sentences that are grammatically correct and sound more authentic to native speakers.

In the present work, we do not set out to explicitly mark the errors made by the learners or suggest corrections to each of the errors separately. Rather, for each sentence produced by the non-

Mathias Creutz and Eetu Sjöblom 2019. Toward automatic improvement of language produced by non-native language learners. *Proceedings of the 8th Workshop on Natural Language Processing for Computer Assisted Language Learning (NLP4CALL 2019)*. Linköping Electronic Conference Proceedings 164: 20–30.

native language user, we propose an alternative, corrected sentence. The proposed sentence can differ significantly, or not at all, from the original sentence, depending on the quality of the original input. By comparing the original and altered sentence, the language learner can identify errors and learn new expressions.

Our work is closely related to the field of grammatical error correction (GEC), although our focus is broader. We are not only interested in *grammar*, but also in fluency and naturalness in a broader sense. Furthermore, the concepts of *error* and *correction* are too narrow, in our opinion, since we are interested in better, or more effective, ways of conveying a message.

Nonetheless, from our point of view, GEC can provide us with useful data sets, methods, as well as evaluation guidelines and metrics. Dahlmeier et al. (2013) introduce the NUCLE corpus, which was used in the CoNLL-2014 shared task on Grammatical Error Correction (Ng et al., 2014). NUCLE is an annotated corpus of English texts written by non-native English speakers. Twenty-eight error types have been annotated manually, such as incorrect preposition or verb tense. Napoles et al. (2017) present JFLEG, an English parallel corpus incorporating fluency edits, in order not only to correct grammatical errors but also make the original text more native sounding. Anastasopoulos et al. (2019) add Spanish translations to the JFLEG corpus.

Grammatical error correction systems are typically evaluated using metrics that compare the corrections suggested by the system to a set of gold standard corrections. The MaxMatch (M^2) algorithm (Dahlmeier and Ng, 2012) matches the system output to the gold standard and computes the sequence of edit operations that has maximal overlap with the gold standard annotation. This set of corrections is then scored using the F_1 measure. In the CoNLL-2014 shared task (Ng et al., 2014), the M^2 scorer is revised. In order to emphasize the precision of the suggested corrections twice as much as recall, the $F_{0.5}$ measure is used instead of F_1. Felice and Briscoe (2015) propose another metric, the I measure, which addresses some shortcomings of M^2, such as not distinguising between not proposing an edit versus proposing the wrong edit. Napoles et al. (2015) develop the Generalized Language Evaluation Understanding metric (GLEU) inspired by BLEU (Papineni et al., 2002), which seems to correlate better with the human ranking than the F and I measures.

When it comes to methods utilized in GEC, a broad range of approaches exist. The participants in the CoNLL-2014 shared task (Ng et al., 2014) propose systems based on classifiers (Naïve Bayes, averaged perceptron, maximum entropy), statistical language models, phrase-based and factored translation models, rule-based approaches, as well as combinations of these methods. More recently, machine translation has been the predominant framework. Sentences containing errors are translated into corrected sentences. Neural machine translation (NMT) generally requires large amounts of training data and has been shown to be sensitive to noisy data (Belinkov and Bisk, 2018). Therefore approaches have been suggested where "noise" of the desired characteristics are incorporated in the training data, such that the system learns to remove the noise in the translation (Belinkov and Bisk, 2018; Michel and Neubig, 2018; Anastasopoulos et al., 2019). Combining neural machine translation with statistical machine translation (SMT) is also claimed to produce better results (Grundkiewicz and Junczys-Dowmunt, 2018). Furthermore, GEC can be studied as a low-resource machine translation task, where in addition to adding source-side noise other techniques are used: domain adaptation, a GEC-specific training-objective, transfer learning with monolingual data, and ensembling of independently trained GEC models and language models (Junczys-Dowmunt et al., 2018), noisy channel models (Flachs et al., 2019) and unsupervised SMT (Katsumata and Komachi, 2019).

We are interested in the Nordic languages Finnish and Swedish. In addition, we perform experiments on English data. We use neural machine translation to produce paraphrases of original sentences written by non-native language learners. We are especially interested in the low-resource scenario, where in-domain, task-specific training data is scarce or non-existent, which is the case with Finnish and Swedish. Our approach uses multilingual character-level NMT in combination with out-of-domain machine translation data to deal with the lack of task-specific data. The data sets used for training and testing are described in Section 2. Our machine translation model and training process are described in Section 3. We then turn to our experiments in Section 4. The models are evaluated using qualitative analysis and manual annotation, and the results are described in Section 5. Finally we conclude with a discussion in Section 6.

2 Data

We test our models on genuine text produced by non-native language learners. For training we use a large collection of subtitles.

2.1 Test data

As our test data we use parts of the YKI Corpus.[1] The corpus has been compiled from the examinations of the Finnish National Certificates of Language Proficiency, which is a language testing system for adults. Examinations can be taken in nine languages: English, Finnish, German, Italian, North Sami, Russian, Spanish, and Swedish. There are three test levels (basic, intermediate and advanced), which offer six levels of proficiency (1–2, 3–4, 5–6). The corpus contains data from all nine languages and levels. The YKI corpus is intended for research purposes. Access is provided by request.[2]

For each of our languages of study (Finnish, Swedish, and English) we have extracted the texts produced by twelve different language learners at random.[3] We have used the so-called "new material (2011–)". The learners are on proficiency levels 1–2 and the writing assignments given to them are on the basic level. The texts in the data represent the genres "informal letter or message", "formal letter or message", "opinion", "feedback" and "announcement". Examples of three texts in the data are shown in Table 1. The full extracted Finnish set contains 376 unique sentences, Swedish 332, and English 315. The data sets do not contain corrected versions of the sentences.

The backgrounds of the learners of Finnish and Swedish are quite diverse, whereas the English data is produced by a more homogeneous group of people. The Finnish learners consist of nine women and three men. Their native languages are: Russian (3), English (2), Chinese (2), German (1), Spanish (1), Turkish (1), and other (2). Among

the Swedish learners there are ten women and two men. Their native languages are: Finnish (3), English (2), Estonian (2), Russian (1), French (1), German (1), Thai (1), and other (1). The English learners consist of eight men and four women. Eleven are native Finnish speakers and one is a Swedish speaker.

2.2 Training data

Our models are trained on data extracted from subtitles from movies and TV episodes. Large numbers of subtitles have been collected from `http://www.opensubtitles.org/` and aligned across languages to produce the OpenSubtitles corpus (Lison and Tiedemann, 2016; Lison et al., 2018). We have used the parallel subcorpora English–Finnish (23 million sentence pairs), English–Swedish (15 million sentence pairs), and Finnish–Swedish (12 million sentence pairs). These corpora allow us to train multilingual machine translation systems between the three languages, but it is also possible to perform so-called "zero-shot" translation from one language to itself.

The style of the subtitle data is not a perfect match for our test data. However, the conversational nature of subtitles make them suitable for modeling dialogues and everyday colloquial language (Lison et al., 2018). Our test data is produced by language learners at a basic level, who are mostly trying to express themselves in everyday language. In that sense it makes sense to use OpenSubtitles as training data. Furthermore, the subtitles are not restricted to a narrow genre or domain. The movies and TV series span from light-hearted productions for toddlers to historic dramas targeting older audiences, involving quite varied and distinct vocabulary (Paetzold and Specia, 2016).

In some of our experiments we use additional, monolingual data from the Opusparcus corpus (Creutz, 2018). Opusparcus consists of sets of sentential paraphrases, that is, pairs of sentences in the same language that mean essentially the same thing. The paraphrases of Opusparcus have been extracted from the OpenSubtitles corpus, so this monolingual data is similar in style to our bilingual training data. We use the Finnish, Swedish and English subsets of Opusparcus.

---

[1] `http://yki-korpus.jyu.fi/?lang=en`
[2] E-mail: `yki-info@jyu.fi`
[3] The participant IDs are: fi: 75798, 75946, 76023, 76030, 76354, 76357, 76361, 76362, 76365, 80504, 85081, 86465; sv: 70094, 70096, 70489, 72570, 72919, 76606, 76686, 76757, 76758, 76759, 77974, 77975; en: 68079, 68112, 69336, 69632, 69635, 69874, 72098, 72099, 72262, 76537, 76705, 77616.

Moi Maija: Minä olen kiinassa lomamatkalla. Olen ollut Kiinassa kahden viikoon. Minä jo kävi monissa kaupungissa. Se oli tosi mukavaa matkaa. Tavataan paljon ystäviä. Olen syönyt paljon kiinalaista herkuiset ystäviäni mukaan. Tosi hauskaa! Minä vielä haluan käymään Shanghaissa ja ostan jotaikin Shanghaista. Toivottavasti, nähdään pian! Terveisin, Matti
Hejsan Tove! Nu har jag äntligen kommit till mitt nya stad Vaasa. Jag mår verkligen bra men litet trött är jag. Flyttningen till bostaden tog fyra timmar och de var två män som hjälpte mig att bära tunna möbler. Bostaden är ljus och här finns stora fönster som ger dagljus till rummet. Det finns två rum, kök och WC, 56m alltså ganska stor lokalen åt mig. Kom och hälsa mig nästa månad. Vi ska ringa. Varma hälsningar åt er alla, Maija
Dear Bob! Thank you for a gift. It was beatufull! You still remember even we haven't met for long time. We celebreat with family our home. Parents, brothers, sisters were there. Family things... We had one thing which I don't Forget never. We take a photo where were Mum and Dad, both sisters and my brother all together the one picture! All peoples same place. Awsome. Please visit to us Bob. I would like to see You very soon! Yours, Matti

Table 1: Examples of three texts of the genre "informal letter" from the YKI Corpus (fi, sv, en). All of these particular three texts contain errors, but in comparison the Swedish text seems to be on the most advanced level, followed by English and Finnish. Despite the errors the texts are intelligible.

3 Model and Training

We adopt the neural machine translation (NMT) approach to paraphrase generation, using a standard encoder-decoder architecture. In an encoder-decoder model, the encoder maps an input sentence to a sequence of continuous vectors. The decoder then generates an output sentence based on the vector representations. Multiple different encoder and decoder choices can be used in the overall encoder-decoder architecture. Architectures based on recurrent neural networks (Luong et al., 2015) or self-attention (Vaswani et al., 2017) are the most common.

For our experiments, we choose the Transformer model by Vaswani et al. (2017). The Transformer has achieved state-of-the-art results in NMT and has found wide use in different sequence-to-sequence problems. It is based solely on self-attention within the encoder and the decoder, as well as attention between the encoder and the decoder, discarding the recurrent connections found in many earlier NMT architectures (Bahdanau et al., 2014; Luong et al., 2015). We train all our models as character-based models in an attempt to make the models more robust to typos and other noise present in the data. For training the multilingual models, we follow Johnson et al. (2017) by prefixing each source sentence with a target-language flag.

The hyperparameter choices for the Trans-

former model follow the recommended setup of OpenNMT-py (Klein et al., 2017), which we use for all experiments. We use 6 layers in both the encoder and the decoder, hidden states and character embeddings with 512 dimensions with separate embeddings for the encoder and decoder, 8 attention heads, and a feed-forward network with 2048 dimensions within the layers. We use a dropout probability of 0.1 between layers. All models are trained for 300k steps or until convergence, with a validation score as the convergence criterion. We use the Adam optimizer (Kingma and Ba, 2014) with a learning rate of 0.0001 and a token batch size of 4096. At inference time we use beam search with beam size 12 to produce the outputs.

4 Experiments

We perform experiments on translation models trained in five different setups. All setups are built on our baseline model, which can translate from any of the three languages Finnish, Swedish or English to any of the same three languages.

4.1 Baseline model trained on bitexts

Our baseline model is trained on all of the Open-Subtitles parallel data (bitexts) for the three languages. This amounts to a total of approximately 50 million unique sentence pairs. We use both directions for all language pairs, but do not train on monolingual data (that is, the source and target sentences are never in the same language). We use this model to produce paraphrases in two ways:

i) Zero-shot translation within the same language: For instance, the model translates from Finnish to Finnish although it has never seen training data where both the source and target sentence have been Finnish sentences. However, the training data does contain Finnish source and target sentences, but always aligned with a sentence in another language.

ii) Pivoting via a second language: The source sentence is translated into another language and then back to the source language. For example, a Finnish sentence is translated into English and then back to Finnish.

4.2 Baseline + Clones

As the baseline model does not see monolingual data during training, paraphrases have to be generated either using zero-shot translation or pivoting. Because zero-shot translation generally suffers from lower performance compared to language pairs seen during training, we attempt to improve the model by adding monolingual data. We do this by simply using copies of sentences from the OpenSubtitles training sets in addition to the full parallel data. We randomly sample 10 million sentences per language and use the same sentence as the source and target during training.

4.3 Baseline + Opusparcus

Because we are interested in generating fluent and natural paraphrases for the input sentences, we also experiment using paraphrase pairs as monolingual data instead of cloned sentences. In this case the model sees alternative ways of formulating sentences, phrases and lexical items. An example of an English source/target pair is: *"He believes in you." ↔ "He has faith in you."* Our paraphrase pairs come from the Opusparcus paraphrase corpus. We use 20 million pairs for English, 3.5 million for Finnish, and 1.8 million for Swedish. These data set sizes have been shown to perform well in a paraphrase detection task in earlier work (Sjöblom et al., 2018).

4.4 Baseline + Error-augmented monolingual data

The OpenSubtitles data consists of mostly clean sentences and proper language, although some noise, such as misspellings or optical character recognition errors, is present (Tiedemann, 2016).

This is in contrast to our test data, where the majority of sentences contain errors. In our fourth setup we introduce artificial noise to our training data in an attempt to improve performance on noisy test sentences. We sample one million sentences for each language from the OpenSubtitles data, and for each sentence generate an erroneous pair using two types of errors: 1) Typos are introduced by randomly deleting a character from a word, swapping two adjacent characters, inserting an extra character or duplicating a character. 2) Inflection errors are introduced by randomly changing the inflection of a noun or a verb within the sentence using the UralicNLP toolkit for Finnish (Hämäläinen, 2019) and HFST tools for English and Swedish (Lindén et al., 2013). We randomly introduce 1–3 errors from either category to each sentence. The erroneous sentence is used as the source and the original as the target during training. Examples 1 and 2 show source sentences with typos and inflection errors respectively, with the corresponding correct targets:

1. *Ae taskuussa näköjään **voittsa tikarrin** saappaassa. → Ase taskussa näköjään voittaa tikarin saappaassa.*

2. *After she **attacks** you, perhaps you **had see** her? → After she attacked you, perhaps you have seen her?*

4.5 Baseline + Error-augmented bilingual data

Finally, in an attempt to improve the pivot-based method without monolingual data, we augment bilingual data for all language pairs with errors. We sample one million sentences pairs for each language pair, and use the same sentence pairs for both translation directions. The pipeline for generating the erroneous data is identical to the previous setup. The source sentences contain artificially introduced errors, whereas the target sentences are correct, as in: *"I had to **got the bigger one's**." → "Piti saada isompi."*

5 Evaluation

Our test sets do not contain gold standard reference sentences, and therefore we cannot use automated metrics to evaluate our models. Instead we will attempt to analyze the output of our models qualitatively and we also perform manual annotation of the generated sentences in two of the setups.

5.1 Qualitative evaluation

As expected, the baseline model (Section 4.1) performs poorly in a zero-shot translation scenario. The model is generally unable to produce a paraphrase with the same semantic content as the source sentence, and many of the produced sentences contain artifacts that can be traced back to one of the other languages, and the multilingual nature of the model. Examples of such artifacts are producing mixed language or incorrectly translating false friends, such as: *"Siinä on Teidän perheen valokuva."* → *"Siinä on erään **familjen** valokuva.",* *"Thank you for a gift."* → *"Thank you for a **poison**."* (The Swedish word for *family* has been inserted into a Finnish sentence, and the English word *gift* means poison in Swedish.)

Pivoting through another language works better as the model now only needs to translate between language pairs explicitly trained on. Examples of the intermediate steps (pivot languages) and the final paraphrases can be seen in Table 2. Many of the errors in the original source sentences have been corrected, although some sentences retain incorrect sentence structure or word forms from the source. Distortion of the source sentence semantics can also be seen in some cases. In the pivot scenario we also deal with the problem of compounding errors because of the two separate translation steps.

We now turn to the models trained on monolingual data in addition to bilingual parallel data. A general trend emerges with all three models where monolingual data was used (Sections 4.2, 4.3, and 4.4). The models will most of the time simply copy the source, including the errors present in the sentence. While this is somewhat expected of the model where clones were used, it is surprising that even the model with paraphrase data exhibits this behavior. The Opusparcus paraphrase corpus does not contain pairs with identical source and target sentences. The error-augmented monolingual data seems to aid in correcting some typographical errors in the source sentences but does not correct bad inflection to the same extent. The sentence structure of the generated paraphrase is generally identical to that of the source sentence: *"I **wiss** that you move the other **plase** and you can sleep very well"* → *"I **wish** that you move the other place and you can sleep very well"*

Guided by the results from pivot-based methods and the attempts to use monolingual data in training, our final setup incorporates error-augmented bilingual data instead of monolingual data (Section 4.5). A look at the generated phrases does not reveal consistent improvements over the baseline model, as shown in Table 3. The baseline model already corrects most typos, and while there are examples of phrases where the baseline model generates an incorrect word or inflection and the error-augmented model a correct one, the converse is true in other cases. We will compare the quality of the two models using manual annotations in the next section.

5.2 Manual annotation

Based on the qualitative assessment in the previous section, we have chosen to manually annotate paraphrases generated by two models using the pivot-based method. The models selected for annotation are the baseline model as well as the model with added error-augmented bilingual data. Annotators were shown one sentence pair at a time. The annotation task was to compare the original sentence to the generated paraphrase and assess the correctness and semantic adequacy of the parapahrase using a single four-grade scale. The annotation categories were the following: 1 (Bad paraphrase, erroneous language), 2 (Mostly bad paraphrase, multiple errors), 3 (Mostly good paraphrase, minor errors), and 4 (Good paraphrase, correct language).

For English and Finnish, two independent annotations were collected for each paraphrase. The inter-annotator agreement as measured by Cohen's Kappa is 0.43 (Moderate) for English and 0.50 (Moderate) for Finnish. Only one person annotated Swedish and consequently no inter-annotator agreement score can be calculated.

The manual annotation results are shown in Table 4. The results show an overall trend of the error augmented model performing better. For all languages the percentage of phrases annotated as 1 decreases, that is, the models generate less completely incorrect paraphrases. On the other end of the scale, the percentage of phrases annotated as category 4 decreases slightly for English, increases very slightly for Finnish, and increases significantly for Swedish.

6 Discussion and Conclusion

We have shown that a straight-forward character-based neural machine translation model trained on

Hey, Mary. I'm in China on vacation. I've been in China in two weeks. I already went to many towns. It was a really nice trip. Meet a lot of friends. I've eaten a lot of Chinese friends with my delicious friends. That's really funny! I still want to go to Shanghai and buy something from Shanghai. I hope I'll see you soon! Hello, Matt. $\rightarrow$ *Hei, Mary. Olen Kiinassa lomalla. Olen ollut Kiinassa kahden viikon päästä. Kävin jo monissa kaupungeissa. Se oli mukava matka. Tässä on paljon ystäviä. Olen syönyt paljon kiinalaisia ystäviäni. Todella hauskaa! Haluan yhä ostaa jotain Shanghailta. Toivottavasti näen sinut pian! Hei, Matt.*
Hi, Tove! Now I've finally come to my new city Vaasa. I'm really fine, but I'm a little tired. The moving to the house took four hours and they were two men who helped me carry thin furniture. The house is light and here are big windows that give daylight to the room. There are two rooms, kitchen and kitchen, 56 metres of the local for me. Come and tell me next month. We're gonna call. Warm greetings for all of you. Maija. $\rightarrow$ *Hej, Tove! Nu har jag äntligen kommit till min nya stad Vaasa. Jag mår bra, men jag är lite trött. Att flytta till huset tog fyra timmar och de var två män som hjälpte mig att bära tunna möbler. Huset är ljust och här är stora fönster som ger dagsljus till rummet. Det finns två rum, kök och kök , 56 meter för mig. Kom och berätta nästa månad. Vi ringer. Varma hälsningar för er alla. Maja.*
Hyvä Bob! Kiitos lahjasta. Se oli hienoa! Muistat vieläkin, ettemme ole tavanneet pitkään. Juhlimme perhettämme. Vanhemmat, veljet, siskot olivat siellä. Perheasioita... Meillä oli yksi asia, jota en koskaan unohda. Otamme kuvan, missä äiti ja isä olivat, molemmat siskoni ja veljeni yhdessä. Kaikki ihmiset samaan paikkaan. Mahtavaa. Käykää Bobin luona. Haluaisin nähdä sinut pian! Sinun, Matti. $\rightarrow$ *Good Bob! Thank you for the gift. That was great! You still remember we haven't met long. We're celebrating our family. Parents, brothers, sisters were there. Family things. We had one thing I'll never forget. We'll take a picture where Mom and Dad were, both my sisters and my brother together. All people in the same place. That's great. Go to Bob's. I 'd like to see you soon! Yours, Matti.*

Table 2: Illustration of the baseline pivoting method for the three source texts in Table 1. The Finnish and Swedish texts have been translated to English (in small font) and back to Finnish and Swedish (in larger font). The English text has been translated to Finnish (small font) and back to English (larger font).

out-of-domain parallel data can effectively correct a multitude of different error types in text without the explicit modeling of these errors. Some further examples of corrected errors are shown in Table 5.

This is an important finding, as language is complex and hard to handle successfully in a "silo manner", fixing typos, grammar and naturalness isolated from each other in separate steps. We initially had an idea of using existing proofing tools (spell checkers) in a preprocessing phase. However, many errors are not unambiguously spelling mistakes, as they may produce valid word forms, but which are wrong in context. We also considered an "oracle" approach for comparison, in which we would fix all the typos manually before applying our automatic methods, but it turned out difficult to decide what exactly were plain typos

and how far the "oracle" would stretch.

We have chosen character-based models in order for these models to be less sensitive to noisy data. Using full words or longer word fragments would introduce numerous out-of-vocabulary words, when words in source sentences contain spelling mistakes. Comparing to Google Translate (Table 6) it seems that Google is more sensitive to noise related to typos and largely leaves such errors unfixed (for instance, the "English" words *beatufull* and *awsome*).

In line with earlier work on translation of non-native text (Anastasopoulos et al., 2019), we find that augmenting clean parallel data with artificially-introduced errors can make a system more robust and improve performance. In our case we find a discrepancy between different lan-

Hello, Mary. I'm on a vacation. I've been in China in two weeks. I already went to many cities. It was a really nice journey. Meet a lot of friends. I've eaten a lot of Chinese friends with me. That's really funny. I want to go to Shanghai and buy something about Shanghai. Hopefully, I'll see you soon! Hello, Matt.

$\rightarrow$

Hei, Mary. Olen lomalla. Olen ollut Kiinassa kahden viikon päästä. Menin jo moneen kaupunkiin. Se oli mukava matka. Tavataan paljon ystäviä. Olen syönyt paljon kiinalaisia ystäviä kanssani. Todella hauskaa. Haluan mennä Shanghaihin ostamaan jotain Shanghaista. Toivottavasti nähdään pian. Hei, Matt.

Hey, Tove! Now I've finally come to my new town Vaasa. I'm really good, but I'm tired. The movement to the residence took four hours and they were two men who helped me wear thin furniture. The residence is light and here are big windows that give daylight to the room. There's two rooms, kitchen and WC, so there's pretty big local for me. Come and tell me next month. We're gonna call. Hot greetings for all of you. Maija

$\rightarrow$

Tove! Nu har jag äntligen kommit till min nya stad Vaasa. Jag är verkligen bra, men jag är trött. Rörelsen tog fyra timmar och de var två män som hjälpte mig att bära möbler. Bostaden är ljus och här är stora fönster som ger dagsljus till rummet. Det finns två rum, kök och WC, så det finns ganska stort lokalt för mig. Kom och berätta nästa månad. Vi ringer. Varma hälsningar för er alla. Maija

---

Rakas Bob! Kiitos lahjasta. Se oli hämmästyttävää! Muistat vielä, ettemme ole tavanneet pitkään aikaan. Juhlimme perheemme kanssa. Vanhemmat, veljet, siskot olivat siellä. Perheasioita... Meillä oli yksi asia, jota en unohda. Otamme kuvan, jossa äiti ja isä olivat, molemmat siskot ja veljeni yhdessä yhdessä kuvassa! Kaikki ihmiset samassa paikassa. Mahtavaa. Käy luonamme, Bob. Haluaisin nähdä sinut pian! Sinun, Matti.

$\rightarrow$

Dear Bob ! Thank you for the gift. It was amazing! You remember that we haven't met in a long time. We're celebrating with our family. Parents, brothers, sisters were there. Family things... We had one thing I won't forget. We'll take a picture where Mom and Dad were, both sisters and my brothers in one picture! All people in the same place. That's great. Come to us, Bob. I'd like to see you soon! Yours, Matti.

Table 3: Illustration of the baseline pivoting method augmented with artificial errors for the three source texts in Table 1. The Finnish and Swedish texts have been translated to English (in small font) and back to Finnish and Swedish (in larger font). The English text has been translated to Finnish (small font) and back to English (larger font).

	Model	1	2	3	4
en	Baseline	28.7	23.0	18.9	29.4
	+Errors	23.5	25.2	23.5	27.8
fi	Baseline	33.1	24.1	16.0	26.8
	+Errors	30.4	25.1	17.3	27.2
sv	Baseline	19.1	25.6	17.1	38.2
	+Errors	11.8	25.3	16.8	46.2

Table 4: Manual annotation results for the Baseline model and the Baseline model with error-augmented bilingual data (+Errors). Proportion [%] of generated sentences annotated as one of the four categories.

guages, with English improving the least and Swedish the most. Differences in translation quality between the different language pairs can be a contributing factor, as there is the least amount of Swedish data for training, which may explain the proportionally larger benefit of additional training data. However, we also note that the degree of inter-annotator agreement is rather low, which may call for clearer annotation guidelines in the future.

A potential bottleneck in our approach is the pivoting method. When two different translation steps are included in the pipeline, the risk of compounding errors increases, and the model is dependent on the quality of two translation directions. We leave for future work further investi-

<table>
<tr><td>

Minä löydäin pientä koiraa kadulla. → *Löysin pienen koiran kadulta.*
Siella on hyvää kaverit. → *Siellä on hyviä tyyppejä.*
Minä asun toisella puolella kaupungilla. → *Asun kaupungin toisella puolella.*
1. opettaja oli kärsiväinen → *Ensimmäinen opettaja oli kärsivällinen.*

</td></tr>
<tr><td>

Det finns inte länge bort här. → *Det är inte långt härifrån.*
darfor att jag glommde i dag är min mamas fodelsedag, och jag behöver går där. → *Jag glömde att idag är min mammas födelsedag och jag måste gå dit.*
Jag hopas du är inte arg! → *Jag hoppas att du inte är arg!*
Jag måste hjälpa min systorna på en school-projekten. → *Jag måste hjälpa mina systrar på ett skolprojekt.*   (Here a small error remains. The preposition should be: ... **med** *ett skolprojekt.*)

</td></tr>
<tr><td>

Other chance is not. → *There's no other chance.*
Depence if you take with new tires or with old one's. → *Depends if you take new tires or old tires.*
They have very funny. → *They're having fun.*
The first you must to talk to these young people for this problem. → *First you have to talk to these young people about this problem.*

</td></tr>
</table>

Table 5:   Examples of successful corrections of sentences in the test data. These translations have been produced using the baseline pivoting approach. Typical errors in the Finnish input are incorrect inflections, incorrect word choices and omissions of umlauts. Similar errors occur in the Swedish data with additional challenges related to word order, agreement and foreign words. The native language of the authors of the English sentences is revealed by the Finnish sentence structure of the English sentences.

gations into how monolingual data could be used effectively to circumvent the need for pivoting and increase performance.

In addition to fixing obvious grammatical errors in source sentences, we find cases where our model introduces fluency edits. This can be seen, for instance, in more idiomatic choices of words: it is typical for non-native Swedish speakers to use the verb *finna*, which resembles *to find* in English and means the same thing, but a more natural choice would be the verb *hitta*. Our models do change *finna* to *hitta*. Similarly, the Finnish expression *mennä takaisin* (go back) is replaced by *palata* (return).

Together our results show promise for using a standard NMT approach to improving and paraphrasing noisy language learner text. As test data we have used Finnish, Swedish and English portions of the YKI corpus, which to our knowledge have not been studied in this setting before, and could be of special interest to a Nordic audience. As far as computer-assisted language learning is concerned, we find the fluency edits introduced by the models especially encouraging. The models go beyond simple grammatical error-correction and can help language learners improve their skills toward more fluent and native-like language production. We believe that our approach is particularly beneficial to more advanced learners, who want to be able to use their new language more autonomously, in situations where no human teacher is available.

Acknowledgment

The authors wish to acknowledge CSC, the Finnish IT Center for Science, for providing the computational resources needed to carry out the experiments in this study.

References

Antonios Anastasopoulos, Alison Lui, Toan Nguyen, and David Chiang. 2019. Neural machine translation of text from non-native speakers. In *Proceedings of NAACL-HLT 2019*, pages 3070–3080, Minneapolis, Minnesota.

Dzmitry Bahdanau, Kyunghyun Cho, and Yoshua Bengio. 2014. Neural machine translation by jointly learning to align and translate. *arXiv preprint arXiv:1409.0473*.

Fatemeh Behjat. 2011. Teacher correction or word processors: Which is a better option for the improvement of EFL students writing skill? *Journal of Language Teaching and Research*, 2(6):1430–1434.

Yonatan Belinkov and Yonatan Bisk. 2018. Synthetic and natural noise both break neural machine translation. In *International Conference on Learning Representations*.

Moi Mai: Olen Kiinan loma-matka. Olen ollut Kiinassa kaksi viikoonia. Menin jo moniin kaupunkeihin. Se oli todella mukava matka. Nähdään paljon ystäviä. Olen syönyt paljon kiinalaisia ystäviä herkuisetiin. Todella hauskaa! Haluan edelleen käydä Shanghaissa ja ostaa jotain Shanghaissa. Toivottavasti nähdään pian! Ystävällisin terveisin Matti

Hejsan Tove! Nu har jag äntligen kommit till min nya stad Vaasa. Jag känner mig väldigt bra men lite trött är jag. Flyttet till hemmet tog fyra timmar och de var två män som hjälpte mig att bära tunna möbler. Boendet är ljust och här finns stora fönster som ger dagsljus till rummet. Det finns två rum, kök och toalett, 56 m så ganska stort rum för mig. Kom och se mig nästa månad. Vi ringer. Varma hälsningar till er alla Maija

Good Bob! Thank you for the gift. It was beatufull! You still remember that we haven't met for a long time. We celebrate with our family with our family. Parents, brothers, sisters were there. Family matters ... We had one thing I would never forget. We take a photo of mother and father, both sisters and brothers together in one picture! All nations in the same place. Awsome. Visit us Bob. I'd like to see you soon! You, Matti

Table 6: Applying the pivoting method using Google Translate (as of June, 2019). The Finnish and Swedish texts have been translated to English and then back. The English text has been translated to Finnish and back. In comparison to our own results in Tables 2 and 3 it is not obvious which method is the most effective, as Google Translate does not seem to cope well with errors in the source sentences.

Mathias Creutz. 2018. Open Subtitles Paraphrase Corpus for Six Languages. In *Proceedings of the 11th International Conference on Language Resources and Evaluation (LREC 2018)*, Miyazaki, Japan. European Language Resources Association (ELRA).

Daniel Dahlmeier and Hwee Tou Ng. 2012. Better evaluation for grammatical error correction. In *2012 Conference of the North American Chapter of the Association for Computational Linguistics: Human Language Technologies*, pages 568–572, Montreal, Canada.

Daniel Dahlmeier, Hwee Tou Ng, and Siew Mei Wu. 2013. Building a large annotated corpus of learner English: The NUS corpus of learner English. In *Proceedings of the Eighth Workshop on Innovative Use of NLP for Building Educational Applications*, pages 22–31, Atlanta, Georgia. Association for Computational Linguistics.

Mariano Felice and Ted Briscoe. 2015. Towards a standard evaluation method for grammatical error detection and correction. In *Human Language Technologies: The 2015 Annual Conference of the North American Chapter of the ACL*, pages 578–587, Denver, Colorado.

Simon Flachs, Ophélie Lacroix, and Anders Søgaard. 2019. Noisy channel for low resource grammatical error correction. In *Proceedings of the Fourteenth Workshop on Innovative Use of NLP for Building Educational Applications*, pages 191–196, Florence, Italy. Association for Computational Linguistics.

Roman Grundkiewicz and Marcin Junczys-Dowmunt. 2018. Near human-level performance in grammatical error correction with hybrid machine translation. In *Proceedings of NAACL-HLT 2018*, pages 284–290, New Orleans, Louisiana.

Mika Hämäläinen. 2019. UralicNLP: An NLP library for Uralic languages. *Journal of Open Source Software*, 4(37):1345.

Melvin Johnson, Mike Schuster, Quoc V Le, Maxim Krikun, Yonghui Wu, Zhifeng Chen, Nikhil Thorat, Fernanda Viégas, Martin Wattenberg, Greg Corrado, et al. 2017. Google's multilingual neural machine translation system: Enabling zero-shot translation. *Transactions of the Association for Computational Linguistics*, 5:339–351.

Marcin Junczys-Dowmunt, Roman Grundkiewicz, Shubha Guha, and Kenneth Heafield. 2018. Approaching neural grammatical error correction as a low-resource machine translation task. In *Proceedings of NAACL-HLT 2018*, page 595606, New Orleans, Louisiana.

Satoru Katsumata and Mamoru Komachi. 2019. (Almost) unsupervised grammatical error correction using synthetic comparable corpus. In *Proceedings of the Fourteenth Workshop on Innovative Use of NLP for Building Educational Applications*, pages 134–138, Florence, Italy. Association for Computational Linguistics.

Diederik P Kingma and Jimmy Ba. 2014. Adam: A method for stochastic optimization. *arXiv preprint arXiv:1412.6980.*

Guillaume Klein, Yoon Kim, Yuntian Deng, Jean Senellart, and Alexander M. Rush. 2017. OpenNMT: Open-source toolkit for neural machine translation. In *Proc. ACL*.

Krister Lindén, Erik Axelson, Senka Drobac, Sam Hardwick, Juha Kuokkala, Jyrki Niemi, Tommi A Pirinen, and Miikka Silfverberg. 2013. HFST – a system for creating NLP tools. In *International Workshop on Systems and Frameworks for Computational Morphology*, pages 53–71. Springer.

Pierre Lison and Jörg Tiedemann. 2016. OpenSubtitles2016: Extracting large parallel corpora from movie and TV subtitles. In *Proceedings of the 10th International Conference on Language Resources and Evaluation (LREC 2016)*, Portorož, Slovenia.

Pierre Lison, Jörg Tiedemann, and Milen Kouylekov. 2018. OpenSubtitles2018: Statistical Rescoring of Sentence Alignments in Large, Noisy Parallel Corpora. In *Proceedings of the 11th International Conference on Language Resources and Evaluation (LREC 2018)*, Miyazaki, Japan. European Language Resources Association (ELRA).

Minh-Thang Luong, Hieu Pham, and Christopher D Manning. 2015. Effective approaches to attention-based neural machine translation. *arXiv preprint arXiv:1508.04025*.

Paul Michel and Graham Neubig. 2018. MTNT: A testbed for machine translation of noisy text. In *Proceedings of the 2018 Conference on Empirical Methods in Natural Language Processing*.

Courtney Napoles, Keisuke Sakaguchi, Matt Post, and Joel Tetreault. 2015. Ground truth for grammatical error correction metrics. In *Proceedings of the 53rd Annual Meeting of the Association for Computational Linguistics and the 7th International Joint Conference on Natural Language Processing (Short Papers)*, pages 588–593, Beijing, China.

Courtney Napoles, Keisuke Sakaguchi, and Joel Tetreault. 2017. JFLEG: A fluency corpus and benchmark for grammatical error correction. In *Proceedings of the 15th Conference of the European Chapter of the Association for Computational Linguistics*, volume 2.

Hwee Tou Ng, Siew Mei Wu, Ted Briscoe, Christian Hadiwinoto, Raymond Hendy Susanto, and Christopher Bryant. 2014. The CoNLL-2014 shared task on grammatical error correction. In *Proceedings of the Eighteenth Conference on Computational Natural Language Learning: Shared Task*, pages 1–14.

Gustavo Henrique Paetzold and Lucia Specia. 2016. Collecting and exploring everyday language for predicting psycholinguistic properties of words. In *Proceedings of COLING 2016, the 26th International Conference on Computational Linguistics: Technical Papers*, pages 669–1679, Osaka, Japan.

Kishore Papineni, Salim Roukos, Todd Ward, and Wei-Jing Zhu. 2002. BLEU: a method for automatic evaluation of machine translation. In *Proceedings of the 40th Annual Meeting of the Association for Computational Linguistics (ACL)*, pages 311–318, Philadelphia, Pennsylvania.

Eetu Sjöblom, Mathias Creutz, and Mikko Aulamo. 2018. Paraphrase detection on noisy subtitles in six languages. In *Proceedings of W-NUT at EMNLP*, Brussels, Belgium.

Jörg Tiedemann. 2016. Finding alternative translations in a large corpus of movie subtitles. In *Proceedings of the 10th International Conference on Language Resources and Evaluation (LREC 2016)*, Portorož, Slovenia.

Ashish Vaswani, Noam Shazeer, Niki Parmar, Jakob Uszkoreit, Llion Jones, Aidan N Gomez, Łukasz Kaiser, and Illia Polosukhin. 2017. Attention is all you need. In *Advances in neural information processing systems*, pages 5998–6008.

Linguistic features and proficiency classification in L2 Spanish and L2 Portuguese

Iria del Río

University of Lisbon, Center of Linguistics - CLUL
`igayo@letras.ulisboa.pt`

Abstract

This work explores the relationship between L2 proficiency levels and certain linguistic features through experiments in automatic proficiency classification. We use L2 Spanish and L2 Portuguese data and perform monolingual and cross-lingual experiments. We also compare native and leaner Spanish texts. To the best of our knowledge, this is the first work that performs automatic proficiency classification for L2 Spanish, as well as cross-lingual proficiency classification between L2 Portuguese and L2 Spanish. Our results for L2 Spanish are similar to the state-of-the-art, while our cross-lingual experiments got lower results than similar works. In general, all the experiments suggest new insights about the relationship between linguistic features and proficiency levels in L2 Portuguese and L2 Spanish.

1 Introduction

Proficiency classification is a common task in second language learning. The linguistic development of the learner is usually defined through a scale that accounts for different levels of linguistic complexity. One of the most common scales is the one described in the Common European Framework of Reference for Languages (CEFR) (Europe et al., 2009). The CEFR defines 3 broad divisions: A, basic user; B, independent user; C, proficient user. These classes are subdivided into 6 development levels: A1 (beginner), A2 (elementary), B1 (intermediate), B2 (upper intermediate), C1 (advanced) and C2 (proficient). Each level relates

to specific linguistic features and skills, and the whole scale establishes a progression from a very rudimentary language to a performance close to a native production. CEFR has become the most common framework for second language learning in Europe, and in this context, it is common that learners perform placement tests that define their proficiency level according to the CEFR scale. The interest of an automatic system that can perform this task is, therefore, evident.

Automatic proficiency classification is considered as a type of Automatic Essay Scoring (AES) task. AES has been explored mainly for English (Burstein, 2003; Burstein and Chodorow, 2012; Yannakoudakis, 2013), but recent approaches have dealt with other languages (Vajjala and Loo, 2013). Researchers have modeled AES as a regression (Yannakoudakis et al., 2011), a ranking (Taghipour and Ng, 2016) or a classification problem (Pilán et al., 2016). Different types of features have been used in the task, from Bag-of-words (BOW) to more abstract representations that use higher levels of linguistic information (morphological, syntactic or even discursive). It is also very common the use of metrics that have been linked to proficiency development and/or linguistic complexity in the area of Second Language Acquisition (SLA), like lexical richness or syntactic complexity. Automatic proficiency classification has been approached mainly as a monolingual task, but recent approaches like (Vajjala and Rama, 2018) have explored multi and cross-lingual perspectives.

In our experiments, we use the main levels of the CEFR scale (A, B, C) and supervised machine learning techniques to classify L2 Portuguese and L2 Spanish texts. As features, we test different linguistic representations, from BOW to syntactic dependencies, and some complexity features. We perform monolingual and cross-lingual experiments, and we compare native to L2 productions

Iria del Río 2019. Linguistic features and proficiency classification in L2 Spanish and L2 Portuguese. *Proceedings of the 8th Workshop on Natural Language Processing for Computer Assisted Language Learning (NLP4CALL 2019)*. Linköping Electronic Conference Proceedings 164: 31–40.

in Spanish. Furthermore, we try to answer the following questions: which linguistic features capture better the proficiency of a L2 text in Spanish and Portuguese? Are those features similar between these two close languages? When comparing L1 and L2 Spanish, which linguistic characteristics allow for predicting the level of linguistic development of a text? We present relevant related work in section 2, and our methodology in section 3. In section 4 we describe the experiments performed and discuss our results, while in section 5 we summarize our conclusions and future directions of work.

2 Related Work

In this section we focus on two types of research: SLA studies that have analyzed the relationship between certain linguistic features and proficiency levels, and approaches that have used machine learning to predict L2 proficiency using the CEFR scale.

Lu (2012) analyses in detail the relationship between proficiency in L2 English and several lexical dimensions, concluding that the features linked to lexical variation (like Type-Token ratio) are the most correlated to the quality of a L2 essay. Several features identified as relevant in this work have been used by automatic approaches afterwards. Crossley and McNamara (2011) and more recently Eckstein and Ferris (2018) compare L1 and high proficiency L2 English texts through different metrics of lexical sophistication, syntactic complexity and cohesion. Both studies conclude that L2 texts can be clearly differentiated from L1 texts, and (Crossley and McNamara, 2011) shows also homogeneity between L2 learners with different native languages (L1). Other characteristics like error patterns have been studied too, mainly for English (Tono, 2000), (Lu, 2012), (Vyatkina, 2012), but also for other languages (Gyllstad et al., 2014).

Yannakoudakis et al. (2018) is one of the most recent works for automatic proficiency classification of L2 English. The authors use a subset of the Cambridge Learner Corpus with human proficiency annotations (levels A1 to C2), and model the task as a ranking function. They use features as character sequences, POS, phrase structure rules or errors rates. The best model gets a Pearson r of 0.765 and a Spearman ρ of 0.773, with a κ of 0.738 (the standard error is 0.026) which indicates high agreement between the predicted CEFR scores and those assigned by humans. In another recent study, Vajjala and Rama (2018) present the first multi and cross-lingual approach for proficiency classification. They use 2,286 manually graded texts (five levels, A1 to C1) from the MERLIN learner corpus (Boyd et al., 2014). It is an unbalanced dataset, with the following distribution: German, 1,029 texts; Italian, 803 texts, and Czech, 434 texts. They use a wide range of features: word and POS n-grams; task-specific word and character embeddings trained through a softmax layer; dependency n-grams (not used before); domain features mainly linked to lexical aspects (Lu, 2012); and error features. In their experiments, monolingual and multilingual models achieve similar performance, and cross-lingual classification yields lower, but comparable results to monolingual classification. For monolingual experiments, the best result (F1-score) is achieved with word n-grams plus domain features (German=0.686; Italian 0.837; Czech= 0.734). (Vajjala and Lõo, 2014) performs proficiency classification for Estonian. They use a corpus of 879 texts, with four proficiency levels (A2 to C1) and also a balanced version of this dataset with 92 texts per category. They compare classification and regression models, and use a set of 78 features that considers morphological aspects and lexical richness features inspired by (Lu, 2012). Interestingly, POS models achieved a poor performance and were not considered in the feature set. The best model is classification, with an accuracy of 79% in the whole dataset and 76.9% in the balanced one. For both datasets, the category with the poorest performance is B2. The authors perform a feature analysis and show that 10 of the 27 best features they identified are lexical (like Corrected Type Token Ratio) and morphological.

3 Methodology

3.1 Corpus

For our experiments we used two different datasets: NLI-PT (del Río et al., 2018) for L2 Portuguese and CEDEL2 corpus (Lozano, 2009) for L2 Spanish. While CEDEL2 is a learner corpus with a planned design, NLI-PT is a compilation of learner texts that belong to four different L2 corpora. Because of this, CEDEL2 is more homogeneous in terms of L1, task and topic than NLI-PT. CEDEL2 has also native texts that constitute a control corpus. We have used these texts for some experiments too, as we will see below. NLI-PT contains annotated versions of learners' texts with two types of linguistic information: morphological (POS) and syntactic (constituency and dependencies). CEDEL2 corpus is not annotated so, to extract the linguistic features that we needed for our experiments, we added similar annotations as the ones in NLI-PT. We incorporated fine-grained POS information using the Spanish tagger of Freeling (Padró and Stanilovsky, 2012), and syntactic dependencies using the DepPattern toolkit (Otero and González, 2012) for L2 and native texts. We also extracted several complexity metrics from both datasets using our own scripts (see section 3.2).

The way to conceptualize proficiency levels is also different in NLI-PT and CEDEL2. While NLI-PT texts are classified according to the CEFR scale, CEDEL2 uses a different classification system. In CEDEL2 the level of the text is determined through a placement test that uses a scale from 0 to 100. Since we are interested in using the CEFR scale as our reference, we converted the CEDEL2 scale to CEFR using the equivalences that the CEDEL2 team has established.[1] In our experiments, we consider the three major levels of the CEFR scale: A, basic user; B, independent user; C, proficient user.

In total, NLI-PT dataset contains 3,069 L2 Portuguese texts, and CEDEL2 1,778 L2 Spanish essays and 796 native Spanish texts. Tables 1 and 2 show the distribution of learner texts by proficiency level in each dataset.

Proficiency Level	Number of Texts
A - Beginner	1,388
B - Intermediate	1,215
C - Advanced	466
Total	**3,069**

Table 1: Distribution of texts by CEFR proficiency level in NLI-PT.

3.2 Features

We were interested in investigating the impact of different linguistic features in the classification task. As a first approach to the task in L2 Spanish and cross-lingual L2 Spanish-Portuguese, we

Proficiency Level	Number of Texts
A - Beginner	456
B - Intermediate	675
C - Advanced	647
Total	**1,778**

Table 2: Distribution of learner texts by CEFR proficiency level in CEDEL2.

were interested in testing basic linguistic representations like BOW or POS n-grams. These features have been proved as useful in previous experiments like (Vajjala and Rama, 2018) or (Yannakoudakis et al., 2018), and they are already available in NLI-PT dataset (and they are easy to get for CEDEL2). Considering the evident importance of complexity features, we included some of them in our experiments too but, due to time and space limitations, we did not explore the wide spectrum of linguistic complexity.[2] We defined the following sets of features for our experiments:

1. **General linguistic features:**

    (a) **Bag-of-words**: this is the simpler representation of a text. We used the original word form, keeping the case. Previous experiments in proficiency classification with NLI-PT for L2 Portuguese (del Río, 2019) showed that using tokens, word forms[3] or lemmas lead to similar results in the classification task. Considering this and the fact that the original word forms may indicate patterns of orthographic deviations in the L2 texts, we kept the original word forms for the BOW representation.

    (b) **POS n-grams**: we used the fine-grained POS representation from Freeling, which contains the main POS and also morphological information, like gender or number. We consider that this information could be especially interesting because Portuguese and Spanish have a rich morphology, and this is problematic for some learners, especially at

---

[1] We thank professor Cristóbal Lozano for providing us the equivalence table.

[2] There is almost not research in linguistic complexity for Spanish or Portuguese and, therefore, there are not available tools to extract lexical or syntactic complexity measures automatically.

[3] The difference between word form and token applies in special cases like contractions or verbal forms with clitics. For example, with the verb "ligar-te" ("to call you"), we have one word form "ligar-te", but two tokens: "ligar" and "te".

the initial stages. Agreement errors like *aréia branco* (*white*-MasculineSingular *sand*-FeminineSingular) can be captured with a POS 2-gram representation, and therefore we wanted to measure the impact of this feature. We evaluated n-grams of different sizes in the experiments.

(c) **Dependency triplets n-grams**: we extracted dependency triplets with the form *relationship, head, dependent* generated with DepPattern. Dependency relationships are not commonly used in proficiency classification, and we were interested in checking their impact. We also evaluated different sizes for the dependency n-grams.

2. **Complexity features**: as we have seen, complexity features have been proved to be useful to differentiate native and learner texts. Moreover, these type of features are commonly used in the task of proficiency classification. We have selected a set of 20 descriptive, morphological and lexical features linked to linguistic complexity (see related work). We have implemented different scripts to extract the features from NLI-PT and CEDEL2.[4] This group includes different types of metrics:

(a) **Morphological metrics**: number of nouns, number of verbs, number of lexical words, etc.[5]

(b) **Lexical metrics**: type-token ratio (ttr) (with different variations: rooted ttr, corrected ttr, mean segmental ttr...), hypergeometric distribution diversity (McCarthy and Jarvis, 2010), etc.

(c) **Descriptive metrics**: average syllables per word, syllable count, word count, readability score (we used the Portuguese adaptation of the Flesch reading index (Martins et al., 1996)).

3.3 Classification and Evaluation

As we have seen, the task of proficiency testing can be considered as a classification or a regression problem, depending on the way we consider the proficiency levels, that is, as discrete or continuous units. In this work we are interested in conceptualizing proficiency levels in the same way that the CEFR scale does, that is, as discrete entities. Therefore, we modeled the problem as a classification task. Another reason to choose classification over regression is presented in (Vajjala and Lõo, 2014), who compared both approaches and got better results with the classification model.

We used the scikit-learn package (Pedregosa et al., 2011) for training and testing the models and for feature selection. We split both datasets in training and test sets (20% of data) for all the experiments. In general, for each experiment we performed initial tests to check which algorithm worked better with each set of features. In these previous experiments, we performed 10-fold cross-validation with the training set, training a different classifier for each set of features to support a comparison of them. We evaluated a varied group of linear and nonlinear algorithms: Logistic Regression (LR), Linear Discriminant Analysis (LDA), KNeighborsClassifier (KNN), DecisionTreeClassifier(CART), GaussianNB (NB), Support Vector Clustering (SVC), LogitBoost (LB) and Random Forests (RF). For each set of features, we selected the best performing model and we evaluated it against the test set.[6]

We use accuracy as the main measure to evaluate the performance of our trained models. We also report weighted-F1 score because the datasets are unbalanced. Weighted-F1 score is computed as the weighted average of the F1 score for each label, taking label support (i.e., number of instances for each label in the data) into account. We also show F1 score per class, to analyze in detail the performance of the classifiers by level. We use text length as the general baseline.

4 Experiments and results

We have performed different classification experiments to investigate the relationship between the linguistic features selected and the main CEFR proficiency levels. We investigate this relationship in three different scenarios. First, we study the interaction of features and proficiency levels for L2 Spanish, using CEDEL2 texts. Our main research question is: which linguistic features in our two sets allow for an accurate classification of CEFR

---

[4]We will make the scripts available after the publication of the paper.

[5]Counts are normalized by text length with the following formula: number of nouns/total words in text*1000.

[6]We indicate the algorithm used for each model in the tables with the results.

proficiency levels in L2 Spanish? This is a monolingual approach similar to the ones presented in the related work section. Secondly, we investigate the same interaction in a cross-lingual scenario, from Spanish to Portuguese and vice versa. With this experiment, we try to reply to two research questions: (i) are the linguistic patterns linked to each proficiency level in our two L2 languages similar to the extent that a model trained in one language can be transferred to the other?; (ii) if so, which features work better in the cross-lingual model? This is an experiment similar to the one presented in (Vajjala and Rama, 2018), where a model trained with German texts is applied to a Czech and an Italian test set. From the typological point of view, German is not close to Czech or Italian, while Portuguese and Spanish are similar languages, with a close morphology and Latin vocabulary. Considering this fact, a priori we could expect good results in the cross-lingual experiments. Finally, we study the relationship between learner and native texts, using our sets of features. For those experiments, we were interested in replying to the following research question: which are the best linguistic features to differentiate a learner text from a native one? We present our results in the sections below.

4.1 L2 Spanish

For the monolingual scenario our best result is 74% accuracy and F1 score, a result similar to the ones we can find in the current literature for other languages.[7]

Comparing the two general types of features (linguistic and complexity), all the sets of features perform better than the baseline (text length), and the linguistic features perform better than the complexity ones. All the linguistic one-feature sets get a 70% of accuracy or more, while for the complexity group only the descriptive features achieve a 70%. Among the linguistic features, the best result is for POS, which in fact achieves an accuracy similar to the best result (73% for POS and 74% for the best result). The assembled set of linguistic features perform better than the assembled set of complexity features, but worse than the POS features individually. The best result is for the combination of POS and complexity fea-

---

[7]It is important to note that, due to the unbalanced structure of our datasets, we were forced to use three classes that correspond to the main CEFR levels, while previous works generally use four or more classes.

Features	Accuracy	F1-Score
Baseline_RF	0.60	0.58
BOW_LB	0.70	0.70
POS_RF	**0.73**	**0.72**
Dep_LB	0.70	0.70
LING_LR	0.72	0.71
CoLex_LR	0.63	0.61
CoMor_NB	0.49	0.47
CoDesc_LR	0.70	0.70
COMP_LDA	**0.70**	**0.70**
POS+Co_RF	**0.74**	**0.74**
POS+Dep+Co_LR	0.74	0.73
ALL_LR	0.72	0.72

Table 3: General results for L2 Spanish.

tures (POS+Co_RF) with a 74% of accuracy and weighted F1 score. This set performs even better than all the features together. Concerning the algorithms we can see that from the initial list of eight three got the best results: RF, LR and LB.

Features	A-F1	B-F1	C-F1
Baseline_RF	0.68	0.33	0.69
BOW_LB	0.71	0.59	0.79
POS_RF	**0.76**	**0.60**	**0.82**
Dep_LB	0.72	0.61	0.78
LING_LR	0.77	0.59	0.80
CoLex_LR	0.71	0.43	0.73
CoMor_NB	0.44	0.34	0.61
CoDesc_LR	0.74	0.60	0.77
COMP_LDA	**0.73**	**0.61**	**0.77**
POS+Co_RF	**0.77**	**0.62**	**0.83**
POS+Dep+Co_LR	0.76	0.60	0.80
ALL_LR	0.77	0.62	0.80

Table 4: Results per class for L2 Spanish.

Moving to the performance by class, we can see that the level that gets the best results for all the features is C, and the level with the worst results is B. Interestingly, CEDEL2 has more B texts than C texts (675 vs. 647). The A level, which has significantly less texts than B and C (456), gets in general a similar F1 score to that of level C. This seems to indicate that A and C texts are easy to classify, while B texts are difficult, no matter the number of training texts or the set of features we employ. This result makes sense from the linguistic point of view, because A and C levels are in the extreme of the proficiency development scale, while B is in the middle and, therefore, B texts can be close to A or to C levels.

Attending to the single features as predictors of each class, POS is the best for A and C, while dependencies are the best predictor for B (although very close to POS). POS is especially useful in the classification of the C class, with a 82% of F1 score.

Summing up, our results show that linguistic features are most effective than complexity ones for classifying proficiency levels in CEDEL2, being the POS features the most useful. Among the complexity features, the descriptive ones are the most efficient for all the levels, which a similar performance to the POS set. A and C levels are easy to classify, while B is difficult, no matter what type of feature we are using.

4.2 Cross-lingual experiments: Spanish and Portuguese L2

In this case, we used (L2) CEDEL2 and NLI-PT datasets and we performed cross-lingual experiments. We tested both directions: Spanish to Portuguese and vice versa. We performed the same type of experiments as for the monolingual dataset, with the only difference that, in this case, we use the whole monolingual corpus as the training dataset, and a section of the other dataset as the testing one.

Features	Accuracy	F1-Score
Baseline_LR	**0.57**	**0.54**
BOW_CART	0.47	0.40
POS_RF	**0.57**	**0.51**
Dep_LB	0.47	0.36
LING_RF	0.50	0.40
CoLex_NB	0.43	0.42
CoMor_SVM	0.39	0.22
CoDesc_NB	0.49	0.50
COMP_NB	0.44	0.44
POS+Co_RF	**0.57**	**0.52**
POS+Dep+Co_LR	0.55	0.48
ALL_RF	0.54	0.46

Table 5: General cross-lingual results for Spanish to Portuguese.

We can see that, in general, we get poor results in the cross-lingual models. For Spanish to Portuguese, none of the trained classifiers beats the baseline, and only the combination of POS and complexity features gets close. The only one-

feature set that performs similar to the baseline is the POS one, but if we check table 6 we can see that the F1 score for level C is 0. All the combinations with complexity features get results below the baseline, being the descriptive metrics the ones with the best score. These numbers seem to be in line with the ones obtained for the monolingual dataset, with the POS and descriptive features as the most relevant in the classification task.

Features	A-F1	B-F1	C-F1
Baseline_LR	**0.67**	**0.55**	**0.54**
BOW_CART	0.61	0.33	0
POS_RF	**0.68**	**0.52**	**0**
Dep_LB	0.63	0.19	0
LING_RF	0.65	0.26	0
CoLex_NB	0.40	0.49	0.30
CoMor_SVM	0.48	0.48	0.25
CoDesc_NB	**0.60**	**0.49**	**0.25**
COMP_NB	0.48	0.48	0.25
POS+Co_RF	**0.66**	**0.55**	**0**
POS+Dep+Co_LR	0.65	0.30	0
ALL_RF	0.66	0.40	0

Table 6: Results per class for cross-lingual Spanish to Portuguese.

Concerning the results per class, POS features are the best to predict the A and B level, and lexical-complexity features the best for C. Interestingly, seven of the twelve models get a F1 score of 0 for this level, while they are able to classify the other two levels, and only the complexity features are useful to classify level C. On the other hand, all the models get the best results for the A level. Linguistic features are the more accurate for predicting this level, especially the POS features, which also get a high F1 score predicting the B level. However, they obtain a 0 F1 score predicting the C level. We can see in table 7 that for Portuguese to Spanish, POS features are also the best among linguistic features to predict level A and B, while they are the worst to predict level C. This fact seems to indicate that A and B level show certain recurrent morpho-syntactic patterns that allow for their identification cross-linguistically, while level C does not.

We could consider the different number of texts in both datasets as a possible factor for these poor results. CEDEL2 has almost half of the texts of NLI-PT, although CEDEL2 has more C texts than A texts, for example, and the performance of the classification models for the A level is always better than for the C level. Another possible factor that can impact the results is the homogeneity of CEDEL2 versus the heterogeneity of NLI-PT in terms of L1, task or topic. More experiments are necessary to check the impact of these variables.

For Portuguese to Spanish the results are better, although still lower than expected. Only the complexity models beat the baseline, being the best result for the complexity lexical features, with a 60% of accuracy and a F1 score of 58%. The descriptive-complexity features beat also the baseline, while the morphological ones do not. All the linguistic features show a low performance, being the BOW model the best one. Interestingly, in this case POS features show a low performance. These results are similar to the ones obtained for monolingual L2 Portuguese in (del Río, 2019), where the best results in the classification task were for the BOW model. Unfortunately, that work did not use all the complexity features that we present, which makes difficult a complete comparison of the results.

Features	Accuracy	F1-Score
Baseline_NB	**0.56**	**0.54**
BOW_LB	0.50	0.49
POS_CART	0.47	0.46
Dep_LB	0.46	0.44
LING_RF	0.39	0.29
CoLex_NB	**0.60**	**0.58**
CoMor_NB	0.39	0.30
CoDesc_NB	0.57	0.55
COMP_NB	0.60	0.57
POS+Co_KNN	0.48	0.45
POS+Dep+Co_KNN	0.48	0.25
ALL_KNN	0.49	0.45

Table 7: General cross-lingual results for Portuguese to Spanish.

Analyzing the results per class, for most of the models A and C level perform better than B, being the A level the easiest to identify (as we saw for monolingual and cross-lingual experiments). Among the one-feature sets, lexical-complexity features are clearly the best to predict the A level; POS (as for cross-lingual Spanish to Portuguese) and morphological-complexity features are the best for predicting the B level; and lexical-complexity features are the best to predict the C level.

Features	A-F1	B-F1	C-F1
Baseline_NB	**0.69**	**0.37**	**0.62**
BOW_LB	0.57	0.40	0.52
POS_CART	**0.59**	**0.45**	**0.37**
Dep_LB	0.51	0.31	0.54
LING_RF	0.61	0.36	0
CoLex_NB	**0.74**	**0.38**	**0.67**
CoMor_NB	0.52	**0.45**	0
CoDesc_NB	0.71	0.38	0.63
COMP_NB	0.74	0.36	0.67
POS+Co_KNN	0.65	0.48	0.28
POS+Dep+Co_KNN	0.65	0.30	0
ALL_KNN	0.66	0.40	0

Table 8: Results per class for cross-lingual Portuguese to Spanish.

Considering that NLI-PT has more texts and is less homogeneous than CEDEL2 in terms of L1 languages, topics or even tasks, which theoretically implies more variation, it seems that complexity features are the most robust to support the adaptation from one L2 to another. POS features appear to be especially useful for predicting A and B level.

We would like to note that our results are quite different to the ones obtained by (Vajjala and Rama, 2018), where the cross-lingual model trained with German texts performs similarly when tested in Czech and Italian as the corresponding monolingual models do. There are two differences between our experiments and the ones presented in that work, though: first, all the texts used in their experiments belong to the same multilingual corpus, MERLIN, factor that allows for a higher homogeneity in terms of topic and task; second, they train the model on the language with more texts (German) and test with the languages with less texts (Czech and Italian). However, German Czech and Italian are more distant languages than Spanish and Portuguese, and even so their results are stable when the model performs cross-lingual, contrary to what we found. More tests will be necessary to investigate the possible causes of this difference.

4.3 Learner texts versus Native texts in Spanish

We were interested in measuring to what extent a machine learning algorithm is able to distinguish between a text written by a learner and a text writ-

Proceedings of the 8th Workshop on Natural Language Processing for Computer Assisted Language Learning (NLP4CALL 2019)

ten by a native speaker, and also in knowing which of the features in our two sets are more useful in this task. CEDEL2 has a corpus control with 796 texts written by native speakers, covering the same topics as the L2 corpus. We created a dataset with the L2 and the native texts (L2+NAT), and we labeled the native texts with a new class, "N". Therefore, this time the classification model has to distinguish among four levels: A, B, C and N. For the selection of the algorithms, we used the same approach as before: we tested several algorithms with the training corpus, and we selected the best model to evaluate it against the testing set.

Features	Accuracy	F1-Score
Baseline_LR	0.50	0.43
BOW_RF	**0.73**	**0.73**
POS_NB	0.39	0.33
Dep_LR	0.37	0.30
LING_LR	**0.75**	**0.74**
CoLex_LR	0.62	0.61
CoMor_ NB	0.40	0.40
CoDesc_LR	0.60	0.59
COMP_LR	**0.65**	**0.64**
POS+Co_RF	0.74	0.74
POS+Dep+Co_LR	0.74	0.74
ALL_RF	**0.75**	**0.74**

Table 9: Classification including native texts.

The best result (LING and ALL) is slightly better than the best for the L2 Spanish dataset: 0.75 vs. 0.74 of accuracy. The one-feature set that performs better is BOW, with an accuracy and F1 score similar to the top result. If we compare the results for both experiments by sets of features, we can see that most of the sets get similar results, except for POS and Dep, that clearly got worse results in the L2+NAT dataset.

LING features allow for a increase in accuracy and F1 score using the native texts, while COMP features get worse results. If we analyze the results per class, it seems that the main cause of this is the behaviour of the C class. Using only learner texts, the C class got the best results, together with level A (see Table 4). However, including the native texts, the C level decreases in F1 score for all the sets of features. The combination that allows for a smaller decrease in F1 score for C is LING (80% vs. 70%). If we take a look to the confusion matrices included in Appendix A, we can see that when we include native texts many C instances

Features	A-F1	B-F1	C-F1	N-F1
Baseline_LR	0.64	0.53	0	0.58
BOW_RF	**0.78**	**0.62**	**0.67**	**0.83**
POS_NB	0	0.25	0.52	0.42
Dep_LR	0.45	0.29	0.48	0.06
LING_LR	**0.75**	**0.63**	**0.70**	**0.88**
CoLex_LR	0.75	0.52	0.49	0.70
CoMor_NB	0.47	0.27	0.40	0.46
CoDesc_LR	0.73	0.42	0.48	0.74
COMP_LR	**0.73**	**0.56**	**0.50**	**0.78**
POS+Co_RF	0.75	0.62	0.67	0.88
POS+Dep+Co_LR	0.73	0.63	0.66	**0.90**
ALL_RF	**0.76**	**0.65**	**0.67**	**0.88**

Table 10: Classification including native texts, per level.

are classified as native. However, when we have only learner classes, C texts "compete" only with B texts. In this scenario, linguistic features seem to be more effective to differentiate C texts from native ones than the complexity features, which indicates that C texts are probably more similar to native texts in terms of complexity metrics, but still different when we consider linguistic features.

POS features show a poor performance, especially if we compare them with the L2 model. POS features, which were the most informative feature there, are the less efficient here. Dependencies are not very useful either, although they work better than POS, especially for the A and the C level. None of the texts is classified as A using POS in the L2+NAT model. The system tends clearly to classify all the texts as C or N classes, although is able to classify at least 23 B texts. However, in the L2 model the system is able to correctly differentiate the three levels without favouring any of them.

5   Conclusions and future work

This work presents the first experiments on automatic proficiency classification for L2 Spanish and cross-lingual Spanish-Portuguese. We got similar results to the state-of-the art for L2 Spanish, and lower results for the cross-lingual approach. We investigated the relationship between different types of linguistic features and the three main levels of proficiency of the CEFR framework. We concluded that the linguistic features that work better for the L2 Spanish model are not the same for the cross-lingual models. POS representation performs better for monolingual L2 Spanish and cross-lingual Spanish to Portuguese. Complexity features related to lexical and descriptive aspects perform better for cross-lingual Portuguese to Spanish. Morphological-complexity features show a low performance in all the scenarios. When comparing L2 and L1 Spanish texts, linguistic features work as better predictors than complexity features. The A level is generally the easiest to predict (together with C) and B the most difficult. When we mix native and learner texts, C level is usually confused with the native one, especially when we use complexity features.

In future experiments we would like to investigate in depth the causes for the low results in our cross-lingual experiments. Specifically, we would like to investigate the influence of factors like the homogeneity of CEDEL2 versus the diversity of NLI-PT. Secondly, we would like to explore new features like metrics of syntactic and discourse complexity, as well as the use of neural models in the classification task.

A   Appendix A: Confusion matrices

Confusion matrices for the L2 Spanish monolingual experiment and L2+NAT Spanish experiment.

Comparison of results for the LING model.

	A	B	C	N
A	69	21	0	1
B	23	83	25	4
C	1	20	88	21
N	1	3	10	145

Table 11: LING model in L2+NAT Spanish.

	A	B	C
A	76	15	0
B	31	73	31
C	0	23	107

Table 12: LING model in L2 Spanish.

Comparison of results for the COMP model.

	A	B	C	N
A	65	18	7	1
B	21	72	33	9
C	1	27	63	39
N	2	7	17	133

Table 13: COMP model in L2+NAT Spanish.

	A	B	C
A	68	19	4
B	22	74	39
C	0	21	109

Table 14: COMP model in L2 Spanish.

Comparison of results for the POS model.

	A	B	C	N
A	0	18	6	67
B	0	23	64	48
C	0	1	94	35
N	0	7	70	82

Table 15: POS model in L2+NAT Spanish.

	A	B	C
A	70	20	1
B	23	73	39
C	0	15	115

Table 16: POS model in L2 Spanish.

References

Adriane Boyd, Jirka Hana, Lionel Nicolas, Detmar Meurers, Katrin Wisniewski, Andrea Abel, Karin Schone, Barbora Stindlová, and Chiara Vettori. 2014. The MERLIN corpus: Learner language and the CEFR. In *Proceedings of the Ninth International Conference on Language Resources and Evaluation (LREC'14)*, Reykjavik, Iceland. European Language Resources Association (ELRA).

Jill Burstein. 2003. The E-rater scoring engine: Automated essay scoring with natural language processing. In Mark Shermis and Jill Burstein, editors, *Automated Essay Scoring: A Cross-Disciplinary Perspective*, chapter 9, pages 113–121. Mahwah.

Jill Burstein and Martin Chodorow. 2012. Progress and New Directions in Technology for Automated Essay Evaluation. *The Oxford Handbook of Applied Linguistics*, pages 487–497.

Scott A. Crossley and Danielle McNamara. 2011. Shared features of L2 writing: Intergroup homogeneity and text classification. *Journal of Second Language Writing*, 20(4):271–285.

Iria del Río, Marcos Zampieri, and Shervin Malmasi. 2018. A Portuguese Native Language Identification Dataset. In *Proceedings of the Thirteenth Workshop on Innovative Use of NLP for Building Educational Applications*, pages 291–296, New Orleans, Louisiana. Association for Computational Linguistics.

Grant Eckstein and Dana Ferris. 2018. Comparing L1 and L2 Texts and Writers in First-Year Composition. *TESOL Quarterly*, 52(1):137–162.

Council Europe, Council Cultural Co-operation, Education Committee, and Modern Languages Division. 2009. *Common European Framework of Reference for Languages: Learning, Teaching, Assessment*.

Henrik Gyllstad, Jonas Granfeldt, Petra Bernardini, and Marie Kllkvist. 2014. Linguistic correlates to communicative proficiency levels of the CEFR: The case of syntactic complexity in written L2 English, L3 French and L4 Italian. *EUROSLA Yearbook*, 14(1):1–30.

Cristóbal Lozano. 2009. Cedel2: Corpus escrito del español como L2. In *Applied Linguistics Now: Understanding Language and Mind*, pages 197–212.

Xiaofei Lu. 2012. The relationship of lexical richness to the quality of esl learners oral narratives. *The Modern Language Journal*, 96(2):190–208.

T.B.F. Martins, C.M. Ghiraldelo, M. das Graças Volpe Nunes, and O.N. de Oliveira Júnior. 1996. *Readability Formulas Applied to Textbooks in Brazilian Portuguese*. Icmsc-Usp.

Philip M. McCarthy and Scott Jarvis. 2010. Mtld, vocd-d, and hd-d: A validation study of sophisticated approaches to lexical diversity assessment. *Behavior Research Methods*, 42(2):381–392.

Pablo Gamallo Otero and Isaac González. 2012. DepPattern: a Multilingual Dependency Parser. In *Proceedings of PROPOR*.

Lluís Padró and Evgeny Stanilovsky. 2012. FreeLing 3.0: Towards wider multilinguality. In *Proceedings of the Eighth International Conference on Language Resources and Evaluation (LREC-2012)*, pages 2473–2479, Istanbul, Turkey. European Languages Resources Association (ELRA).

F. Pedregosa, G. Varoquaux, A. Gramfort, V. Michel, B. Thirion, O. Grisel, M. Blondel, P. Prettenhofer, R. Weiss, V. Dubourg, J. Vanderplas, A. Passos, D. Cournapeau, M. Brucher, M. Perrot, and E. Duchesnay. 2011. Scikit-learn: Machine learning in Python. *Journal of Machine Learning Research*, 12:2825–2830.

Ildikó Pilán, Sowmya Vajjala, and Elena Volodina. 2016. A readable read: Automatic assessment of language learning materials based on linguistic complexity. *CoRR*, abs/1603.08868.

Iria del Río. 2019. Automatic proficiency classification in L2 Portuguese. Accepted.

Kaveh Taghipour and Hwee Tou Ng. 2016. A neural approach to automated essay scoring. In *Proceedings of the 2016 Conference on Empirical Methods in Natural Language Processing*, pages 1882–1891. Association for Computational Linguistics.

Yukio Tono. 2000. A corpus-based analysis of interlanguage development: Analysing POS tag sequences of EFL learner corpora. In *PALC'99: Practical Applications in Language Corpora*, Bern, Switzerland. Peter Lang.

Sowmya Vajjala and Kaidi Loo. 2013. Role of Morpho-Syntactic Features in Estonian Proficiency Classification. In *Proceedings of the Eighth Workshop on Innovative Use of NLP for Building Educational Applications*, Atlanta, Georgia. Association for Computational Linguistics.

Sowmya Vajjala and Kaidi Lõo. 2014. Automatic CEFR level prediction for Estonian learner text. In *Proceedings of the third workshop on NLP for computer-assisted language learning*, Uppsala, Sweden. LiU Electronic Press.

Sowmya Vajjala and Taraka Rama. 2018. Experiments with universal CEFR classification. *CoRR*, abs/1804.06636.

Nina Vyatkina. 2012. The development of second language writing complexity in groups and individuals: A longitudinal learner corpus study. *The Modern Language Journal*.

Helen Yannakoudakis. 2013. Automated assessment of English-learner writing. Technical Report UCAM-CL-TR-842, University of Cambridge, Computer Laboratory.

Helen Yannakoudakis, Øistein E Andersen, Ardeshir Geranpayeh, Ted Briscoe, and Diane Nicholls. 2018. Developing an automated writing placement system for ESL learners. *Applied Measurement in Education*, 31(3):251–267.

Helen Yannakoudakis, Ted Briscoe, and Ben Medlock. 2011. A New Dataset and Method for Automatically Grading ESOL Texts. In *Proceedings of the 49th Annual Meeting of the Association for Computational Linguistics: Human Language Technologies*, pages 180–189, Portland, Oregon, USA. Association for Computational Linguistics.

Integrating large-scale web data and curated corpus data in a search engine supporting German literacy education

Sabrina Dittrich[a] **Zarah Weiss**[a] **Hannes Schröter**[c] **Detmar Meurers**[a,b]

[a] Department of Linguistics, University of Tübingen
[b] LEAD Graduate School and Research Network, University of Tübingen
[c] German Institute for Adult Education – Leibniz Centre for Lifelong Learning
{dittrich,zweiss,dm}@sfs.uni-tuebingen.de schroeter@die-bonn.de

Abstract

Reading material that is of interest and at the right level for learners is an essential component of effective language education. The web has long been identified as a valuable source of reading material due to the abundance and variability of materials it offers and its broad range of attractive and current topics. Yet, the web as source of reading material can be problematic in low literacy contexts.

We present ongoing work on a hybrid approach to text retrieval that combines the strengths of web search with retrieval from a high-quality, curated corpus resource. Our system, *KANSAS Suche 2.0*, supports retrieval and reranking based on criteria relevant for language learning in three different search modes: unrestricted web search, filtered web search, and corpus search. We demonstrate their complementary strengths and weaknesses with regard to coverage, readability, and suitability of the retrieved material for adult literacy and basic education. We show that their combination results in a very versatile and suitable text retrieval approach for education in the language arts.

1 Introduction

Low literacy skills are an important challenge for modern societies. In Germany, 12.1% of the German-speaking working age population (18 to 64 years), approximately 6.2 million people, cannot read and write even short coherent texts; another 20.5% cannot read or write coherent texts of medium length (Grotlüschen et al., 2019), falling short of the literacy rate expected after nine years of schooling. While these figures are lower than those reported in previous years (Grotlüschen and Riekmann, 2011), there seems to be no significant change in the proportion of adults with low literacy skills when taking into account demographic changes in the composition of the population from 2010 to 2018 (Grotlüschen and Solga, 2019, p. 34), such as the risen employment rate and average level of education.

Literacy skills at such a low level impair the ability to live independently, to participate freely in society, and to compete in the job market. To address this issue, the German federal and state governments launched the *National Decade for Literacy and Basic Skills (AlphaDekade) 2016–2026*.[1] One major concern in the efforts to promote literacy and basic education in Germany is the support of teachers of adult literacy and basic education classes, who face particular challenges in ensuring the learning success of their students. Content-wise, teaching materials should be of personal interest to them and closely aligned with the demands learners face in their everyday and working life (BMBF and KMK, 2016, p. 6). Language-wise, reading materials for low literacy and for language learning in general should be authentic (Gilmore, 2007) and match the individual reading skills of the learners so that they are challenged but not overtaxed (Krashen, 1985; Swain, 1985; Gilmore, 2007). This demand for authentic, high-quality learning materials is currently not met by publishers, making it difficult for teachers to address the needs of their diverse literacy classes. Relatedly, there is a lack of standardized didactic concepts and scientifically evaluated materials, despite first efforts to address this shortage (Löffler and Weis, 2016). What complicates matters fur-

---

[1] https://www.alphadekade.de

Sabrina Dittrich, Zarah Weiss, Hannes Schröter and Detmar Meurers 2019. Integrating large-scale web data and curated corpus data in a search engine supporting German literacy education. *Proceedings of the 8th Workshop on Natural Language Processing for Computer Assisted Language Learning (NLP4CALL 2019).* Linköping Electronic Conference Proceedings 164: 41–56.

ther is that literacy and basic education classes are comprised of learners with highly heterogeneous biographic and education backgrounds. This includes native and non-native speakers, the latter of whom may or may not be literate in their native language. Low literacy skills sometimes are also associated with neuro-atypicalities such as intellectual disorders, dyslexia, or Autism Spectrum Disorders (ASD; Friedman and Bryen, 2007; Huenerfauth et al., 2009).

Given the shortage of appropriate reading materials provided by publishers, the web is an attractive alternative source for teachers seeking reading materials for their literacy and basic education classes. There is an exceptional coverage of current topics on the web, and a standard web search engine provides English texts at a broad range of reading levels (Vajjala and Meurers, 2013), though the average reading level of the texts is quite high. For German, most online reading materials appear to target native speakers with a medium to high level of literacy. Offers for low literate readers are restricted to a few specialized web pages presenting information in simple language or simplified language for language learners or children. These may or may not be suited in content and presentation style for low literate adults. Web materials specifically designed for literacy and basic education do not follow a general standard indicating how the appropriateness of the material for this context was assessed. This makes it difficult for teachers of adult literacy and basic education classes to verify the suitability of the materials. As we argued in Weiss et al. (2018), this challenge extends beyond the narrow context of literacy classes, as it also pertains to the question of web accessibility for low literate readers who perform their own web queries.

We address this issue by presenting our ongoing work on *KANSAS Suche 2.0*, a hybrid search engine for low literacy contexts that offers three search modes: free web search, filtered web search exclusively on domains providing reading materials for low levels of literacy (henceforth: *alpha sites*), and a corpus of curated, high-quality literacy and basic education materials we are currently compiling. The corpus will come with a copyright allowing teachers to adjust and distribute the materials for their classes. We thus considerably extend the original *KANSAS Suche* system (Weiss et al., 2018), which only supported web search. Differ-

ent from previous text retrieval systems for language learning, focusing on either web search or compiled text repositories (Heilman et al., 2010; Collins-Thompson et al., 2011; Walmsley, 2015; Chinkina et al., 2016), our approach instantiates a hybrid architecture in the spectrum of potential strategies (Chinkina and Meurers, 2016, Figure 4) by combining the strengths of focused, high-quality text databases with large-scale, more or less parameterized web search.

The remainder of the article is structured as follows: First, we briefly review research on readability and low literacy and compare previous approaches to text retrieval systems for education contexts (section 2). Then, we describe our system in section 3, before providing a quantitative and qualitative comparison of the three different search modes supported by our system in section 4. Section 5 closes with some final remarks on future work.

2 Related Work

Text retrieval for low literate readers or language learners at its core consists of two tasks: text retrieval, and readability assessment of the retrieved texts. We here provide some background on previous work on these two tasks as well as on the German debate on how to characterize low literacy skills. We start by reviewing work on readability analysis for language learning and low literacy contexts (section 2.1), before discussing the characterization of low literacy skills (section 2.2), and ending with an overview of text retrieval approaches for language learning (section 2.3).

2.1 Readability Assessment

Automatic readability assessment matches texts to readers with a certain literacy skill such that they can fulfill a predefined reading goal or task such as extracting information from a text. Early work on readability assessment started with readability formulas (Kincaid et al., 1975; Chall and Dale, 1995) which are still used in some studies (Grootens-Wiegers et al., 2015; Esfahani et al., 2016) despite having been widely criticized for being too simplistic and unreliable (Feng et al., 2009; Benjamin, 2012). In answer to this criticism, more advanced methods supporting broader linguistic modeling using Natural Language Processing (NLP) were established. For example, Vajjala and Meurers (2012) showed that measures of language complexity originally devised in Second Language Acquisition (SLA) research can successfully be adopted to the task of readability classification. An increasing amount of NLP-based research is being dedicated to the assessment of readability for different contexts, in particular for English (Feng et al., 2010; Crossley et al., 2011; Xia et al., 2016; Chen and Meurers, 2017b), with much less work on other languages, such as French, German, Italian, and Swedish (François and Fairon, 2012; Weiss and Meurers, 2018; Dell'Orletta et al., 2011; Pilán et al., 2015).

Automatic approaches to readability assessment at low literacy levels are less common, arguably also due to the lack of labeled training data for the highly heterogeneous group of adults with low literacy in their native language (Yaneva et al., 2016b). But there is research in this domain bringing in eye-tracking evidence to identify challenges and reading strategies for neuro-atypical readers with low literacy skills, such as people with dyslexia (Rello et al., 2013a,b) or ASD (Yaneva et al., 2016a; Eraslan et al., 2017). Two approaches should be mentioned that overcome the lack of available training data by implementing rules determined in previously developed guidelines for low literacy contexts. Yaneva (2015) presents a binary classification approach to determine the adherence of texts to Easy-to-read guidelines. Easy-to-read guidelines are designed to promote accessibility of reading materials for readers with cognitive disabilities such as 'Make It Simple' by Freyhoff et al. (1998) and 'Guidelines for Easy-to-read Materials' by Nomura et al. (2010). Yaneva (2015) applies this algorithm to web materials labeled as Easy-to-Read to investigate their compliance to the guidelines by Freyhoff et al. (1998). She shows that providers of Easy-to-Read materials overall adhere to the guidelines. This is an important finding since not all self-declared 'simple' reading materials on the web actually are suitable for readers with lower reading skills. For example, Simple Wikipedia was found to not be systematically simpler than Wikipedia (see, for example, Štajner et al., 2012, Xu et al., 2015, and Yaneva et al., 2016b), though Vajjala and Meurers (2014) illustrate that an analysis at the sentence level can identify relative complexity differences. While such research on the adherence of web materials to guidelines is an important contribution to the evaluation of web accessibility, it is less suit-

able for our education purposes, as it does not differentiate degrees of readability within the range of low literacy. In Weiss et al. (2018), we propose a rule-based classification approach for German following the analysis of texts for low literate readers in terms of the so-called Alpha Readability Levels introduced in the next section. As far as we are aware, this currently is the only automatic readability classification approach that differentiates degrees of readability at such low literacy levels.

2.2 Characterizing Low Literacy Skills

According to recent large-scale studies, there is a high proportion of low literate readers in all age groups of the population in Germany (Schröter and Bar-Kochva, 2019). For the German working age population (18–64 years), three major studies further focused on investigating the parts of the working population with the lowest level of literacy skills. The *lea. – Literalitätsentwicklung von Arbeitskräften* [literacy development of workers] study carried out from 2008 to 2010, supported by the Federal Ministry of Education and Research, was the first national survey on reading and writing competencies in the German adult population.[2] In this context, a scale of six *Alpha Levels* was developed to allow a fine grained measure of the lowest levels of literacy. These levels were empirically tested in the first *leo. – Level-One* study (Grotlüschen and Riekmann, 2011), which was updated in 2018 (Grotlüschen et al., 2019).[3]

At Alpha Level 1, literacy is restricted to the level of individual letters and does not extend to the word level. At Alpha Level 2, literacy is restricted to individual words and does not extend to the sentence level. At Alpha Level 3, literacy is restricted to single sentences and does not extend to the text level. At Alpha Levels 4 to 6, literacy skills are sufficient to read and write increasingly longer and more complex texts. The descriptions of Alpha Levels in the *lea.* and *leo.* studies are ability-based, i.e., they focus on what someone at this literacy level can and cannot read or write. Weiss and Geppert (2018) used these descriptions to derive annotation guidelines for the assessment of texts rather than people, focusing on the Levels 3 to 6 relevant for characterizing texts. Based on those annotation guidelines, Weiss et al. (2018)

---

[2]`https://blogs.epb.uni-hamburg.de/lea`
[3]`https://blogs.epb.uni-hamburg.de/leo`

developed a rule-based algorithm supporting the automatic classification of reading materials for low literacy contexts. They demonstrate that the classifier successfully approximates human judgments of Alpha Readability Levels as operationalized in Weiss and Geppert (2018).

While Alpha Levels 4 and higher still describe very low literacy skills, only Alpha Levels 1 to 3 constitute what has previously been referred to as *functional illiteracy* in the German adult literacy discourse: literacy skills at a level that only permits reading and writing below the text level. Literacy at this level is not sufficient to fulfill standard social requirements regarding written communication in the different domains of working and living (Decroll, 1981). Grotlüschen et al. (2019) argue that the term functional illiteracy is stigmatizing and therefore ill-suited for use in adult education. Instead, they refer to *adults with low literacy skills* and *low literacy*. In the following, we will use the term *low literacy* in a broad sense to refer to literacy skills up to and including Alpha Level 6. To discuss literacy below the text level, i.e., Alpha Levels 1 to 3, we will make this explicit by referring to *low literacy in a narrow sense*.

2.3 Text Retrieval for Language Learning

A growing body of research is dedicated to the development of educational applications that provide reading materials for language and literacy acquisition. Many of them are forms of leveled search engines, i.e., information retrieval systems that perform some form of content-based web query and analyze the readability of the retrieved materials on the fly, often by using readability formulas as discussed in section 2.1. The readability level of the results is then displayed to the user as additional criterion for the text choice, the results are ranked according to the level, or a readability filter allows exclusion of hits with undesired readability levels. The majority of these systems are designed for English (Miltsakaki and Troutt, 2007; Collins-Thompson et al., 2011; Chinkina et al., 2016), although there are some notable exceptions for a few other languages (Nilsson and Borin, 2002; Walmsley, 2015; Weiss et al., 2018). One of the main advantages of leveled web search engines is that they allow access to a broad bandwidth of texts that are always up-to-date. These are important features for the identification of interesting and relevant reading materials in educational contexts. Be-

yond the educational domain, leveled web search engines also contribute to web accessibility by allowing web users with low literacy skills to query web sites that are at a suitable reading level for their purposes. One example for such a system for literacy training is the original *KANSAS Suche* (Weiss et al., 2018). The system analyses web search results and assigns reading levels to them based on a rule-based algorithm which is specifically designed for low literate readers. Linguistic constructions can be (de-)prioritized to re-rank the search results.

The main drawback of such web-based approaches, however, is the lack of control of the quality of the content. This may lead to results that include incorrect or biased information or inappropriate materials, such as propaganda, racist or discriminating contents, or fake news. This issue may require the attentive eye of a teacher during the selection process. Query results may also include picture or video captions, forum threads, or shopping pages, which are unsuited as reading texts. To avoid such issues, many applications rely on restricted web searches on pre-defined websites, as is the case for FERN (Walmsley, 2015) or net-Trekker (Huff, 2008), which may also be crawled and analyzed beforehand, as in SyB (Chen and Meurers, 2017a).

Some systems extend their functionality beyond a leveled search engine and incorporate tutoring system functions. For example, the FERN search engine for Spanish (Walmsley, 2015) provides an enhanced reading support by allowing readers to flag and look up unknown words and train new vocabulary in automatically generated training material. This relates to another type of educational application that provides reading materials for language and literacy acquisition: reading tutors. Such systems generally provide access to a collection of texts that have been collected and analyzed beforehand (Brown and Eskenazi, 2004; Heilman et al., 2008; Johnson et al., 2017). The collections are usually a curated selection of high-quality texts that are tailored towards the specific needs of the intended target group. To function as tutoring systems, the systems support interaction for specific tasks, e.g., reading comprehension or summarizing tasks. One example for such a system in the domain of literacy and basic education is iSTART-ALL, the Interactive Strategy Training for Active Reading and Thinking for Adult Literacy Learners (Johnson et al., 2017). It is an intelligent tutoring system for reading comprehension with several practice modules, a text library, and an interactive narrative. It contains a set of 60 simplified news stories sampled from the California Distance Learning Project.[4] They are specifically designed to address the interests and needs of adults with low literacy skills (technology, health, family). It offers summarizing and question asking training for these texts as well as an interactive narrative with integrated tasks and immediate corrective feedback. The greater quality of curated reading materials in reading tutors comes at the cost of drawing from a considerably more limited pool of reading materials, which may become obsolete quickly. Thus, leveled web search engines as well as reading tutors have complementary strengths and weaknesses. As we will demonstrate in the following, combining the two approaches can help obtain the best of both worlds.

3 Our System

We present *KANSAS Suche 2.0*, a hybrid search system for the retrieval of appropriate German reading materials for literacy and basic education classes. While these classes are typically designed for low literate native speakers, in practice, they are comprised of native- and non-native speakers of German.[5] As the original *KANSAS Suche* (Weiss et al., 2018), which was inspired by *FLAIR* (Chinkina and Meurers, 2016; Chinkina et al., 2016), the updated system operates on the premise that users want to select reading materials in a way combining content queries with a specification of the linguistic forms that should be richly represented or not be included in the text. But *KANSAS Suche 2.0* is a hybrid system in the sense that it combines different search modes in order to overcome the individual weaknesses of web-based and corpus-based text retrieval outlined in the previous section.

More specifically, our system offers three different search modes: a) an unrestricted web search option to perform large-scale content queries on the web, b) a filtered web search to perform content queries on web pages specifically designed for low literacy and basic education purposes, and c) a corpus search mode to retrieve edited materials that have been pre-compiled specifically for the purpose of literacy and basic education courses. Users may flexibly switch between search modes if they find that for a specific search term the chosen search mode does not yield results satisfying their needs. In all three search modes, the new system allows users to re-rank search results based on the (de-)prioritization of linguistic constructions, just as in the original *KANSAS Suche*. The results are automatically leveled by readability in terms of an Alpha Level-based readability scale specifically tailored towards the needs of low literacy contexts following Kretschmann and Wieken (2010) and Gausche et al. (2014), as detailed in Weiss et al. (2018). This readability classification may be used to further filter results, to align them with the reading competencies of the intended reader. Users can also upload their own corpora to re-rank the texts in them based on their linguistic characteristics and automatically compute their Alpha Readability Levels. We understand this upload functionality as an additional feature rather than a separate search mode because it does not provide a content search and does not differ from the corpus search mode in terms of its strengths and weaknesses. Accordingly, it will not receive a separate mention in the discussion of search modes below.

3.1 Workflow & Technical Implementation

KANSAS Suche 2.0 is a web-based application that is fully implemented in Java. Its workflow is illustrated in Figure 1. The basic architecture remains similar to the original *KANSAS Suche*, see Weiss et al. (2018) for comparison, but has been heavily extended in order to accommodate the additional search options offered by our system. The user can enter a search term and start a search request which is communicated from the client to the server using Remote Procedure Calls.

The front end, based on the Google Web Toolkit (GWT)[6] and GWT Material Design[7], is shown in Figure 2.[8] It allows users to choose between the three search modes: unrestricted web search, filtered web search on *alpha sites*, and corpus search

---

[4] http://www.cdlponline.org

[5] There also are literacy and basic education classes specifically designed to prepare newly immigrated people and refugees for integration courses. Our system is being designed with a focus on traditional literacy and basic education classes. While our system is not specifically targeting German as a second language learners, it is plausible to assume that our target readers include native and non-native speakers.

[6] http://www.gwtproject.org

[7] https://github.com/GwtMaterialDesign

[8] Note that the actual front end is in German. For illustration purposes, we here translated it into English.

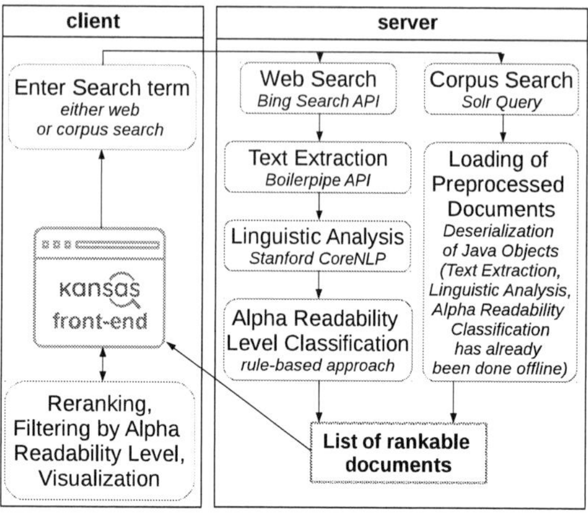

Figure 1: System workflow including web search and corpus search components

as well as the option to upload their own corpus. In the case of an unrestricted or filtered web search, the request is communicated to Microsoft Azure's BING Web Search API (version 5.0)[9] and further processed at runtime. The text content of each web page is then retrieved using the Boilerpipe Java API (Kohlschütter et al., 2010).[10] We remove links, meta information, and embedded advertisements. The NLP analysis is then performed using the Stanford CoreNLP API (Manning et al., 2014). We identify linguistic constructions with TregEx patterns (Levy and Andrew, 2006) we defined. The linguistic annotation is also used to extract all information for the readability classification. We use the algorithm developed for *KANSAS Suche* (Weiss et al., 2018), currently the only automatic approach we are aware of for determining readability levels for low literate readers in German. The resulting list of analyzed and readability-classified documents is then returned to the client side. The user can re-rank the results based on the (de-)prioritization of linguistic constructions, filter them by Alpha Readability Level, or use the system's visualization to inspect the search results. For re-ranking we use the BM25 IR algorithm (Robertsin and Walker, 1994).

The corpus search follows a separate workflow on the server side which will be elaborated on in more detail in section 3.3 after discussing the filtered web search in section 3.2.

[9]https://azure.microsoft.com/
en-us/services/cognitive-services/
bing-web-search-api
[10]https://boilerpipe-web.appspot.com

3.2 The Filtered Web Search

While the web provides access to a broad variety of up-to-date content, an unrestricted web search may also retrieve various types of inappropriate material. Not all search results are reading materials (sales pages, advertisement, videos, etc.), many reading materials on the web require high literacy skills, and some of the sufficiently easy reading materials contain incorrect or biased information. However, there are several web pages specialized in providing reading materials for language learners, children, or adults with low literacy skills in their native language. One option to improve web search results thus is to ensure that queries are processed so that they produce results from such web pages.

We provide the option to focus the web search on a pre-compiled list of *alpha sites*, i.e., web pages providing reading materials for readers with low literacy skills. For this, we use BING's built-in search operator `site`, which restricts the search to the specified domain. The `or` operator can be used to broaden the restriction to multiple domains. The following example illustrates this by restricting the web search for *Bundestag* ("German parliament") to the web pages of the German public international broadcaster *Deutsche Welle* (DW) and the web pages of the German Federal Agency for Civic Education *Bundeszentrale für politische Bildung* (BPB):

```
(site:www.dw.com or
site:www.bpb.de) Bundestag
```

The `site` operator is a standard operator of most major search engines and could be directly specified using exactly this syntax by the users. In *KANSAS Suche 2.0* we integrate a special option to promote its use for a series of specific websites for three reasons. First, the `site` operator and the use of operators in search engine queries overall are relatively unknown to the majority of search engine users. Allowing users to specify a query with a `site` operator through a check box in our user interface makes this feature more accessible. Second, while specifying multiple sites is possible using the `or` operator, it becomes increasingly cumbersome the more domains are added. Having a shortcut for suitable web sites considerably increases ease of use. Third, there are a number of web pages that offer materials for low literacy classes, but many of them will not be know to the

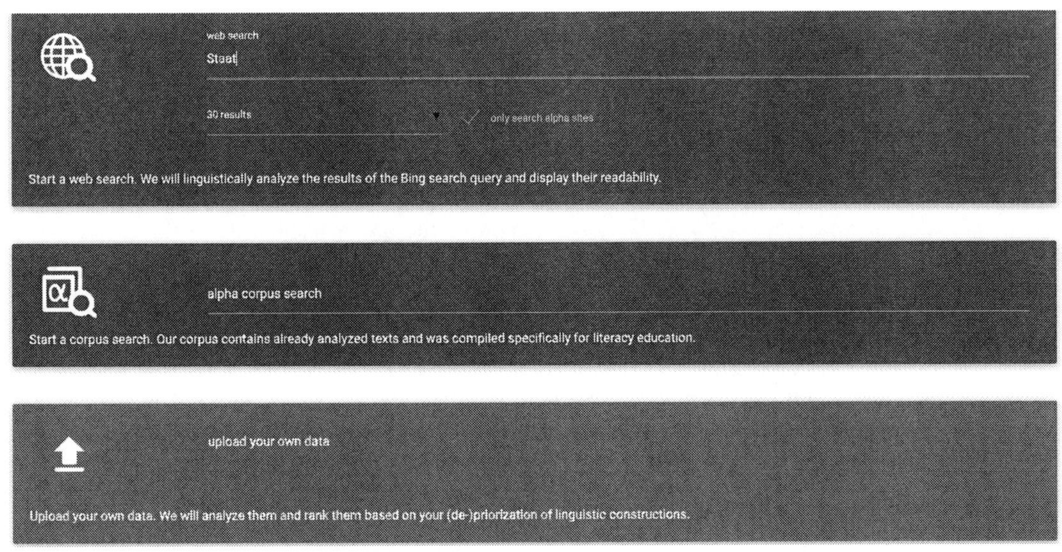

Figure 2: *KANSAS Suche 2.0* search mode options set to web query for *Staat* ("state") on 30 *alpha sites*.

user and some cannot be directly accessed by a search engine, as discussed in more detail below. Our list of *alpha sites* makes it possible to quickly access a broad selection of relevant web sites that are compatible with the functionality of *KANSAS Suche 2.0*.

To compile our list of *alpha sites*, we surveyed 75 web sites that provide reading materials for low literacy contexts. Not all of them are well-suited for the envisioned use case. We excluded web pages that offer little content (fewer than three texts), require prior registration, or predominantly offer training exercises at or below the word level rather than texts. While the latter may in principle be interesting for teachers of literacy and basic education classes, they are ill-suited for the kind of service provided by our system. The linguistic constructions that we allow the teacher or user to (de-)prioritize often target the phrase or clause level and do not make sense for individual words. However, by far the biggest drop in the number of potentially relevant web sites resulted from the fact that many web sites are designed in such a way that the materials they offer are not crawled and indexed by search engines at all. Since the material on these web sites cannot be found by search engines, it makes no sense to include them as *alpha sites* in our system.

At the end of our survey, we were left with six domains that are both relevant as accessible. This includes lexicons, news, and magazine articles in simple German (`lebenshilfe.`

`de/de/leichte-sprache, hurraki.de/ wiki, nachrichtenleicht.de`), texts written for children (`klexikon.zum.de, geo. de/geolino`), and texts for German as a Second Language learners (`deutsch-perfekt.com`). While this is a relatively short list compared to the number of web sites in our initial survey, these sites provide access to 34,100 materials, as identified by entering a BING search using the relevant operator specification without a specific content search term. The fact that we found so few suitable domains also showcases that the search functionality with a pre-compiled list goes beyond what could readily be achieved by a user thinking about potentially interesting sites and manually spelling out a query using the `site` operator. We are continuously working on expanding the list of *alpha sites* used by the system and welcome any information about missing options.

3.3 The Corpus Search

While there are some web sites dedicated to the distribution of reading materials for low literate readers, high-quality open source materials for literacy and basic education classes are relatively scarce. Even where materials are available, the question under which conditions teachers may alter and distribute materials often remains unclear. We want to address this issue by providing the option to specifically query for high-quality materials that have been provided as open educational resources with a corresponding license. For this, we are currently assembling a collection of such materials in collaboration with institutions creating materials for literacy and basic education.

In our system, this collection may be accessed through the same interface as the unrestricted and the filtered web search. On the server side, however, a separate pipeline is involved, as illustrated in Figure 1. Unlike the web search processing the retrieved web data on the run, the corpus search accesses already analyzed data. For this, we first perform the relevant linguistic analyses on the reading materials offline using the same NLP pipeline and readability classification as for the web search.

We use an Apache Solr index to make the corpus accessible to content queries.[11] Solr is a query platform for full-text indexing and high-performance search. It is based on the Lucene search library and can be easily integrated into Java applications. When a query request for the corpus search is sent by the user, the search results are fetched from that local Apache Solr index. In order to load the preprocessed documents into a Solr index, we transform each document into an XML file. We add a `metaPath` element which contains the name of the project responsible for the creation of the material, the author's name and the title. Additionally, we assign a `text_de` attribute to each text element, which ensures that Solr recognizes the text as German and applies the corresponding linguistic processing. The following tokenizer and filter factories, which are provided by Solr, have been set in the schema file of the index:

StandardTokenizerFactory splits the text into tokens.

LowerCaseFilterFactory converts all tokens into lowercase to allow case-insensitive matching.

StopFilterFactory removes all the words given in a predefined list of German stop words provided by the Snowball Project.[12]

GermanNormalizationFilterFactory normalizes the German special characters ä, ö, ü, and ß.

GermanLightStemFilterFactory stems the tokens using the light stemming algorithm implemented by the University of Neuchâtel.[13]

This ensures that the texts are recognized, processed, and indexed as German, which will improve the query results. Given a query, Solr returns the relevant text ids and the system can then deserialize the documents given the returned ids. Just as for the web search, the list of documents then is passed to the front-end, where the user can rerank, filter, and visualize the results.

We are still in the process of compiling the collection of high quality reading materials specifically designed for low literacy contexts. To be able to test our pipeline and evaluate the performance of the different search modes already at this stage, we use a test corpus of 10,012 texts crawled from web sites providing reading materials for low literate readers, compiled for the original *KANSAS Suche* (Weiss et al., 2018). We cleaned the corpus in a semi-automatic approach, in which we separated texts that had been extracted together and excluded non-reading materials. While we are confident that the degree of preprocessing is sufficient to demonstrate the benefits of our future corpus when compared to the web search options, it should be kept in mind that the current results are only a first approximation. The pilot corpus was only minimally cleaned so that it may still contain, for example, advertisement that would not be included in the high quality corpus being built. The pilot corpus also lacks explicit copyright information and thus is unsuitable outside of scientific analysis and demonstration purposes.

4 Comparison of Search Modes

Our system combines three search modes that have complementing strengths and weaknesses. Unrestricted web search can access a vast quantity of material, yet, most of it is not designed for low literate readers. Also, the lack of quality control may yield many unsuitable results for certain search terms, for example, those prone to elicit advertising. In contrast, restricted searches or corpus searches draw results from a considerably smaller pool of documents. Thus, although it stands to reason that the retrieved text results are of more consistent, higher quality and more likely to be at ap-

---

[11] http://lucene.apache.org/solr
[12] http://snowball.tartarus.org

[13] http://members.unine.ch/jacques.savoy/clef

propriate reading levels for our target users, there may be too few results.

To test these assumptions and see how the strengths and weaknesses play out across several queries, we compared the three search modes with regard to three criteria:

Coverage Does the search mode return enough results to satisfy a query request?

Readability Are the retrieved texts readable for low literate readers?

Suitability Are the retrieved texts suitable as teaching materials?

While the first criterion addresses a question of general interest for text retrieval systems, the other two are more specifically tailored towards the needs of our system as a retrieval system for low literacy contexts. We expect all three search modes to show satisfactory performance in general, but to exhibit the strengths and weaknesses hypothesized above.

4.1 Set-Up

For each search mode, we queried ten search terms requesting 30 results per term. The ten search terms were obtained by randomly sampling from a list of candidate terms that was compiled from the basic vocabulary list for illiteracy teaching by Bockrath and Hubertus (2014). The selection criterion for candidate terms was to identify nouns that in a wider sense relate to topics of basic education such as finance, health, politics, and society. The final list consists of the intersection of candidate terms selected by two researchers. The final ten search terms used in our evaluation are: *Alkohol* ("alcohol"), *Deutschkurs* ("German course"), *Erkältung* ("common cold"), *Heimat* ("home(land)"), *Internet* ("internet"), *Kirche* ("church"), *Liebe* ("love"), *Polizei* ("police"), *Radio* ("radio"), and *Staat* ("state"). In the following, all search terms will be referred to by their English translation.

All texts were then automatically analyzed and rated by the readability classifier used in our system. We calculated their Alpha Readability Level – both including and excluding the text length criterion of Weiss et al. (2018) based on Gausche et al. (2014); Kretschmann and Wieken (2010), since we found that many materials for low literate readers available on the web do not adhere to

the text length criterion. Since texts may be relatively easily shortened by teachers before using them for literacy and basic education classes, we include both sets in our evaluation.

4.2 Coverage of Retrieved Text

Our first evaluation criterion concerns the coverage of retrieved material across search terms. While the unlimited web search (referred to as "www") draws from a broad pool of available data, the restricted web search ("filter") and the corpus search ("corpus") are based on a considerably more restricted set of texts. Therefore, we first investigated to which extent the different search modes are capable of providing the requested number of results across search terms.

Overall, we obtained 817 texts for the requested 900 results. While the unrestricted web search returned the requested number of 30 results for each search term (i.e., overall 300 texts), the corpus search only retrieved 261 texts and the filtered web-search 256 texts. The latter search modes struggled to provide enough texts for the search terms *Deutschkurs* ("German course"), *Erkältung* ("common cold"). As shown in Figure 3, the corpus search returns only nine for the former and 12 results for the latter term, while the filtered search identifies seven and nine results, respectively. For the other eight search terms, all three search modes retrieve the requested 30 results.

The results indicate that with regard to plain coverage, the web search outperforms the two re-

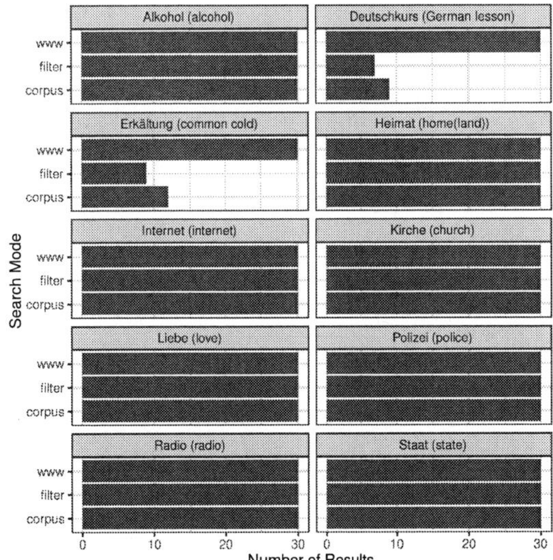

Figure 3: Results per term across search modes

stricted search modes. This is expected since neither the filtered web search nor the corpus search have access to the vast number of documents accessible to the unrestricted web search. However, they do provide the requested number of results for the majority of queries, illustrating that even the more restrictive search options may well provide sufficient coverage for many likely search terms.

4.3 Readability of Retrieved Texts

The second criterion that is essential for our comparison is the readability of the retrieved texts on a readability scale for low literacy. For this, we used the readability classifier integrated in our system to assess the Alpha Level of each text, once with and once without the text length criterion. Tables 1 and 2 show the overall representation of Alpha Readability Levels aggregated over search terms for each search mode including and ignoring text length as a rating criterion.

Alpha Level	WWW	Filter	Corpus
Alpha 3	0.00%	0.39%	4.98%
Alpha 4	19.00%	15.23%	35.25%
Alpha 5	14.33%	8.20%	14.56%
Alpha 6	10.00%	7.42%	8.43%
No Alpha	56.67%	68.75%	36.78%

Table 1: Distribution of Alpha Readability Levels *including* text length across search modes

Alpha Level	WWW	Filter	Corpus
Alpha 3	1.00%	4.30%	13.41%
Alpha 4	49.67%	53.91%	50.19%
Alpha 5	21.00%	22.66%	18.77%
Alpha 6	2.00%	10.16%	7.28%
No Alpha	26.33%	8.98%	10.34%

Table 2: Distribution of Alpha Readability Levels *ignoring* text length across search modes

As expected, the unrestricted web search elicits a high percentage of texts that are above the level of low literate readers. 56.67% of texts are rated as No Alpha and not a single text receives the rating Alpha 3. When ignoring text length, the rate of No Alpha texts drops to 26.33% but there are still only 1.00% Alpha 3 texts. It should be noted, though, that 49.67% of results are rated as Alpha 4 when ignoring text length, indicating that the unrestricted web search is not completely unsuitable

for the retrieval of low literacy reading materials even though there is clear room for improvement.

The filtered web search does not seem to perform much better at first glance. On the contrary, with 68.75% it shows the overall highest rate of No Alpha labeled texts when including the text length criterion and it retrieves only 0.39% Alpha 3 texts. However, when ignoring text length, the rate of No Alpha texts drops to 8.98% – the lowest rate of No Alpha texts observed across all three search modes. It also retrieves 4.30% of Alpha 3 texts and 53.91% of Alpha 4 texts. This shows that while many of the texts found by the filtered web search seem to be too long, they are otherwise better suited for the needs of low literate readers than texts found with the unrestricted web search.

The corpus search exhibits the lowest rate of No Alpha texts (36.78%) and the highest rate of Alpha 3 and Alpha 4 texts (4.98% and 35.25%, respectively) when including the text length criterion. Without it, the rate of Alpha 3 texts even rises to 13.41%. Interestingly, though, it has a slightly higher rate of No Alpha texts than the filtered web search. That the corpus contains texts that are beyond the Alpha Levels at first may seem counterintuitive. However, the test corpus also includes texts written for language learners which may very well exceed the Alpha Levels. Considering that the majority of texts identified by this search mode are within the reach of low literate readers, this is not an issue for the test corpus. The selection of suitable materials does yield more fitting results in terms of readability.

Figure 4 shows the distribution of Alpha Readability Levels ignoring text length across search terms. It can be seen that for all search terms, Alpha Level 4 is systematically the most commonly retrieved level. A few patterns relating search terms and elicited Alpha Levels can be observed. *Deutschkurs* ("German course"), *Erkältung* ("common cold") elicit notably fewer Alpha 4 texts, which is due to the lack of coverage in the filtered web and the corpus search. Other than that, *Polizei* ("police") elicits by far the least No Alpha texts and among the most Alpha 3 and Alpha 4 texts, indicating that texts retrieved for this topic are overall better suited for low literacy levels. In contrast, *Radio* ("radio") elicits most No Alpha texts and among the least Alpha 3 texts. However, it also exhibits the highest rate of Alpha 4 texts. Thus, overall it seems that the distribution

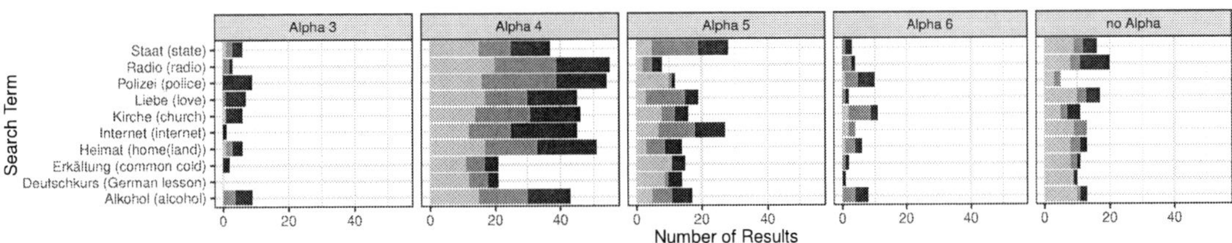

Figure 4: Distribution of query results across search terms by Alpha Level (ignoring text length)

of Alpha Readability Levels is comparable across search terms. This is in line with our expectations, given that all terms were drawn from a list of basic German vocabulary.

4.4 Suitability of Retrieved Texts

Our final criterion concerns the suitability of texts for reading purposes. As mentioned, some materials from the web are ill-suited as reading materials for literacy and basic education classes. Search results may not be reading materials but rather sales pages, advertisement, or videos. Certain search terms, such as those denoting purchasable items, such as *Radio* ("radio"), are more likely to yield such results than others. Other terms, such as those relating to politics, may be prone to elicit biased materials or texts containing misinformation. The challenge of suitability has already been recognized in previous web-search based systems, such as FERN (Walmsley, 2015) or netTrekker (Huff, 2008), where it was addressed by restricting the web search to manually verified web pages.

We investigated to which extent suitability of contents is an issue for our search modes by manually labeling materials as suitable or unsuitable on a stratified sample of the full set of queries that samples across search modes, search terms, and Alpha Readability Levels (N=451). Note that since Alpha Readability Levels are not evenly distributed across search modes, the stratified sample does not contain the same number of hits for each search term. However, each search mode is represented approximately evenly with 159 results for the corpus search, 142 for the filtered web search, and 150 for the unrestricted web search.

On this sample, we let two human annotators flag search results as unsuitable, if they were a) advertisement, b) brief captions of a video or figure, c) or a hub for other web pages on the topic. Such hub pages linking to relevant topics are not unsuitable per se, in the way advertisement or brief

captions are. However, since the point of a search engine such as *KANSAS Suche 2.0* is to analyze the web resource itself rather than the pages being linked to on the page, such pages are unsuitable. Since the reliable evaluation of bias and misinformation is beyond the scope of this paper, we excluded this aspect from our evaluation. We also discarded materials as not suitable if they neither contained the search term nor a synonym to the search term. Since the information retrieval algorithm used in our corpus search is less sophisticated than the one used by BING, stemming mistakes can lead to such unrelated and thus unsuitable results. Finally, we restricted texts to 1,500 words and flagged everything beyond that as unsuitable. This is based on the practical consideration that it would take teachers too much time to review such long texts for suitability – but this rule only became relevant for six texts from the corpus, which contained full chapters from booklets on basic education matters written in simplified language.

Based on this definition of suitability that we specifically fitted for the needs of our system, our two annotators show a prevalence and bias corrected Cohen's kappa of $\kappa = 0.765$. For the following evaluation of suitability, we only considered texts as not suitable if both annotators flagged them as such. Results that have been classified as unsuitable by only one annotator were treated as suitable materials. This resulted in overall 137 texts being flagged as not suitable, i.e., 30.38% of all search results. When splitting these results across search modes, we find that the unrestricted web search has the highest rate of unsuitable results: 52.70% of all retrieved materials were identified as not suitable. In contrast, only 8.80% of the corpus search results were labeled as unsuitable. For the filtered web search, the percentage of unsuitable materials lies between these two extremes, at 31.00%. Figure 5 shows the distribution

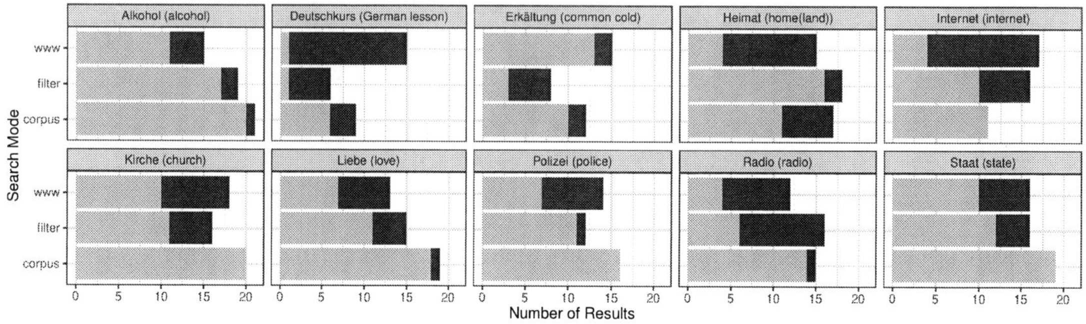

Figure 5: Suitability of sample texts (N=451) across search modes by query term

of suitable and not suitable materials across search modes split by search terms. As can be seen, some search terms elicit more unsuitable materials than others. *Deutschkurs* ("German course"), for example, contains by far more unsuitable than suitable materials for both web searches. This puts our previous findings into perspective that the unrestricted web search has higher coverage for this term than the corpus search. At least for the sample analyzed here, the corpus search retrieves considerably more suitable texts than either web search, despite its lower overall coverage.[14] The terms *Heimat* ("home(land)"), *Internet* ("internet"), and *Radio* ("radio") also seem to be particularly prone to yield unsuitable materials in an unrestricted web search.

But not all search terms elicit high numbers of unsuitable results in the unrestricted web search, see for example *Alkohol* ("alcohol"), *Erkältung* ("common cold"), and *Staat* ("state"). With for some exceptions, such as *Erkältung* ("common cold") and *Heimat* ("home(land)"), the filtered corpus search behaves similar to the unrestricted corpus search with regard to retrieving suitable materials. The corpus search clearly outperforms both web-based approaches in terms of suitability. The only term that elicits a notable quantity of unsuitable materials is *Heimat* ("home(land)"), for which the corpus includes some advertisement texts expressed in plain language. For all other search terms, corpus materials flagged as unsuitable were so based on their length.

Figure 6 displays the distribution of suitable and unsuitable materials across search modes split by readability level ignoring text length. It shows, that more than half of the Alpha Level 4 texts found in the unrestricted web search as well as approximately half of those found in the filtered web search are actually unsuitable. Similarly, a considerable number of Alpha Level 5 and nearly all Alpha Level 6 texts retrieved by the unrestricted web search in our sample are flagged as unsuitable. This puts the previous findings concerning the readability of search results into a new perspective. After excluding unsuitable results, both web searches yield considerably fewer results that are readable for low literacy levels as compared to the corpus search.

4.5 Discussion

The comparison of search modes confirmed our initial assumptions about the strengths and weaknesses of the different approaches. The unrestricted web search has the broadest plain coverage but elicits considerably more texts which require too high literacy skills or contain unsuitable materials. Although it retrieves a high proportion of Alpha 4 texts, the majority of these consist of unsuitable material. After correcting for this, it becomes apparent that users may struggle to obtain suitable reading materials at low literacy levels when solely relying on an unrestricted web search. However, depending on the search term, the rate of unsuitable materials widely differs. Thus, it stands to reason that the unrestricted web search works well for some queries while others will be less fruitful for low literacy contexts.

In these cases, the filtered web search or the corpus search can be of assistance. They both have been shown to retrieve more texts suitable for low literacy levels despite struggling with coverage

---

[14]This does not hold for the other term for which low coverage for all but the unrestricted web search was reported. For the search term *Erkältung* ("common cold"), the unrestricted web search finds a high number of suitable results.

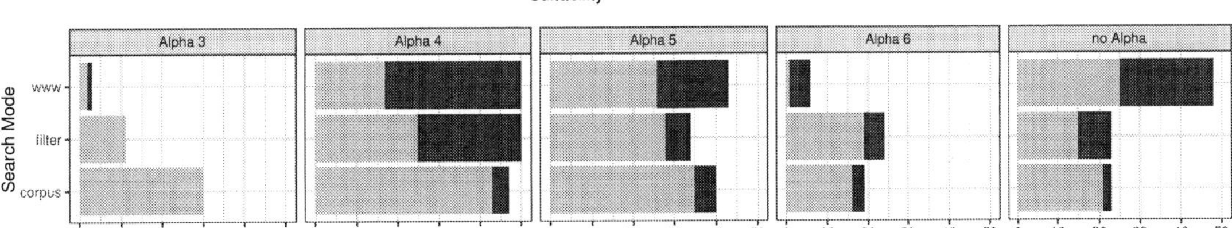

Figure 6: Suitability of sample texts (N=451) across search modes by Alpha Levels (ignoring text length)

for some search terms. Interestingly, the corpus search was shown to exceed the web search in coverage after subtracting unsuitable results for one search term. This demonstrates that raw coverage may be misleading depending on the suitability of the retrieved results. All in all, the restricted web search showed fewer advantages than the other two search modes as it suffered from both, low coverage and unsuitable materials. However, it does elicit a considerably lower ratio of unsuitable materials than the unrestricted web search, while keeping the benefit of providing up-to-date materials. Thus, we would still argue that it is a valuable contribution to the overall system.

Overall, the results show that depending on the search term and targeted readability level, it makes sense to allow users to switch between search modes so that they can identify the ideal configuration for their specific needs, as there is no single search mode that is superior across contexts.

5 Summary and Outlook

We presented our ongoing work on *KANSAS Suche 2.0*, a hybrid text retrieval system for reading materials for low literate readers of German. Unlike previous systems, our approach makes it possible to combine the strengths of unrestricted web search, broad coverage of current materials, with those of more restricted searches in curated corpora, high quality materials with clear copyright information. We demonstrated how, depending on the search term, the suitability and readability of results retrieved by an unrestricted web search can become problematic for users searching for materials at low literacy levels. Our study showed that a restricted web search and the search of materials in our corpus are valuable alternatives in these cases. Overall, there is no single best solution for all searches, so our hybrid solution allows users to choose themselves which search

mode suits their needs best for a given query.

While the system itself is fully implemented, we are still compiling the corpus of reading materials for low literacy contexts and work on expanding the list of domains for our restricted web search. We are also conducting usability studies with teachers of low literacy and basic education classes and with German language teachers in training. We plan to expand the functionality of the corpus search to also support access to the corpus solely based on linguistic properties and reading level characteristics, without a content query. This will make it possible to retrieve texts richly representing particular linguistic properties or constructions that are too infrequent when having to focus on a subset of the data using the content query. We are also considering development of a second readability classifier targeting CEFR levels to accommodate the fact that German adult literacy and basic education classes are not only attended by low literate native speakers but also by German as a second language learners.

Acknowledgments

KANSAS is a research and development project funded by the Federal Ministry of Education and Research (BMBF) as part of the *AlphaDekade*[15] ("Decade of Literacy"), grant numbcr W143500.

References

Rebekah George Benjamin. 2012. Reconstructing readability: Recent developments and recommendations in the analysis of text difficulty. *Educational Psychology Review*, 24:63–88.

BMBF and KMK. 2016. *General Agreement on the National Decade for Literacy and Basic Skills 2016-2026. Reducing functional illiteracy and raising the level of basic skills in Germany.* Bundesministerium für Bildung und Forschung

---

[15]https://www.alphadekade.de

(BMBF), Ständige Konferenz der Kultusminister der Länder in der Bundesrepublik Deutschland (KMK). `https://www.alphadekade.de/img/EN_General_Agreement_on_the_National_Decade_for_Literacy_and_Basic_Skills.pdf`.

Angela Bockrath and Peter Hubertus. 2014. *1.300 wichtige Wörter. Ein Grundwortschatz*, 5th edition. Bundesverband Alphabetisierung und Grundbildung e.V., Münster, Germany.

Jonathan Brown and Maxine Eskenazi. 2004. Retrieval of authentic documents for reader-specific lexical practice. In *InSTIL/ICALL 2004 Symposium on Computer Assisted Learning, NLP and speech technologies in advanced language learning systems*, Venice, Italy. International Speech Communication Association (ISCA). `http://reap.cs.cmu.edu/Papers/InSTIL04-jonbrown.pdf`.

Jeanne S. Chall and Edgar Dale. 1995. *Readability revisited: the new Dale-Chall Readability Formula*. Brookline Books.

Xiaobin Chen and Detmar Meurers. 2017a. Challenging learners in their individual zone of proximal development using pedagogic developmental benchmarks of syntactic complexity. In *Proceedings of the Joint 6th Workshop on NLP for Computer Assisted Language Learning and 2nd Workshop on NLP for Research on Language Acquisition at NoDaLiDa 2017*, Linköping Electronic Conference Proceedings 134, pages 8–17, Gothenburg, Sweden. ACL. `http://aclweb.org/anthology/W17-0302.pdf`.

Xiaobin Chen and Detmar Meurers. 2017b. Word frequency and readability: Predicting the text-level readability with a lexical-level attribute. *Journal of Research in Reading*, 41(3):486–510.

Maria Chinkina, Madeeswaran Kannan, and Detmar Meurers. 2016. Online information retrieval for language learning. In *Proceedings of ACL-2016 System Demonstrations*, pages 7–12, Berlin, Germany. Association for Computational Linguistics. `http://anthology.aclweb.org/P16-4002`.

Maria Chinkina and Detmar Meurers. 2016. Linguistically-aware information retrieval: Providing input enrichment for second language learners. In *Proceedings of the 11th Workshop on Innovative Use of NLP for Building Educational Applications (BEA)*, pages 188–198, San Diego, CA. ACL.

K. Collins-Thompson, P. N. Bennett, R. W. White, S. de la Chica, and D. Sontag. 2011. Personalizing web search results by reading level. In *Proceedings of the Twentieth ACM International Conference on Information and Knowledge Management (CIKM 2011)*.

Scott A. Crossley, David B. Allen, and Danielle McNamara. 2011. Text readability and intuitive simplification: A comparison of readability formulas. *Reading in a Foreign Language*, 23(1):84–101.

Frank Decroll. 1981. Funktionaler Analphabetismus – Begriff, Erscheinungsbild, psycho-soziale Folgen und Bildungsinteressen. In *Für ein Recht auf Lesen: Analphabetismus in der Bundesrepublik Deutschland*, pages 29–40.

Felice Dell'Orletta, Simonetta Montemagni, and Giulia Venturi. 2011. Read-it: Assessing readability of Italian texts with a view to text simplification. In *Proceedings of the 2nd Workshop on Speech and Language Processing for Assistive Technologies*, pages 73–83.

Sukru Eraslan, Victoria Yaneva, and Yeliz Yelisada. 2017. Do web users with autism experience barriers when searching for information within web pages? In *Proceedings of the 14th Web for All Conference on The Future of Accessible Work*, pages 20–23. ACM. `https://doi.org/DOI:10.1145/3058555.3058566`.

B. Janghorban Esfahani, A. Faron, K. S. Roth, P. P. Grimminger, and J. C. Luers. 2016. Systematic readability analysis of medical texts on websites of german university clinics for general and abdominal surgery. *Zentralblatt fur Chirurgie*, 141(6):639–644.

Lijun Feng, Noémie Elhadad, and Matt Huenerfauth. 2009. Cognitively motivated features for readability assessment. In *Proceedings of the 12th Conference of the European Chapter of the ACL (EACL 2009)*, pages 229–237, Athens, Greece. Association for Computational Linguistics. `http://aclweb.org/anthology/E09-1027`.

Lijun Feng, Martin Jansche, Matt Huenerfauth, and Noémie Elhadad. 2010. A comparison of features for automatic readability assessment. In *In Proceedings of the 23rd International Conference on Computational Linguistics (COLING 2010), Beijing, China*.

Thomas François and Cedrick Fairon. 2012. An "AI readability" formula for French as a foreign language. In *Proceedings of the 2012 Joint Conference on Empirical Methods in Natural Language Processing and Computational Natural Language Learning*. `https://www.aclweb.org/anthology/D12-1043`.

Geert Freyhoff, Gerhard Hess, Linda Kerr, Elizabeth Menzell, Bror Tronbacke, and Kathy Van Der Veken. 1998. *Make It Simple, European Guidelines for the Production of Easy-to-Read Information for People with Learning Disability for authors, editors, information providers, translators and other interested persons*. International League of Societies for Persons with Mental Handicap European Association, Brussels.

Mark G. Friedman and Diane Nelson Bryen. 2007. Web accessibility design recommendations for people with cognitive disabilities. *Technology and Disability*, 19(4):205–2012.

S. Gausche, A. Haase, and D. Zimper. 2014. *Lesen. DVV-Rahmencurriculum*, 1 edition. Deutscher Volkshochschul-Verband e.V., Bonn.

Alex Gilmore. 2007. Authentic materials and authenticity in foreign language learning. *Language teaching*, 40(02):97–118.

Petronella Grootens-Wiegers, Martine C. De Vries, Tessa E. Vossen, and Jos M. Van den Broek. 2015. Readability and visuals in medical research information forms for children and adolescents. *Science Communication*, 37(1):89–117.

Anke Grotlüschen, Klaus Buddeberg, Gregor Dutz, Lisanne Heilmann, and Christopher Stammer. 2019. LEO 2018 – living with low literacy. Press brochure, Hamburg, Germany. `http://blogs.epb.uni-hamburg.de/leo/files/2019/06/LEO_2018_Living_with_Low_Literacy.pdf`.

Anke Grotlüschen and Wibke Riekmann. 2011. leo. - level-online studie. Press brochure, Hamburg, Germany. `http://blogs.epb.uni-hamburg.de/leo/files/2011/12/leo-Press-brochure15-12-2011.pdf`.

Anke Grotlüschen and Heike Solga. 2019. Leben mit geringer Literalität. Hauptergebnisse der LEO-studie 2018. Presentation.

Michael Heilman, Kevyn Collins-Thompson, Jamie Callan, Maxine Eskenazi, Alan Juffs, and Lois Wilson. 2010. Personalization of reading passages improves vocabulary acquisition. *International Journal of Artificial Intelligence in Education*, 20:73–98.

Michael Heilman, Le Zhao, Juan Pino, and Maxine Eskenazi. 2008. Retrieval of reading materials for vocabulary and reading practice. In *Proceedings of the Third Workshop on Innovative Use of NLP for Building Educational Applications (BEA-3) at ACL'08*, pages 80–88, Columbus, Ohio.

Matt Huenerfauth, Lijun Feng, and Noémie Elhadad. 2009. Comparing evaluation techniques for text readability software for adults with intellectual disabilities. In *Proceedings of the 11th international ACM SIGACCESS conference on Computers and accessibility*, Assets '09, pages 3–10, New York, NY, USA. ACM. `http://doi.acm.org/10.1145/1639642.1639646`.

Leslie Huff. 2008. Review of nettrekker di. *Language Learning & Technology*, 12(2):17–25.

Amy M. Johnson, Tricia A. Guerrero, Elizabeth L. Tighe, and Danielle S. McNamara. 2017. iSTART-ALL: Confronting adult low literacy with intelligent tutoring for reading comprehension. In *International Conference on Artificial Intelligence in Education*, pages 125–136. Springer.

J. Peter Kincaid, Robert P. Fishburne, Richard L. Rogers, and Brad S. Chissom. 1975. Derivation of new readability formulas (Automated Readability Index, Fog Count and Flesch Reading Ease formula) for Navy enlisted personnel. Research Branch Report 8-75, Naval Technical Training Command, Millington, TN.

Christian Kohlschlütter, Peter Frankhauser, and Wolfgang Nejdl. 2010. Boilerplate detection using shallow text features. In *Proceedings of the Third ACM international conference on web search and data mining*, pages 441–450. ACM.

Stephen D Krashen. 1985. *The input hypothesis: Issues and implications*. Longman, New York.

R. Kretschmann and P. Wieken. 2010. *Lesen. Alpha Levels*. lea., Hamburg.

Roger Levy and Galen Andrew. 2006. Tregex and tsurgeon: tools for querying and manipulating tree data structures. In *5th International Conference on Language Resources and Evaluation*, Genoa, Italy.

Cordula Löffler and Susanne Weis. 2016. Didaktik der Alphabetisierung. In Cordula Löffler and Jens Korfkamp, editors, *Handbuch zur Alphabetisierung und Grundbildung Erwachsener*, pages 365–382. Waxmann, Münster, New York.

Christopher D. Manning, Mihai Surdeanu, John Bauer, Jenny Finkel, Steven J. Bethard, and David McClosky. 2014. The Stanford CoreNLP natural language processing toolkit. In *Association for Computational Linguistics (ACL) System Demonstrations*, pages 55–60. `http://aclweb.org/anthology/P/P14/P14-5010`.

Eleni Miltsakaki and Audrey Troutt. 2007. Read-x: Automatic evaluation of reading difficulty of web text. In *Proceedings of World Conference on E-Learning in Corporate, Government, Healthcare, and Higher Education 2007*, pages 7280–7286, Quebec City, Canada. AACE. `http://www.editlib.org/p/26932`.

Kristina Nilsson and Lars Borin. 2002. Living off the land: The web as a source of practice texts for learners of less prevalent languages. In *Proceedings of LREC 2002, Third International Conference on Language Resources and Evaluation, Las Palmas: ELRA*, pages 411–418.

Misako Nomura, Gyda Skat Nielsen, and Bror Tronbacke. 2010. Guidelines for easy-to-read materials. revision on behalf of the ifla/library services to people with special needs section. IFLA Professional Reports 120, International Federation of Library Associations and Institutions, The Hague, IFLA Headquarters.

Ildikó Pilán, Sowmya Vajjala, and Elena Volodina. 2015. A readable read: Automatic assessment of language learning materials based on linguistic complexity. In *Proceedings of CICLING 2015- Research*

in *Computing Science Journal Issue (to appear)*.
`https://arxiv.org/abs/1603.08868`.

Luz Rello, Ricardo Baeza-Yates, Laura Dempere-Marco, and Horacio Saggion. 2013a. Frequent words improve readability and short words improve understandability for people with dyslexia. In *IFIP Conference on Human-Computer Interaction*, pages 203–219, Berlin, Heidelberg. Springer. `https://doi.org/DOI:10.1007/978-3-642-40498-6_15`.

Luz Rello, Susana Bautista, Ricardo Baeza-Yates, Pablo Gervás, Raquel Hervás, and Horacio Saggion. 2013b. One half or 50%? an eye-tracking study of number representation readability. In *IFIP Conference on Human-Computer Interaction*, pages 229–245, Berlin, Heidelberg. Springer. `https://doi.org/DOI:10.1007/978-3-642-40498-6_17`.

Stephen Robertsin and Steve Walker. 1994. Some simple effective approximations to the 2-poissin model for probabilistic weighted retrieval. In *Proceedings of the 17th annual international ACM SIGIR conference on Research and development in information retrieval*, pages 131–241.

Hannes Schröter and Irit Bar-Kochva. 2019. Keyword: Reading literacy. Reading competencies in Germany and underlying cognitive skills. *Zeitschrift für Erziehungswissenschaft*, 22(1):17–49.

Sanja Štajner, Richard Evans, Constantin Orasan, and Ruslan Mitkov. 2012. What can readability measures really tell us about text complexity? In *In Proceedings of the First Workshop on Natural Language Processing for Improving Textual Accessibility*. European Language Resources Association (ELRA).

Merrill Swain. 1985. Communicative competence: Some roles of comprehensible input and comprehensible output in its development. In Susan M. Gass and Carolyn G. Madden, editors, *Input in second language acquisition*, pages 235–253. Newbury House, Rowley, MA.

Sowmya Vajjala and Detmar Meurers. 2012. On improving the accuracy of readability classification using insights from second language acquisition. In *Proceedings of the 7th Workshop on Innovative Use of NLP for Building Educational Applications (BEA)*, pages 163–173, Montréal, Canada. ACL. `http://aclweb.org/anthology/W12-2019.pdf`.

Sowmya Vajjala and Detmar Meurers. 2013. On the applicability of readability models to web texts. In *Proceedings of the Second Workshop on Predicting and Improving Text Readability for Target Reader Populations*, pages 59–68.

Sowmya Vajjala and Detmar Meurers. 2014. Readability assessment for text simplification: From analyzing documents to identifying sentential simplifications. *International Journal of Applied Linguistics*, *Special Issue on Current Research in Readability and Text Simplification*, 165(2):142–222.

Michael Walmsley. 2015. *Learner Modelling for Individualised Reading in a Second Language*. Ph.D. thesis, The University of Waikato. `http://hdl.handle.net/10289/10559`.

Zarah Weiss, Sabrina Dittrich, and Detmar Meurers. 2018. A linguistically-informed search engine to identifiy reading material for functional illiteracy classes. In *Proceedings of the 7th Workshop on Natural Language Processing for Computer-Assisted Language Learning (NLP4CALL)*. Association for Computational Linguistics.

Zarah Weiss and Theresa Geppert. 2018. Textlesbarkeit für Alpha-Levels. Annotationsrichtlinien für Lesetexte. Version 1.1. `http://www.sfs.uni-tuebingen.de/~zweiss/rsrc/textlesbarkeit-fur-alpha.pdf`.

Zarah Weiss and Detmar Meurers. 2018. Modeling the readability of German targeting adults and children: An empirically broad analysis and its cross-corpus validation. In *Proceedings of the 27th International Conference on Computational Linguistics (COLING)*, Santa Fe, New Mexico, USA. `https://www.aclweb.org/anthology/C18-1026`.

Menglin Xia, Ekaterina Kochmar, and Ted Briscoe. 2016. Text readability assessment for second language learners. In *Proceedings of the 11th Workshop on Innovative Use of NLP for Building Educational Applications*, pages 12–22.

Wei Xu, Chris Callison-Burch, and Courtney Napoles. 2015. Problems in current text simplification research: New data can help. *Transactions of the Association for Computational Linguistics*, 3:283–297.

Victoria Yaneva. 2015. Easy-read documents as a gold standard for evaluation of text simplification output. In *Proceedings of the Student Research Workshop associated with RANLP 2015*, pages 30–36, Hissar, Bulgaria.

Victoria Yaneva, Irina Temnikova, and Ruslan Mitkov. 2016a. Accessible texts for autism: An eye-tracking study. In *Proceedings of the 17th International ACM SIGACCESS Conference on Computers & Accessibility*, pages 49–57.

Victoria Yaneva, Irina P. Temnikova, and Ruslan Mitkov. 2016b. Evaluating the readability of text simplification output for readers with cognitive disabilities. In *Proceedings of the 10h International Conference on Language Resources and Evaluation (LREC)*, pages 293–299.

Formalism for a language agnostic language learning game and productive grid generation

Sylvain Hatier and **Arnaud Bey**
Univ. Grenoble Alpes
Litt&Arts
F-38000 Grenoble
sylvain.hatier@univ-grenoble-alpes.fr
arnaud.bey@univ-grenoble-alpes.fr

Mathieu Loiseau
Univ. Grenoble Alpes
Lidilem
F-38000 Grenoble
mathieu.loiseau@univ-grenoble-alpes.fr

Abstract

In this article, we describe the modifications of MagicWord, a language learning game focused on accuracy, in order to allow the integration of new languages. We first describe the motivations behind the design of the game. Then we explain the modifications performed before exploring the consequences both game-wise and language learning-wise.

In order to improve their replay-value, language learning games need to rely on language resources of diverse complexity depending on their rules and objectives. In this paper, we tackle the issue of providing multi-language resources for a language learning letter game, MagicWord. Before exploring the technical difficulties as well as their intricacies both in terms of language representation, learning and gaming, we will explain the game, its objectives and the design process.

1 Issues of Game-Based Language Learning

Game-based learning gained momentum in the last decade to become a hot topic (Sharples et al., 2013, 29–31) with promises of improved motivation and self-esteem (Cerezo, 2012, 134), and hopes good pedagogy (Gee, 2003; Oblinger, 2004). At the same time that serious games have fostered high hopes, they also brought criticism

regarding their actual learning outcomes (Girard et al., 2013) and even their ludicity (Lavigne, 2014; Bruckman, 1999; Söbke et al., 2013).

To us, rather than questioning the concept of serious game, these criticisms underlie the difficulty of creating such games. In this article we will not delve into the complexity and intricate viewpoints on the concepts of "game" and "play" and settle for Brougère's utterance: "Gaming is a dual reality which interweaves a gaming structure and a playful attitude"[1](Brougère, 2012, 127). The importance of the "playful attitude" inside this sentence underlines one of the central issues towards the creation of a serious game: to be a serious game, the object has to be a game. And to be one, it needs to provoke in the learner a playful attitude. In other words:

> "A good rule of thumb for determining the degree to which a CALL activity is a game [is] the degree to which students want to play it for the pleasure it brings rather than for some external reason. What a teacher or courseware designer calls an activity is not important; it is how the learner views it that will determine whether it is used as one." (Hubbard, 1991, 221).

Another issue of the design of serious games, that could serve as an explanation of the previous issue, is the cost of developing video games (espe-

[1]"Le jeu est une réalité double qui articule une structure ludique (l'aspect *game* ou *gameplay*) et une attitude ludique (le *play*)." (our translation)

Sylvain Hatier, Arnaud Bey and Mathieu Loiseau 2019. Formalism for a language agnostic language learning game and productive grid generation. *Proceedings of the 8th Workshop on Natural Language Processing for Computer Assisted Language Learning (NLP4CALL 2019)*. Linköping Electronic Conference Proceedings 164: 57–64.

cially those to which the learners are accustomed to playing[2]). Even casual games reportedly require a budget between 100 000 and 1 million dollars (Casual Games Association, 2015), successful games costing more than 500 000 dollars (Handrahan, 2014).

2 Design strategy

In order to try to overcome this issue we have resorted to the following design strategy (Zampa et al., 2017) in various projects:

- adapt Söbke, Bröker and Kornadt's strategy (2013) and select successful commercial-off-the-shelf games which inherently rely on some language competence;

- make sure they allow replayability through generic game mechanics that can be interfaced with language ressources;

- adapt these mechanics so that the language element at the core of the game is made more accessible to the learner (trying not to undermine the playfulness by doing so);

- all this done through various iterations to cut the cost and allow us to get feedback from learners and teachers.

3 Issues of multilingualism in a letter game

MagicWord is one of the (open-source) games designed and implemented using this strategy. Before entering the details of the present iteration of its development, it seems necessary to document the previous stages of the project.

3.1 MagicWord v1

MagicWord is a word game based on the same set of *metaludic* rules (pertaining to a game genre) (Silva Ochoa, 1999, 277) as games like Boggle, Ruzzle, Wordament (and others): 16 letters are set in a 4×4 grid; the goal of the game is to create words (or more precisely word-forms); to do that, the player uses contiguous letters, in every direction (up, down, left, right & diagonally, *cf.* fig. 1), using each letter cell at most once per word form.

We chose this set metaludic rules, because they allow replayability, many forms of the game are

successful and those rules rely on the players vocabulary. But what interested us most is that good players tend to try to find all the inflected forms associated with the lemmas they find in the game. And in learning languages with rich stemming mechanisms, such as French, Spanish or German, the learning of the various forms can be considered tedious (Castañeda and Cho, 2016, 1195).

The first version we created was available in Italian, French and English, allowed players to engage in duels. Some games allowed free play and others came with a constraint, that when respected granted extra points (*e.g.* English words ending with "-er"). This version was presented to teachers in a focus group (Montaufier, 2016) and later tested against another version devised in collaboration with the University of Bologna that focused solely on vocabulary (Roccetti et al., 2016). This experiment (Loiseau et al., 2016) and the focus group allowed us to conclude that:

- Our version with duels between two players was better received *playful attitude*-wise than the one player Bologna version;

- That both learners and teachers saw the potential of the game in terms of lexicon rather than in terms of inflections.

3.2 MagicWord v2

Based on this feedback, we created a new version of MagicWord, that built upon the first version but added new rules and functionalities to expand the affordances of the game.

3.2.1 "Massive" games

Without erasing the duel mode, we decided to create a mode where players would compete against the whole community on the same grids in order to create more emulation within the class.

3.2.2 C-c-c-combo

Considering the fact that the *normative* rules (which are followed by experimented players of the game) (Silva Ochoa, 1999, 277) — in this case, trying to find as many forms of each word as possible — are hardly accessible to teachers and learners, we decided to make them part of the *constitutive* rules (explicit rules of a specific game) (Silva Ochoa, 1999, 277) of our game and added a new way to earn points: "combos" (*cf.* fig. 1, left). Combos, short for "combination", are triggered whenever the player selects two words in a

---

[2]See for instance the notion of AAA game.

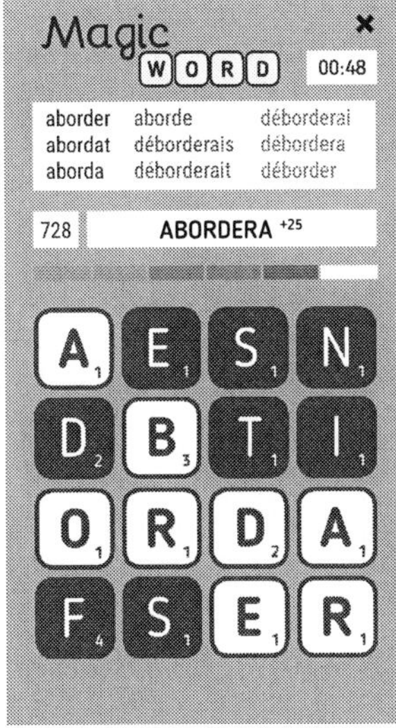

Figure 1: Presentation of the game modes introduced in MagicWord v2 (Loiseau et al., 2017)

row that stem from the same lemma (*e.g.* "play", "playing" in English). The bonus is increased with each new form and broken, whenever the player selects a form that does not exist or that is not linked to the same lemma.

3.2.3 "Conquer" mode and authoring tool

We did not want to overlook the lexical aspect of the game and wanted to give teachers more control over the grid when they wanted to work on specific lexicon items. So we used the algorithm created for the Bologna version (Roccetti et al., 2016) to allow a mode in which players would not score points based on how many words they would find in a limited time, but how little time they would need to find specific words (*cf.* fig. 1, right). Three types of objectives are available in this mode. The user can be asked to: find a word based on a clue written by another user; realize a combo with a minimum of n forms; or find n forms based on their morphological category. This type of play comes with an authoring tool that allow users to create their own "conquer" grids (or sets of grids).

3.3 Towards a generic multilingual game

While the first version only used a list of inflected forms, the functionalities of version 2 require links between inflected form and their lemmas (*cf.* Combo, section 3.2.2) and access to the morphological features of each inflected form (both machine interpretable and human readable, for the authoring tool). The development time alloted to the project forced us to base the lexicon on the traits of the French language, thus making the structure hardly usable for other languages.

Based on this assumption we undertook the task of creating a data structure and the associated software that will allow administrators to import their own lexicon into MagicWord. The issues raised by this task are manyfolds and intertwine the linguistic nature of the material handled by Magic-Word, its game nature, the learning objectives and the overall usability of the software.

4 Updating the datastructure

The first issue is to provide a lexicon structure that will make the game as open as possible, widely and easily used.

4.1 Formalism for the lexicons

We therefore resorted to a rather standard formalism for the lexicon, to wit, tab-separated values (TSV). Given that the lexicon files are encoded in UTF-8, the game should be able to handle most alphabets.

A lexicon row is organized in three columns :

- **Form**: the first column represents the lexical form.

- **Root**: the second column contains a label which connects forms among themselves and which is used for the combo rule (*cf.* section 3.2.2) that was also revamped to make it more generic. We named the column "root" but it can used for anything and the displayed name can be customized, depending on the pedagogical intents, and the language involved. To make full use of the combo rule, that columns could contain the lemma for inflected languages, but it could also, for example, contain an archilexeme, a root word, or even the phonetic transcription if the aim is to work on homophony.

- **Features**: The third column contains features (morphological, grammatical or other), organized in label-value pairs, separated with semi-colons. There are no constraints about the content, the software takes the input as it is formulated.

As a consequence, some perl scripts have been developed to format lexicons from different sources[3] into our formalism. This makes the integration of new languages easier. It is even possible to have several lexicons for a same language coexisting in a MagicWord instance. An administrator can thus provide teachers and learners with a lexicon putting the emphasis on basic vocabulary for instance and another one focusing verbs conjugations, etc.

The "features" column is associated with their transcription in natural language. This is necessary to provide the learner with information on the

---

[3]Use of free lexical resources:

- English lexicon: dela (Courtois, 2004);

- French lexicon: morphalou 3 (ATILF, 2019);

- Russian, Spanish, Galician, French & English lexicons: FreeLing (Padró and Stanilovsky, 2012).

forms found, but also for anyone who would create a grid for a "conquer" game (*cf.* section 3.2.3) and add a morphological objective. It is planned to add a nesting dimension to the features, which would allow authors and players to adopt a finer approach, manipulating feature classes and subclasses. We also intend to make features label and value translatable in every interface language, either in the specifications file (*cf.* section 4.2) or in the administration panel.

4.2 Game/lexicon specifications

Having defined a generic formalism for the import of the lexicon does not make it useable for the system. Indeed, the game relies on various linguistic elements that will constitute metadata for the import of the lexicon. We will describe in this section the additional information necessary for the system to successfully create a game based on the imported lexicon. This information is to be provided to the system in a text file.

4.2.1 Character rewriting rules

Considering the way words are constructed in the game (*cf.* section 3.1), if the alphabet used contains to many different signs there is a high probability that the number of words to find in grids will be lower, thus making the game more difficult to play. For instance, in French, most letter games (crossword puzzles, boggle, scrabble, etc.) traditionally ignore diacritics. In these games "E" represents at the same time all variations of "E" (case & diacritics): "e", "E", "É", "é", "È", etc.

To allow such behavior, the system can be provided with a set of rules to rewrite the forms only using a subset of the alphabet of the lexicon. After rewriting occurs, whenever the game is played all characters are displayed in uppercase in the interface.

The system gives the administrator the possibility to declare a set of rules that to any given string of letters (made of 1 to n letters) associates a replacement string (empty, single letter or n-gram). E.g. a simple rule to rewrite uppercase 'Œ' and "œ" to the lowercase "oe" would be `RW:Œ,œ=oe`.

Administrators must be aware that the rules are applied in the same order as they are written in the file to avoid side effects. But that gives them the power to shift the balance between accuracy and productivity (number of words in the grids) based on their learning objectives. They can even create 1337 grids if they carefully craft the rewriting rules[4], thanks to the character rewriting rules.

4.2.2 "Rush" mode scoring

In the same way that scrabble is scored differently from one language to the other, MagicWord needs to adapt its scoring system based on the loaded lexicon. The scoring system works around three components to associate to each inflected form found a certain number of points added to the user's score:

- **Letters**: each letter has an inherent value in the game, the base of the word score is the sum of the letters' values;

- **Wordlength**: longer words score more points than shorter words;

- **Combo**: a bonus is attributed if the word is part of a combo and in which position (the 5th word in a combo scores more points than the 3rd).

All these number of scores need to take into account the language. For instance, the English language leaves very little room for (inflection related) combos compared to French, Spanish or German and this should be addressed by putting more weight on the first words in a combo. The frequency of the letters can also be taken into account in the same way as in Scrabble. The length can be neutralized or not depending on the decisions of the administrator, who can specify all the values.

Samples of rules about scoring are given in the specification file model within the game. The administrator can refer to this file in order to write his own rules.

The default value for each **letter** is one point if not defined in the specification file. The interface also allows the administrator to change those values in the administration lexicon section.

Further work is currently planned to attribute automatically a number of points to each letter depending on its frequency in the 'form column' of the lexicon file (after the application of the rewriting rules). The most frequent letters should be associated to the lowest score and vice versa.

By default, the "wordlength" score is set at the size of the word minus one (*i.e.* a four letter word

has a "wordlength" score of three). It is also possible to parameter those values in the lexicon specification file but also in the application in the lexicon administration section.

Likewise combo bonus values — established for any length from 2 to 7 words — can be modified by the administrator either through the lexicon specification file or online by using the lexicon administration interface.

By defining a generic formalism both for the entries of the lexicon and the metadata that will allow to create a game out of it, we have explained the influence and control over the game that is granted to the administrator through the import of a new lexicon. Still, the playability of the game depends on the ability of the system to provide grids with sufficient forms available.

4.3 Grid generation

One of the attractive game features of Ruzzle and Wordament is that they are *"fast-paced"*[56]. In order not to ruin one of the central aspects of such games, the grid generation should therefore produce letters configuration ensuring a minimum of foundable forms thus keeping grid interest and playability. It is especially important for learners not to feel discouraged. Another issue is to find strategies that will not limit exaggeratedly the coverage of the lexicon.

In this section, we present our strategy to generate grids with sufficient forms available. Our strategy is based on bigrams. In order to quantify our algorithm, we introduce two metrics computed across multiple grids:

- **productivity**: average number of forms and/or combos available in a grid;

- **diversity**: number of distinct lemmas available across generated grids.

4.3.1 Use of bigrams

The letters configuration should depend on the language and *i.e.* the lexicon used. We thus resorted to the use of bigrams. The rationale behind this choice is that depending on their position in the grids each letter is part of 3 (corner), 5 (edge) or 8 (center) bigrams. Is it complicated to have full control over the content of the grid, yet if the bigrams represented in the grid are frequent in the

---

[4]That will not include the words invented by the *"leet"* community but just the way words are transcribed

[5]"Ruzzle is a fast-paced and addictively fun word game" (Presentation of the game by the mag interactive).

[6]"Wordament is rather fast-paced" (Game review).

language, there is higher probability that the grid contains more words.

In consequence, throughout lexicon import, we list every bigram that occur at least once in a form and calculate bigrams frequency. Then, when a grid is generated, the algorithm organizes the letters in the grid, after randomly drawing them. Rather than resorting to the "scrabble bag" algorithm, like in v1 and v2, we decided to weigh the drawing of letters based on the frequency of bigrams. Once the first letters have been disposed in the grid, letters that are part of more frequent bigrams involving existing letters in the grid are more likely to be selected.

One of the issues of such an algorithm is that the sheer diversity of existing bigrams might produce noise regarding our objectives (high productivity without lowering too much diversity). We therefore introduce a frequency threshold[7] under which bigrams are ignored[8]. For example, if the threshold is set to 5, the 5% less frequent bigrams will disregarded. This has consequences on the grids:

- a positive side effect is the exclusion of parasitic characters (mostly due to encoding issues);

- less frequent bigrams withdrawal (thus augmenting the probability that the bigrams in the grid are used in more forms);

- frequent bigrams occurring in frequent morphemes of the specific lexicon are more represented in grids. As a consequence, inflection bigrams[9] are also more represented (which is one of our objectives for languages with rich inflection mechanisms, *cf.* section 3.1).

4.3.2 Forms diversity & productivity in grids

We have tested this algorithm in relation with various threshold values with the *Morphalou3* french lexicon (668 993 entries). We chose to make the bigram threshold vary between 0 and 100, selecting 13 values (*cf.* fig. 2). Foreach value, we generate 2000 grids and evaluate productivity (average score per grid) and diversity (overall score for 2000 grids).

---

[7]The administration panel enables the administrator to temper with this threshold value.

[8]Even if they are ignored, they can still occur through the layout of the grid considering that they share letters with more frequent bigrams.

[9]found in morphemes expressing tense, number, gender, mood, etc.

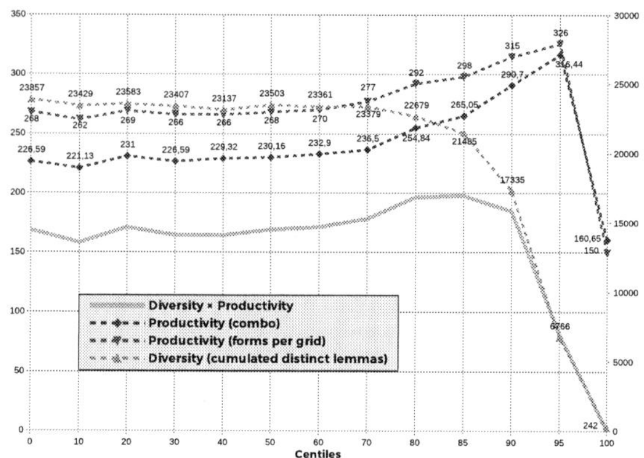

Figure 2: Forms diversity & productivity depending on bigrams centiles

The first element one can note is that combo forms are highly represented. At the ultimate threshold value (99), combos even over come total forms in the grid, which is explainable by the fact that ambiguity can provoke forms to be part of more than one possible combo. For instance, "lit" can be found in a combo about the noun "lit" (bed: "lit", "lits") and the verb "lire" (read: "lit", "lis"). In that example, 3 different forms result in 4 possible (and mutually exclusive) combo forms.

As expected, the gap between combo and form productivity reduces as the threshold value increases, which is consistent with the global reduction of diversity as the threshold value increases.

The best diversity over productivity rates are reached between the exclusion of the 80% and 85% less represented bigrams. Over this specific data, this zone is sensitive as the 70% mark initiates a deep dive in diversity that results in five letters (j, k, w, x, y) being excluded from the game altogether.

With our objectives (working specifically on inflection mechanism), the v3 of MagicWord will be deployed using an 81% threshold value on the morphalou lexicon for "rush" grids generation, in order to maximize productivity, without going to deep in the loss of diversity. It is worth noting that some diversity can be achieved by creating "conquer" grids that will contain specific words.

5   Consequences

From the learner's standpoint, changes in Magic-Word v3 might not seem overwhelming (though the interfaces will be sleeker, especially on mobile devices). All the same we actually underwent a complete overhaul of the data structures that, provided close collaboration between teachers and engineers, can open many doors pedagogically speaking.

The obvious improvement is that MagicWord can now virtually be configured for any alphabetical language. But the generic structure provided to integrate other languages is augmented with modalities that improve drastically the control over the system.

First, all scoring mechanisms can be tuned to focus on certain aspects by putting more or less weight on letters, word length or combos.

More importantly, the data structure, now allows the use of language resources that focus on more diverse phenomena. For instance, if one wants to introduce a more semantic dimension to the game, the resources used to create "Semantic Boggle" (Toma et al., 2017) could be integrated to create semantic combos, thus keeping the fast pace component that some (but not all) players like in Boggle and other derivatives. One can imagine, the same instance of MagicWord could even embark multiple lexicons for the same language to mix rules — *i.e.* viewpoint on the language — inside the same game.

5.1 Future works

In the long run, further improvements will be made to improve administrator control over the game. Two columns might be added to the lexicon.

The first will be scoring information (to be interpreted with a formula provided in the description file). In the long run, frequency lists could be used to refine the scoring process and add a "usage" dimension to it. This will allow a per-word scoring, that could be corpus based (lesser used words scoring more than more widely used words) or even game based (the words more often present in grids and more often found being worth less points).

It should be noted that in the previous iterations of MagicWord, lemmas definitions were automatically retrieved from the wiktionary. In keeping with the genericity, we plan to let administrators define where and how these informations should be collected, by providing urls and regular expressions (or xpath queries). Some institution might have *offline* resources with definitions of the terms in the lexicon written for learners. This information could be provided in the last added column. But the ideal "combo" would be to interface MagicWord with a system of personal lexicon (Mangeot et al., 2016) that would allow to make links between the in-game wordbox[10] with out-of-game more formal activities.

Acknowledgments

The present work has been funded by "Démarre SHS!".

None of this work would have been possible without the many contributiors, most of them volunteers.

References

ATILF. 2019. Morphalou. ORTOLANG (Open Resources and TOols for LANGuage) – `www.ortolang.fr`.

Gilles Brougère. 2012. Le jeu peut-il être sérieux? Revisiter Jouer/Apprendre en temps de serious game. *Australian Journal of French Studies*, 49(2):117–129.

Amy Bruckman. 1999. Can educational be fun? In *Game Developers Conference*, volume 99, page 75–79.

Daniel A. Castañeda and Moon-Heum Cho. 2016. Use of a game-like application on a mobile device to improve accuracy in conjugating spanish verbs. *Computer Assisted Language Learning*, 29(7):1195–1204.

Casual Games Association. 2015. How much does it cost to develop a casual game? FAQ, Casual Games Association.

Catherine Cerezo. 2012. Un serious game junior, vecteur d'estime de soi et d'apprentissages pour des élèves de cm2. *Adolescence*, 30(79):133–143.

Blandine Courtois. 2004. *Dictionnaires électroniques DELAF anglais et français*, volume 24 of *Lingvisticæ Investigationes Supplementa*, page 113–123. John Benjamins, Amsterdam.

James Paul Gee. 2003. What video games have to teach us about learning and literacy. *Computers in Entertainment*, 1(1):20–20.

Coralie Girard, Jean Écalle, and Annie Magnan. 2013. Serious games as new educational tools: how effective are they? a meta-analysis of recent studies. *Journal of Computer Assisted Learning*, 29(3):207–219.

---

[10]Players can store words of their interest in a personal lexicon called "wordbox".

Matthew Handrahan. 2014. Spil: Casual games "just don't pay the bills any more". *gameindustry.biz*.

Philip Hubbard. 1991. Evaluating computer games for language learning. *Simulation & Gaming*, 22(2):220–223.

Michel Lavigne. 2014. Les faiblesses ludiques et pédagogiques des serious games. In *Actes de TiceMed 9*. SFSIC.

Mathieu Loiseau, Cristiana Cervini, Andrea Ceccherelli, Monica Masperi, Paola Salomoni, Marco Roccetti, Antonella Valva, and Francesca Bianco. 2016. *Exploring learners' perceptions of the use of digital letter games for language learning: the case of Magic Word*, page 277–283. Research-publishing.net, Dublin, Voillans.

Mathieu Loiseau, Virginie Zampa, Racha Hallal, Pauline Ballot, Yoann Goudin, Nadia Yassine-Diab, and John Kenwright. 2017. Gamer (gaming applications for multilingual educational resources).

Mathieu Mangeot, Valérie Bellynck, Emmanuelle Eggerss, Mathieu Loiseau, and Yoann Goudin. 2016. Exploitation d'une base lexicale dans le cadre de la conception de l'enpa innovalangues. In *Actes de la conférence conjointe JEP-TALN-RECITAL 2016*, volume 9 : ELTAL, page 48–64, Paris. ATALA/AFCP.

Agnès Montaufier. 2016. Magic word : comment intégrer le jeu dans une classe de langues ? Master's thesis, Grenoble.

Diana Oblinger. 2004. The next generation of educational engagement. *Journal of Interactive Media in Education*, 2004(1):1–16.

Lluís Padró and Evgeny Stanilovsky. 2012. Freeling 3.0: Towards wider multilinguality. In *Proceedings of the Eight International Conference on Language Resources and Evaluation (LREC'12)*, page 2473–2479, Istanbul, Turkey. European Language Resources Association (ELRA).

Marco Roccetti, Paola Salomoni, Mathieu Loiseau, Monica Masperi, Virginie Zampa, Andrea Ceccherelli, Cristiana Cervini, and Antonella Valva. 2016. On the design of a word game to enhance italian language learning. In *2016 International Conference on Computing, Networking and Communications (ICNC)*, Kaui. IEEE Communications Society.

Mike Sharples, Patrick McAndrew, Martin Weller, Rebecca Ferguson, Elizabeth FitzGerald, Tony Hirst, and Mark Gaved. 2013. Innovating pedagogy 2013: Exploring new forms of teaching, learning and assessment, to guide educators and policy makers. Technical Report 2, The Open University, United Kingdom.

Haydée Silva Ochoa. 1999. *Poétiques du jeu. La métaphore ludique dans la théorie et la critique littéraires françaises au XXe siècle*. Thèse, Université Paris 3 — Sorbonne Nouvelle, Paris.

Heinrich Söbke, Thomas Bröker, and Oliver Kornadt. 2013. Using the master copy — adding educational content to commercial video games. In *The Proceedings of The 7th European Conference on Games Based Learning*, volume 2, page 521–530, Reading. Instituto Superior de Engenharia do Porto (ISEP), Academic Conferences and Publishing International Limited.

Irina Toma, Cristina-Elena Alexandru, Mihai Dascalu, Philippe Dessus, and Stefan Trausan-Matu. 2017. Semantic boggle: A game for vocabulary acquisition. In *Data Driven Approaches in Digital Education*, page 606–609, Cham. Springer International Publishing.

Virginie Zampa, Nadia Yassine-Diab, and Mathieu Loiseau. 2017. Des jeux et des mots : stratégies de conception et réalisations. *Recherche et pratiques pédagogiques en langues de spécialité*, 36(2).

Understanding Vocabulary Growth Through An Adaptive Language Learning System

Elma Kerz[1], Andreas Burgdorf[3], Daniel Wiechmann[2], Stefan Meeger[1],
Yu Qiao[1], Christian Kohlschein[1], Tobias Meisen[3]

[1]RTWH Aachen University, Germany
[2]University of Amsterdam, Netherlands
[3]University of Wuppertal, Germany

Abstract

Learning analytics and educational data mining have gained an increased interest as an important way of understanding the way humans learn. The paper introduces an adaptive language learning system designed to track and accelerate the development of academic vocabulary skills thereby generating dense longitudinal data of individual vocabulary growth trajectories. We report on an exploratory study based on the dense longitudinal data obtained from our system. The goal is the study was twofold: (1) to examine the pace and shape of vocabulary growth trajectories and (2) to understand the role various individual differences factors play in explaining variation in such growth trajectories.

1 Introduction

Considerable variability is observed in the rate at which individuals (both children and adults) learn language. From the literature on child development and adult second language development we know that some individuals start slow and speed up, others start fast and continue at a steady pace. This variability is particularly apparent in the area of vocabulary acquisition (see, e.g., Hart and Risley, 1995; Pellicer-Sánchez, 2018). Understanding the acquisition of vocabulary knowledge – i.e. the pace of vocabulary growth – is considered to be of key importance for a number of reasons: Vocabulary skills are shown to be strongly related to a variety of academic, vocational and social outcomes (e.g. Rohde and Thompson, 2007; Dollinger et al., 2008; Verhoeven et al., 2011).

These skills are a crucial component of language competence and language use (Nation, 1993; Milton, 2013) and their development is found to boost the acquisition of other language domains, such as grammar and phonology (e.g., Goodman and Bates, 2013). Vocabulary skills have been recognized as a strong predictor of reading comprehension ability in both first and second language development (e.g., Muter et al., 2004; Tannenbaum et al., 2006; Verhoeven and Van Leeuwe, 2008; Verhoeven et al., 2011; Cain and Oakhill, 2011).

With the emergence of technology-enhanced language learning systems and automatic analyses of educational data obtained by such systems, many efforts have been directed at facilitating the learning experience (e.g., Becker and Nguyen, 2017). These efforts emphasize the effectiveness of adaptive (personalized) language learning as opposed to traditional cohort-based learning (Ismail et al., 2016). The dense longitudinal data generated by such systems open up new avenues for exploring human learning based on learning analytics and educational data mining, an emerging multidisciplinary field closely linked to statistics and machine learning on the one side and the cognitive and language sciences on the other side (Vahdat et al., 2016). These data make it possible to perform learning behavior analytics at many different granularities and behavior categories.

In this paper we introduce an adaptive language learning system – AISLE (short for *Adaptive Statistical Language Learning*) – that was designed with the aim to track and accelerate the development of vocabulary skills and to generate dense, longitudinal data to understand the dynamics of growth of individual learning trajectories. The design of the system was motivated by recent developments in the language sciences in general, and in the area of language learning and processing in particular. These developments are driven, among other things, by the existence of large databases of

Elma Kerz, Andreas Burgdorf, Daniel Wiechmann, Stefan Meeger, Yu Qiao, Christian Kohlschein and Tobias Meisen 2019. Understanding vocabulary growth through an adaptive language learning system. *Proceedings of the 8th Workshop on Natural Language Processing for Computer Assisted Language Learning (NLP4CALL 2019)*. Linköping Electronic Conference Proceedings 164: 65–78.

language use (language corpora), the use of NLP techniques and statistical analyses and computational modeling of language data.

The paper is organized as follows. In a first step, we describe the architecture and design principles of the adaptive language learning system. In a second step, we present first results of a study on vocabulary growth based on the dense longitudinal data obtained by the system. The data come from a group of 46 second language (L2) learners of English who engaged with the AISLE system in a laboratory setting for several hours distributed across three sessions over a period of three weeks. Using a within-subject design embedded in an individual-differences (IDs) framework, the same group of participants was administered a battery of tasks assessing a range of experience-related, cognitive and affective IDs factors that may affect second language acquisition. The study is guided by the following two research questions: (1) What is the best longitudinal model that describes participants' vocabulary growth and how much variation is there in growth rates? and (2) What is the role of a range of IDs factors in explaining variation in participants' vocabulary acquisition?

2 Introducing AISLE: Design Principles and Architecture

The AISLE system is characterized by two design features: [1] 'optimal language input' (see Subsection 2.1) and [2] 'optimal repetition intervals' (see Subsection 2.2). The graphical user interface (GUI) was designed to give users automatic feedback during the learning process (see Subsection 2.3). The interface also includes a number of questionnaires and tasks assessing diverse individual differences across experience-related, cognitive and affective domains.

2.1 Extraction and Representation of Vocabulary Items

Since the target population are university students, we were particularly interested in tracking and accelerating the development of academic vocabulary (AV). As it is the case with the general vocabulary skills, AV knowledge is recognized as an indispensable component of academic reading abilities (e.g., Biemiller, 1999; Nagy and Townsend, 2012), which is and has been directly linked to academic success, economic opportunity, and societal well-being (Ippolito et al., 2008; Jacobs,

2008). The key role of academic vocabulary in educational success is true for both native and non-native speakers of English (e.g., Schmitt et al. 2011). In response to this, a substantial amount of research has been devoted to the compilation of vocabulary lists (Gardner and Davies, 2013). A major advance has been in recognizing that language requires not only knowledge of a vast amount of statistically relevant academic vocabulary but also successful extraction of the statistics of academic multiword sequences (MWS), i.e. variably sized continuous or discontinuous frequently recurring strings of words. In fact, in recent models of language MWS (ngrams) are increasingly recognized as the fundamental building blocks that facilitate anticipatory processing and boost language acquisition (Arnon and Christiansen, 2017). Correspondingly, the term 'vocabulary item' is used here as a cover term for both single words and MWS (ngrams of different orders).

To arrive at 'optimal language input', we extracted 'statistically relevant' vocabulary items – words (unigrams) and n-grams for $n \in \{2, 3, 4\}$ – from a Corpus of Contemporary American English[1], approx. 560 million words of text equally divided among spoken, fiction, popular magazines, newspapers, and academic texts. This extraction involved several preprocessing steps that we performed using the spaCy[2] framework for natural language processing. The whole preprocessing pipeline is written with PySpark[3] and executed on a Hadoop[4] cluster. The pipeline involved the following four consecutive steps:

1. *Lemmatization*: This step is only performed to extract unigrams. The outcome of this step is a sequence of lemmas for a given processed document.

2. *Sentence splitting*: The sentence splitting was performed to ensure that n-grams are not extracted across sentence boundaries, and also to increase the degree of parallelism of the following steps.

3. *N-Gram Extraction*: Next, we extracted n-grams for all for $n \in \{2, 3, 4\}$ for each sentence. The result of this step is a collection

---

[1]`https://corpus.byu.edu/coca/`
[2]`https://spacy.io/`
[3]`https://spark.apache.org/`
[4]`https://hadoop.apache.org/`

of all n-grams along with the number of documents in which an item occurs and its frequency of occurrence in each document.

4. *Metrics Calculation*: The final step concerns the calculation of more sophisticated metrics, used in the identification of statistically relevant vocabulary items. By applying these metrics, only those words relevant for understanding texts - neither too general, nor to specific - are presented to learners.

As a metric for the distribution of a n-gram in the corpus we use dispersion as defined by Gardner and Davies (2013). Formalized, we used the following metrics for frequency f and dispersion d where i_n defines an arbitrary item with n words (n-gram), T_k defines a subcorpus with $k \in \{(a), (b), (c), (d)\}$, $N_n(T_k)$ defines the list of n-grams in subcorpus T_k and $\#i_n(T_k)$ describes the count of the item i_n in the subcorpus T_k. Further, $\sigma i_n(T_k)$ describes the number of documents of subcorpus T_k, i_n appears in. The abbreviation *gen* stands for 'general' and *ac* for 'academic':

$$f_{gen}(i_n) := \frac{\sum\limits_{k \in \{a,b,c\}} \#i_n(T_k)}{\sum\limits_{k \in \{a,b,c\}} |N_n(T_k)|} \quad (1)$$

$$d_{gen}(i_n) := \frac{\sum\limits_{k \in \{a,b,c\}} \sigma i_n(T_k)}{\sum\limits_{k \in \{a,b,c\}} |N_n(T_k)|} \quad (2)$$

$$f_{ac}(i_n) := \frac{\#i_n(T_{(d)})}{|N_n(T_{(d)})|} \quad (3)$$

$$d_{ac}(i_n) := \frac{\sigma i_n(T_{(d)})}{|N_n(T_{(d)})|} \quad (4)$$

A vocabulary item is considered to be 'statistically relevant' if one of the conditions given in (5) and (6) holds, where k_f and k_d are variable thresholds for the frequency and dispersion ratio, respectively, between academic and general corpora that are determined experimentally, depending on value n:

$$\frac{f_{ac}(i_n)}{f_{gen}(i_n)} > k_f \quad (5)$$

$$\frac{d_{ac}(i_n)}{d_{gen}(i_n)} > k_d \quad (6)$$

Further, we calculate a rank that defines how academic a n-gram is as follows where the parameters MIN_D (minimum academic dispersion) and MIN_R (minimum ratio of academic and general dispersion) have to be evaluated experimentally for each item length:

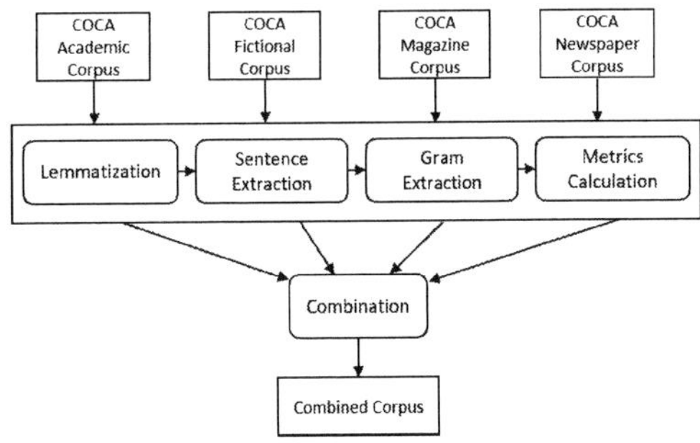

Figure 1: NLP pipeline for extracting statistically relevant vocabulary items

$$rank = \begin{cases} 0 & \text{if } d_{ac} < MIN_D \\ 0 & \text{if } \frac{d_{ac}}{d_{gen}} < MIN_R \\ \frac{f_{ac}}{f_{gen}} \cdot \frac{d_{ac}}{d_{general}} & \text{else} \end{cases} \quad (7)$$

After this pipeline has been executed for all sub-collections (a)-(d) of the COCA corpus a combination step is performed that aggregates the results from the four collections and calculates the defined rank for each item.

The extracted items are represented in a Neo4j[5] graph database. The access to the database was realized in a flask API. This enables the interconnection of each n-gram with all its constitutive lemmas, which is especially useful later on to ensure that the basic building blocks of an n-gram are known to a degree necessary to present it to the user during learning. The graph representation of data consists of three different types of nodes:

- *lemma*-nodes contain a lemma as well as related metrics like frequency and dispersion.

- *n-gram*-nodes contain a n-gram and related metrics like frequency and dispersion.

- *user*-nodes represent a user of the learning application together with some information about his current state of learning.

For relations, we define the following two types:

- *contains*: this directed relation connects n-gram nodes to the lemmas of the words it

---

[5] https://neo4j.com/

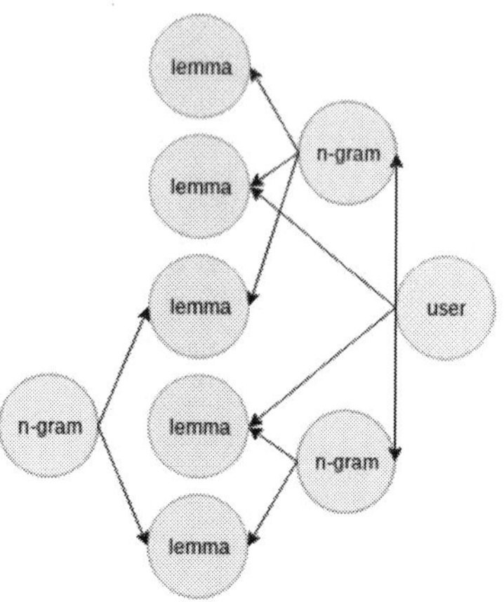

Figure 2: Representation of words and grams in a graph database

consists of. Additionally the relations store the metrics relative item frequency and entropy.

- *has_seen*: this directed relation connects user nodes to the lemmas and n-grams they have already seen while using the learning application. As soon as this relation is established, it further contains information about the current learning progress for this item like learning score, how often it has been presented and how long answers did take.

Lemma and n-gram nodes and their metrics are initially loaded directly from the aggregated corpus list and then connected using *contains*-relations which indicate the position of a lemma in the respective n-gram. Following the equations given in (5) and (6), we only imported academically relevant items into the graph database. The user nodes are populated from the running learning system application and a new node is generated for every user upon registration.

2.2 Learning algorithm

To ensure 'optimal repetition intervals' we developed and implemented an adaptive learning algorithm. The general structure of the learning algorithm is visualized in Figure 3. The algorithm selects a set of items from the graph database, which fall into four different categories: (1) items never seen before, (2) items recently answered incorrectly, (3) items close to be learned and (4) items already learned. The algorithm presents all items to the user one after the other and waits for the user's response. The current knowledge status of

a vocabulary item is represented by 'normalized learning score' that takes the user's prior history of a given item into account. Values between 0 and 0.8 indicate that a given item is not yet part of the user's vocabulary repertoire. Once the learner has reached a normalized learning score for a given item that is greater than 0.8 the item is considered to be learned. The scoring of an individual user response to an item depends on whether or not the item has already been presented to the user. If the item is presented for the first time and the answer is correct, a *has-seen*-relation with the value 0.8 is created in the graph database between the user and the item and the item is treated as already known. If the answer is incorrect, the evaluation of the answer depends on the severity of the error, so that a spelling error is punished less than a completely wrong word. To this end, the user's response – a character string – is compared with the target word(s) based on the Levenshtein distance between the two strings. The evaluation takes the length of the target item into account (1 - *Edit distance/Word length* (*in characters*)) and ranges between between 0 (maximally incorrect) and 1 (maximally correct)).

The primary metric of participants' performance is their cumulative number of items learned during the time of engagement with the system. An vocabulary item was taken to be learned if (i) it is was not marked as 'previously known' and (ii) its 'normalized learning score' – the sum of all scores received for an item normalized by the number of presentations – has reached the threshold value of 0.8. Based on the user's prior performance, the algorithm decides on the next set of items based on their statistical relevance and the learner's current knowledge state of the vocabulary items.

2.3 User Interface

Users interact with the system via a web interface based on the *vue.js*-framework[6]. The web interface provides two major functionalities: user interaction and user tracking. After login, the user has access to the vocabulary learning module as well as to a number of tasks and measures geared to assess a range of learner background and IDs factors. During vocabulary learning, the user performs a cloze test (aka fill-the-gap task) where a sentence is presented in which the target item is

---

[6]`https://vuejs.org/`

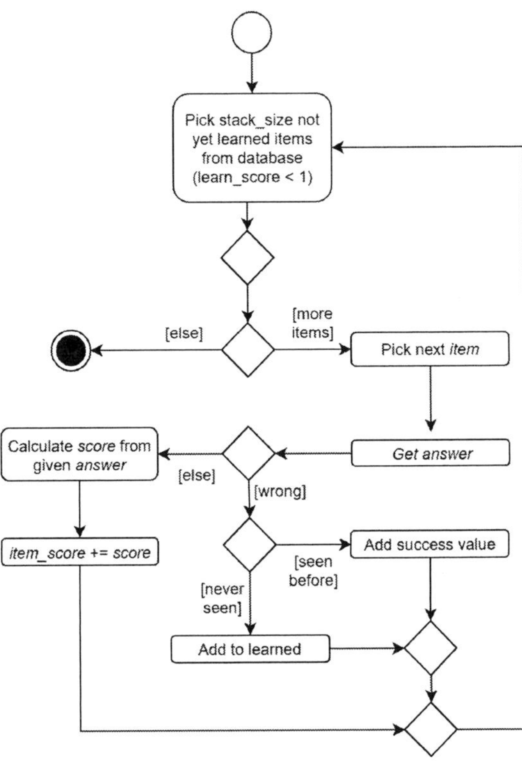

Figure 3: Learning Algorithm

missing and the task is to fill in the gap. The corresponding definition of the target item is presented below the sentence (see Figure 4 (top)). In case the user has entered the target word, the vocabulary item is colored green and displayed for two seconds. In case of a mismatch between the target and the user's input string, the correct string is presented with mismatching characters being highlighted in red font color (see Figure 4 (bottom)). After presentation of the correct answer, the user is prompted to re-enter it and the next item is presented. The interface stores and visualizes multiple relevant performance indicators that are available to the user at any point in time during interaction with the system. These indicators include the number of learned words so far and the longest streaks of consecutive correct inputs in the current session and during the total interaction period with the system (see Figure 5). A number of additional metrics are collected that, while not shown to the user, are useful for subsequent data analyses. These metrics include the number of responses per minute, the average number of repetitions per item, the number of items presented that were already known, the average number of pre-

sentations of an items until the item was learned, mean time until item learned in minutes, and the mean number of words per hour (see Table 1).

2.4 Integrated individual differences tasks and measures

The interface features a range of questionnaires and tasks assessing diverse individual differences (IDs) factors across experience-related, cognitive and affective domains. Upon successful registration, learners can currently complete a total of eight questionnaires and tasks. The group of currently integrated measures includes a two standardized tests designed to assess receptive vocabulary, the 'Lexical Test for Advanced Learners of English' (LexTALE, Lemhöfer and Broersma, 2012) and the 'Vocabulary Levels Test' (VLT, Schmitt et al., 2001) as well as a proxy measure of print exposure, the 'Author Recognition Test' (ART, West et al., 1993), and the 'Need for Cognition' test (NFC, Cacioppo et al., 1984), a personality-based measure indicating the degree to which an individual prefers cognitively engaging activities (see Subsection 3.2. for further details). The battery further contains implementations of two language and social background questionnaires – the LEAP-Q questionnaire (Marian et al., 2007) and the LSBQ-questionnaire (Anderson et al., 2018), as well as the Big Five Inventory (BFI, John et al., 2008) designed to assess five personality dimensions (Extraversion, Neuroticism, Conscientiousness, Openness to Experience, and Agreeableness). The web-based integration of tasks gauging additional cognitive abilities is still under development. At present, such tasks can be integrated using separate applications (see Section 3 for details on how these tasks are currently integrated into the system).

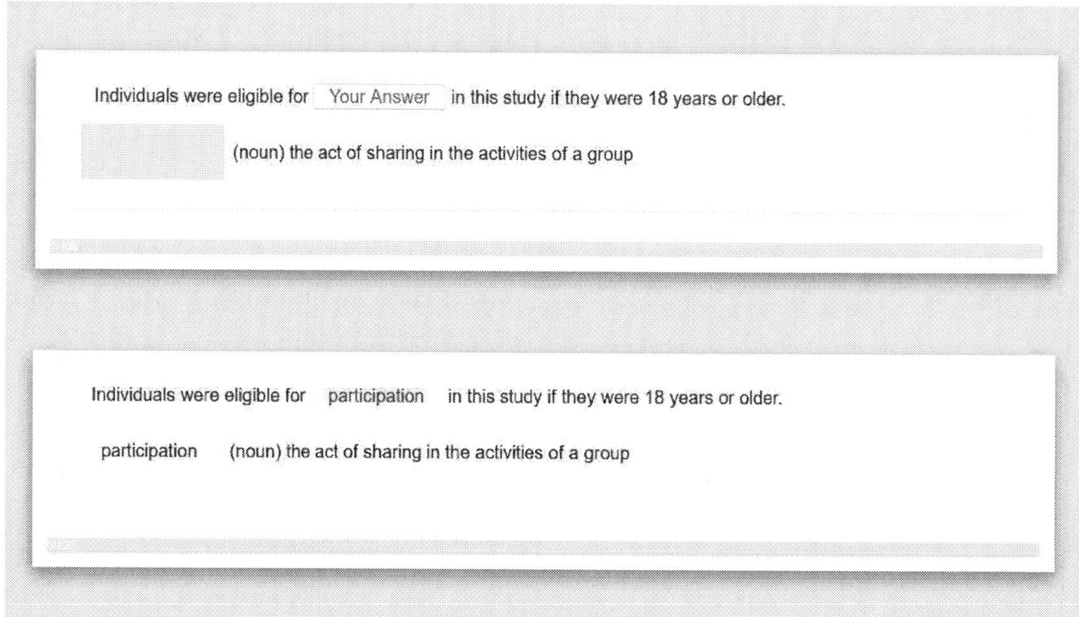

3 Modeling Growth Trajectories

In this section, we report on first results of a study on vocabulary growth based on the dense longitudinal data obtained by the AISLE system. As outlined in the Introduction (Section 1), the study addressed the following two research questions: (1) What is the best longitudinal model that describes participants' vocabulary growth and how much variation is there in growth rates? and (2) What is the role of a range of IDs factors in explaining variation in participants' vocabulary acquisition? We focus here on the acquisition of individual words (1-grams). The number of cumulative word types learned within a four-hour engagement with the AISLE system served as the measure of vocabulary growth. Variability in this performance metric was related to a total of 17 individual difference measures: four experience-based measures, five personality indicators and eight cognitive measures (see Subsection 3.2 for details; an overview of these measures is provided in Table 2).

3.1 Participants

The data come from forty-six second language (L2) learners of English (25 female and 21 male, M = 22.98 years, SD = 3.32). All participants were university students from the RWTH Aachen University studying towards a BA or MA degree.

3.2 Materials

L2-Experience measures: Participants were administered two receptive vocabulary tasks: the 'Lexical Test for Advanced Learners of English' (LexTALE, Lemhöfer and Broersma, 2012) and the 'Vocabulary Levels Test' (VLT, Schmitt et al., 2001). The LexTALE is a short yes/no vocabulary test implemented as a lexical decision task. In it particpants are presented a series of letter strings, some of which are existing English words and some of which are not, and are asked to indicate for each item whether it is an existing English word or not. The test consists of 60 items (40 words, 20 nonwords). Performance on the test is assessed as the percentage of correct responses adjusted for the unequal proportion of words and nonwords (averaged % correct).

The VLT assesses vocabulary knowledge at four frequency levels of English word families targeting the top 2000, 3000, 5000, and 10000 most frequent words in a language plus words from the domain of academic language (based on items from the Academic Word List; Coxhead, 2000). Each level consists of 30 items in a multiple matching format in which single words in the left-hand column need to be matched with a meaning presented in the right-hand column. Performance on the VLT is measured as the number of correct matches.

In addition, participants completed the 'Author Recognition Test' (ART, West et al., 1993) and the 'Need for Cognition' test (NFC, Cacioppo et al., 1984). The ART is a proxy measure of print exposure in which test takers are presented with a series of 81 names and foils and are asked to indicate which ones they recognize as authors. Performance on the task is assessed in terms of the number of correctly identified authors minus the number of foils selected.

The NFC is a personality-based measure indicating the degree to which an individual prefers cognitively engaging activities. Test takers indicate their agreement (based on a 5-point Likert scale) with 18 statements such as 'I really enjoy a task that involves coming up with new solutions to problems' (positive polarity item) or 'Thinking is not my idea of fun' (negative polarity item). Scores on the NFC are determined by averaging the responses to all items (with negative polarity items being reverse scored).

Personality-related measures: Participants were also asked to fill in the Big Five Inventory (BFI, John et al., 2008), a 44-item personality-related questionnaire that measures an individual on the Big Five personality dimensions (Extraversion, Neuroticism, Conscientiousness, Openness to Experience, and Agreeableness). Scores on each dimension are assessed in terms of person-centered z-scores adjusted for differences in acquiescent response styles ('yea-saying' vs. 'nay-saying')

Cognitive measures: We administered a total of eight cognitive IDs measures as indicators three aspects of cognition: (1) four indicators of statistical learning ability (the probabilistic Serial Reaction Time (pSRT) task from Kaufman et al. (2010), along with the Visual-Nonverbal-Adjacent (VNA), Auditory-Verbal-Adjacent (AVA), and the Auditory-Verbal-Nonadjacent (AVN) Artificial Grammar Learning tasks described in Siegelman and Frost (2015)), (2) one indicator of verbal working memory (a modified version of the Reading Span (RSPAN) task as described in Farmer et al. (2017)), and (3) three indicators of cognitive control (the variants of the Simon task and the Eriksen-Flanker task used in Wilhelm et al. (2013) as well as the Stroop Color-Word task described in Linnman et al. (2006)). Performance on all measures was scored following standard procedures. A brief description of each measure is provided in Table 2. For further details on these tasks the reader is referred to the cited literature.

3.3 Procedure

The participants engaged with the adaptive language learning system in a laboratory setting for a total of approximately four hours distributed across three sessions within a period of three weeks. Once they had successfully registered participants completed the experience- and personality-related questionnaires and tasks. The cognitive tasks were interspersed with the vocabulary learning sessions. These tasks were administered in a laboratory setting using PsychoPy[7], an open-source application for the creation of experiments in behavioral science (Peirce et al., 2019). The results obtained from these tasks were automatically exported into the graph database.

3.4 Results

Before turning to the modeling results, we first briefly present an overview of the descriptive statistics of the engagement- and performance-metrics tracked by the AISLE system (Table 1). As shown in Table 1, there was considerable variation in the way users interacted with the system as well as in their learning outcomes. For example, the observed range of the number of items learned was 8 to 84 items, with a mean of 19.18 items learned and a standard deviation of 17.90 items. Normalized by the net amount of time that users engaged with the system these differences corresponded to an observed range in mean learning rates of 0.89 to 23.03 words learned per hour, with a mean of 5.16 words per hour and a standard deviation of 4.36 words per hour. The descriptive statistics of all cognitive, personality-related and L2 experience-related individual difference measures investigated in this study is presented in Table 2.

In finding the best model for vocabulary growth, we began with an empirical plot of participants' cumulative number of words learned (Figure 6:

left panel). As is evident from this plot, participants varied considerably in their rates of vocabulary growth. Growth curve analysis (Mirman, 2017) was used to analyze the word learning trajectories up to the 678th interaction, which was reached by 75% of the participants (i.e. 25% of the participants responded to fewer than 678 items). To obtain the best fitting within-person model for these data, i.e. the 'unconditional growth model (GCM)', we fitted linear, quadratic, and cubic growth models to the data using orthogonal polynomials of 'number of interactions' as our 'Time' variables. All models were fitted using the BOBYQA algorithm for optimization as implemented in the package lme4 (version 1.1-21, Bates et al., 2014) for the R language and environment for statistical computing and graphics (R Core Team, 2018). Model comparisons using Akaike's Information Criterion (AIC) revealed that the cubic unconditional growth model best represented the empirical data. The plot of the cubic model also best mirrored the plot of the empirical data (see Figure 6: center panel). On average, the cubic model indicates that users have an estimated cumulative vocabulary of approximately 15 word types, with an average increase of about 2 words types per 100 presented items. The rightmost plot in Figure 6 shows the predicted vocabulary growth at the 10th, 25th, 50th, 75th, and 90th percentiles.

Next we explored the relationship between vocabulary growth and each of our 17 L2 experience-related, personality-related and cognitive individual differences measures. All IDs variables were dichotomized based on median splits (high vs. low). The best fitting (minimal adequate) model was identified using a forward model selection procedure based on likelihood ratio tests, i.e. we started with the cubic unconditional growth model and evaluated the added value of each IDs predictor. We subsequently included the most significant predictor, re-estimated the model and repeated the procedure until no significant term was left to include. In all models we used the maximal random effects structure justified by our design, which included by-subject random intercepts and slopes on all time terms. The results of the models are summarized in Table 3. Preliminary analyses (data not shown) indicated that – when considered on their own – 9 out of the 17 IDs variables were significant predictors of growth trajectories (L2 experience-related: ART (sig. quadratic

---

[7]https://www.psychopy.org/

Table 1: Descriptive statistics of the AISLE metrics

	mean	sd	obs. range
Total number of responses	828.67	391.34	271 – 1980
Number of responses per minute	3.84	1.92	1.69 – 10.64
Average number of repetitions per item	4.67	1.97	2.24 – 10.54
Number of items already known	58.84	38.99	17 – 172
Number of new items presented	160.80	26.30	111 – 216
Number of items learned	19.18	17.90	4 – 84
Average number of presentations until word learned	2.36	0.99	1.00 – 5.52
Mean time until items learned (in min)	23.00	6.94	10.63 – 49.38
Number of items learned per hour	5.16	4.36	0.89 – 23.03

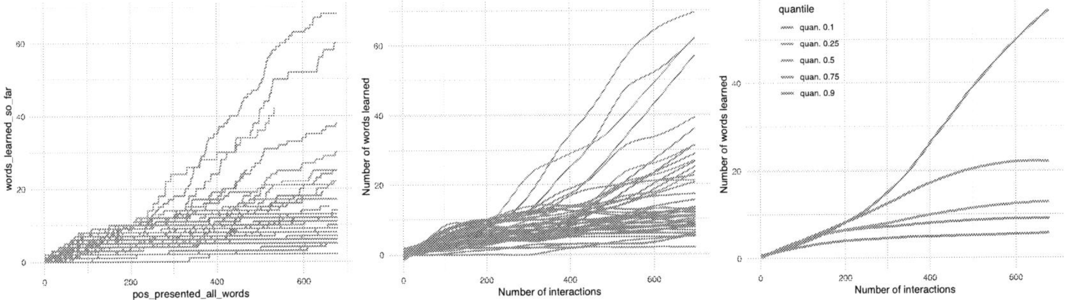

Figure 6: Plots of empirical growth trajectories (left), predicted growth trajectories from cubic model (center), and average predicted vocabulary growth at the 10th, 25th, 50th, 75th, and 90th percentiles.

and cubic change), LexTALE (sig. quadratic change), NFC (sig. linear, quadratic and cubic change); VLT (sig. quadratic change); Cognitive: Ericsen-Flanker (sig. linear, quadratic and cubic change); Personality-related: Openness (sig. linear, quadratic and cubic change), Extraversion (sig. quadratic and cubic change), Agreeableness (sig. quadratic and cubic change), Neuroticsm (sig. linear, quadratic and cubic change). No effects were found for the conscientiousness personality trait and the cognitive predictors AVA, AVN, VNA, pSRT, RSPAN, Simon, and Stroop. The NFC score was the strongest single predictor of linear, quadratic and cubic growth (all $p < .01$, see Table 3), indicating that participants with higher NFC scores exhibited significantly faster rates of increase, relative to participants with lower NFC scores. The best fitting (minimal adequate) model contained the participants scores on the Need for Cognition (NFC) scale as well as scores on the Openness to Experience personality trait. This model indicated that learning rates were significantly associated with the openness personality trait even after controlling for the effects of L2 experience, such that individuals with high openness

scores showed faster learning rates. These effects are visualized in Figure 7, which shows that the trajectories of vocabulary growth began to separate early (around 200 presented items) based on whether or not the participant has a high or low NFC score. The effect of openness became apparent after 400 presentations, where individuals with lower scores level-off while the culmulative vocabulary of individuals with higher scores kept increasing.

4 Discussion and Future Work

It is widely recognized that vocabulary skills play a critical role in people's lives and future prospects as they are shown to be strongly related to individuals' overall educational success and academic achievement (Hart and Risley, 1995; Townsend et al., 2012). As a consequence, research on vocabulary growth has emphasized the importance of understanding not only the causes of individual differences in vocabulary growth rates but also the consequences of acquiring vocabulary at different rates (Rowe et al., 2012; Duff et al., 2015). Much of the cognitive developmental research in the area of vocabulary growth has utilized cross-

Table 2: Descriptive statistics for all cognitive, personality-related and L2 experience-related individual difference measures investigated in this study.

Task	Dependent measure	Mean (SD)	Obs. range
Statistical Learning			
pSRT	Mean reaction time (RT) difference between improbable and probable trials (in sec) ($\Delta RT_{improbable} - RT_{probable}$)	0.04 (0.03)	-0.02 – 0.1
VNA	Percent correct (out of 32 2-alternative forced choice trails)	49.03 (10.01)	31.25 – 71.88
AVA	Percent correct (out of 36 2-alternative forced choice trails)	51.36 (12.77)	16.67 – 86.11
AVN	Percent correct (out of 36 2-alternative forced choice trails)	52.04 (11.94)	33.33 – 80.56
Verbal Working Memory			
RSPAN	Percentage of responses (out of 60) that were accurate*	68.16 (20.13)	11.11 – 96.67
Cognitive Control			
Ericsen-Flanker	Mean reaction time (RT) difference between congruent and incongruent items ($\Delta RT_{incongruent} - RT_{congruent}$)	0.07 (0.1)	-0.14 – 0.42
Simon	$\Delta RT_{incongruent} - RT_{congruent}$	0.07 (0.06)	-0.08 – 0.21
Stroop	$\Delta RT_{incongruent} - RT_{congruent}$	0.18 (0.21)	-0.19 – 1.13
Personality Traits			
Openness	For all 5 indicators: person-centered	0.00 (0.68)	-1.53 – 1.05
Conscientiousnness	z-scores adjusted for differences	0.35 (0.45)	-0.65 – 1.28
Extraversion	in acquiescent response styles	-0.36 (0.59)	-1.28 – 1.20
Agreeablenees	('yea-saying' vs. 'nay-saying')	0.07 (0.56)	-1.34 – 1.18
Neuroticism		0.28 (0.68)	-0.85 – 3.67
L2 Experience			
LexTALE$_{English}$	Average % correct	73.75 (10.16)	53.75 – 93.75
VLT	Num. correct (out of 150 items)	121.25 (20.28)	21.00 – 142.00
ART	Num. correctly identified authors minus foils marked (out of 81)	11.22 (6.59)	0.00 – 26.00
NFC	Avg. of responses to all items (out of 18) with negative polarity items reverse scored	3.60 (0.57)	2.06 – 4.72

NOTE: Responses on the RSPAN task were coded as accurate if participants recalled the final word and judged the sentence in which it had occurred correctly.

Table 3: Results of growth curve analysis - Estimates of fixed effects and Goodness of Fit for the unconditional cubic growth model (left) and models including the L2 experience predictor Need for Cognition (NFC; middle) and Openness to Experience personality trait (right). The variable 'Time' refers to the number of interactions with the AISLE system.

	Dependent variable: Number of words learned		
	Unconditional GCM	added NFC (L2 exp.)	added Openness (Pers.)
			(best-fitting model)
Constant	12.065*** (1.272)	17.657*** (2.073)	19.443*** (2.359)
Linear change	68.295*** (14.492)	193.456*** (34.185)	216.504*** (37.897)
Quadratic change	6.356 (5.780)	81.212*** (12.188)	91.081*** (11.791)
Cubic change	9.733* (5.119)	34.998*** (6.115)	38.739*** (6.912)
NFC		−5.501* (2.997)	−3.815 (3.012)
NFC x Time		−99.283** (46.577)	−59.411 (50.181)
NFC x Time^2		−62.305*** (13.738)	−38.427** (18.165)
NFC x Time^3		−27.749*** (8.498)	−20.236** (9.203)
Openness			−5.267* (2.941)
Openness x Time			−85.196* (47.702)
Openness x Time^2			−41.335*** (15.750)
Openness x Time^3			−13.417 (8.794)
Log Likelihood	−97,698.190	−97,692.140	−97,688.800

Note: *p<0.1; **p<0.05; ***p<0.01

sectional methodologies to capture snapshots of children's competence at different stages. While cross-sectional studies are useful to describe vocabulary growth in the general population over time, only longitudinal studies can shed light on the pace and pattern of vocabulary development, i.e. estimate rates of growth. It is, thus, unfortunate that the bulk of discussions within the field of (both child and second) language acquisition favors a cross-sectional view of vocabulary development and, as a consequence, discussions about longitudinal research are scarce.

In the present paper we introduced an adaptive language learning system (AISLE) designed to track and accelerate academic vocabulary growth in university students. The extraction pipeline relied on NLP techniques to arrive at statistically relevant items ('optimal language input'). The learning algorithm was designed to adapt in real-time during learning sessions to match the student's progress and memory patterns ('optimal repetition intervals').

In a second step, we showcased how the dense, longitudinal data generated by the system can be utilized to understand the dynamics of individual vocabulary growth trajectories. To this end, we presented first results of a study on a group who engaged with the AISLE system in a laboratory setting for several hours across three sessions over a period of three weeks. The goal of the study was twofold. First, we aimed to make use of our dense longitudinal data to examine the pace and shape of vocabulary growth trajectories. Second, we aimed to understand the role that experience-related, cognitive and affective factors play in explaining variation in students' vocabulary acquisition. We began by fitting the best longitudinal model to our dense observational data of vocabulary growth. We found that the empirical data were best represented by a cubic growth curve model. This result is consistent with the results reported in previous studies on children's vocabulary growth (e.g. Ganger and Brent, 2004; Rowe et al., 2012), suggesting that the vocabulary growth trajectories exhibit similar shapes across different learning contexts. The cubic model indicates that, on average, users increased their vocabulary size by approximately two words per 100 presented vocabulary items and increased their vocabulary by about 15 words in the course of a three-hour period of engagement with the system. There was, however, substantial variation in vocabulary growth with in-

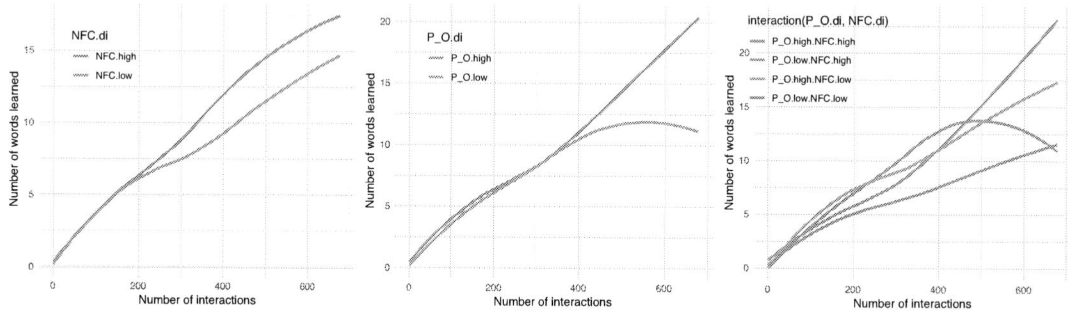

Figure 7: Predicted growth trajectories for participants with higher or lower NFC scores (left) and higher and lower scores on the openness to experience personality dimension (center). The plot on the right displays the results of the final model containing the effects of both NFC and Openness.

dividuals above the 90th percentile reaching an estimated vocabulary growth of about 50 words after 600 presented vocabulary items, whereas individuals below the the 10th percentile acquired about 5 words overall. Considerable between-subject variation was also observed for all other engagement and performance indicators collected by the system (see Table 1). To achieve our second goal, we next incorporated a total of 17 experience-related, cognitive and affective predictors measured into this growth model to examine whether and to what extent they affected the velocity (linear change) and acceleration (quadratic change) of learners' vocabulary growth. We found that - when considered on their own - 9 out of 17 IDs factors (four experience-related, four affective, and one cognitive factor) were significantly associated with vocabulary development. The best-fitting (minimal adequate) model assessing the joint effects of the IDs factors indicated (1) that participants with higher scores on the NFC experience proxy measure exhibited significantly faster rates of increase, relative to participants with lower NFC scores, and (2) that individuals with higher scores on the openness personality scale show faster learning rates – relative to those with lower scores on that scale. These results contribute to and expand the existing literature on the role of individual differences in second language acquisition (Dörnyei and Skehan, 2008; Ellis, 2004; Dewaele, 2009).

In conclusion, advancing our understanding of the dynamics of vocabulary growth is of central importance. There is a growing awareness in the cognitive sciences that an adequate theoretical model of language acquisition should be first and foremost constrained by empirical demonstra-

tions of IDs as well as predict and account for the complex interrelationships between variation in the quantity and quality of language input, cognitive and affective factors in language development and attainment (for a recent review, see Kidd et al., 2017). The data obtained from an adaptive language learning system such as AISLE have the potential to transform our current understanding of vocabulary growth and to provide a new window into the mechanisms and principles underlying language development in general.

References

John AE Anderson, Lorinda Mak, Aram Keyvani Chahi, and Ellen Bialystok. 2018. The language and social background questionnaire: Assessing degree of bilingualism in a diverse population. *Behavior Research Methods*, 50(1):250–263.

Inbal Arnon and Morten H Christiansen. 2017. The role of multiword building blocks in explaining l1–l2 differences. *Topics in Cognitive Science*, 9(3):621–636.

Douglas Bates, Martin Maechler, Ben Bolker, Steven Walker, et al. 2014. lme4: Linear mixed-effects models using eigen and s4. *R package version*, 1(7):1–23.

Kimberly Becker and Phuong Nguyen. 2017. Review of technology-enhanced language learning for specialized domains: Practical applications and mobility. In Elorza I. Martin-Monje, E. and B. G. Riaza, editors, *Technology-enhanced language learning for specialized domains: Practical applications and mobility*, volume 21, page 6771.

Andrew Biemiller. 1999. *Language and reading success*, volume 5. Brookline Books.

John T Cacioppo, Richard E Petty, and Chuan Feng Kao. 1984. The efficient assessment of need for cognition. *Journal of Personality Assessment*, 48(3):306–307.

Kate Cain and Jane Oakhill. 2011. Matthew effects in young readers: Reading comprehension and reading experience aid vocabulary development. *Journal of Learning Disabilities*, 44(5):431–443.

Averil Coxhead. 2000. A new academic word list. *TESOL quarterly*, 34(2):213–238.

Jean-Marc Dewaele. 2009. Individual differences in second language acquisition. In Ritchie W. C. and Bhatia T.K., editors, *The new handbook of second language acquisition*, pages 623–646. Emerald Insight Bingley, England.

Stephen J Dollinger, Anna M Matyja, and Jamie L Huber. 2008. Which factors best account for academic success: Those which college students can control or those they cannot? *Journal of Research in Personality*, 42(4):872–885.

Zoltán Dörnyei and Peter Skehan. 2008. Individual differences in second language learning. In *The handbook of second language acquisition*, chapter 18, pages 589–630. Wiley-Blackwell.

Fiona J Duff, Gurpreet Reen, Kim Plunkett, and Kate Nation. 2015. Do infant vocabulary skills predict school-age language and literacy outcomes? *Journal of Child Psychology and Psychiatry*, 56(8):848–856.

Rod Ellis. 2004. *Individual differences in second language learning*. Blackwell Publishing.

Thomas A Farmer, Alex B Fine, Jennifer B Misyak, and Morten H Christiansen. 2017. Reading span task performance, linguistic experience, and the processing of unexpected syntactic events. *The Quarterly Journal of Experimental Psychology*, 70(3):413–433.

Jennifer Ganger and Michael R Brent. 2004. Reexamining the vocabulary spurt. *Developmental Psychology*, 40(4):621.

Dee Gardner and Mark Davies. 2013. A new academic vocabulary list. *Applied Linguistics*, 35(3):305–327.

Judith C Goodman and Elizabeth Bates. 2013. On the emergence of grammar from the lexicon. In *The emergence of language*, pages 47–98. Psychology Press.

Betty Hart and Todd R Risley. 1995. *Meaningful differences in the everyday experience of young American children*. Paul H Brookes Publishing.

Jacy Ippolito, Jennifer L Steele, and Jennifer F Samson. 2008. Introduction: Why adolescent literacy matters now. *Harvard Educational Review*, 78(1):1–6.

Heba M Ismail, Saad Harous, and Boumediene Belkhouche. 2016. Review of personalized language learning systems. In *2016 12th International Conference on Innovations in Information Technology (IIT)*, pages 1–6. IEEE.

Vickki Jacobs. 2008. Adolescent literacy: Putting the crisis in context. *Harvard Educational Review*, 78(1):7–39.

Oliver P John, Laura P Naumann, and Christopher J Soto. 2008. Paradigm shift to the integrative big five trait taxonomy. *Handbook of Personality: Theory and research*, 3(2):114–158.

Scott Barry Kaufman, Colin G DeYoung, Jeremy R Gray, Luis Jiménez, Jamie Brown, and Nicholas Mackintosh. 2010. Implicit learning as an ability. *Cognition*, 116(3):321–340.

Evan Kidd, Seamus Donnelly, and Morten H Christiansen. 2017. Individual differences in language acquisition and processing. *Trends in Cognitive Sciences*, pages 154–169.

Kristin Lemhöfer and Mirjam Broersma. 2012. Introducing lextale: A quick and valid lexical test for advanced learners of english. *Behavior Research Methods*, 44(2):325–343.

Clas Linnman, Per Carlbring, Åsa Åhman, Håkan Andersson, and Gerhard Andersson. 2006. The Stroop effect on the internet. *Computers in Human Behavior*, 22(3):448–455.

Viorica Marian, Henrike K Blumenfeld, and Margarita Kaushanskaya. 2007. The language experience and proficiency questionnaire (leap-q): Assessing language profiles in bilinguals and multilinguals. *Journal of Speech, Language, and Hearing Research*.

James Milton. 2013. Measuring the contribution of vocabulary knowledge to proficiency in the four skills. *C. Bardel, C. Lindqvist, & B. Laufer (Eds.) L*, 2:57–78.

Daniel Mirman. 2017. *Growth curve analysis and visualization using R*. Chapman and Hall/CRC.

Valerie Muter, Charles Hulme, Margaret J Snowling, and Jim Stevenson. 2004. Phonemes, rimes, vocabulary, and grammatical skills as foundations of early reading development: evidence from a longitudinal study. *Developmental Psychology*, 40(5):665.

William Nagy and Dianna Townsend. 2012. Words as tools: Learning academic vocabulary as language acquisition. *Reading Research Quarterly*, 47(1):91–108.

ISP Nation. 1993. Vocabulary size, growth, and use. *The bilingual lexicon*, pages 115–134.

Jonathan Peirce, Jeremy R Gray, Sol Simpson, Michael MacAskill, Richard Höchenberger, Hiroyuki Sogo, Erik Kastman, and Jonas Kristoffer Lindeløv. 2019. Psychopy2: Experiments in behavior made easy. *Behavior Research Methods*, pages 1–9.

Ana Pellicer-Sánchez. 2018. Examining second language vocabulary growth: Replications of schmitt (1998) and webb & chang (2012). *Language Teaching*, pages 1–12.

R Core Team. 2018. *R: A Language and Environment for Statistical Computing*. R Foundation for Statistical Computing, Vienna, Austria.

Treena Eileen Rohde and Lee Anne Thompson. 2007. Predicting academic achievement with cognitive ability. *Intelligence*, 35(1):83–92.

Meredith L Rowe, Stephen W Raudenbush, and Susan Goldin-Meadow. 2012. The pace of vocabulary growth helps predict later vocabulary skill. *Child Development*, 83(2):508–525.

Norbert Schmitt, Diane Schmitt, and Caroline Clapham. 2001. Developing and exploring the behaviour of two new versions of the vocabulary levels test. *Language Testing*, 18(1):55–88.

Noam Siegelman and Ram Frost. 2015. Statistical learning as an individual ability: Theoretical perspectives and empirical evidence. *Journal of Memory and Language*, 81:105–120.

Kendra R Tannenbaum, Joseph K Torgesen, and Richard K Wagner. 2006. Relationships between word knowledge and reading comprehension in third-grade children. *Scientific Studies of Reading*, 10(4):381–398.

Dianna Townsend, Alexis Filippini, Penelope Collins, and Gina Biancarosa. 2012. Evidence for the importance of academic word knowledge for the academic achievement of diverse middle school students. *The Elementary School Journal*, 112(3):497–518.

Mehrnoosh Vahdat, Luca Oneto, Davide Anguita, Mathias Funk, and Matthias Rauterberg. 2016. Can machine learning explain human learning? *Neurocomputing*, 192:14–28.

Ludo Verhoeven, Jan van Leeuwe, and Anne Vermeer. 2011. Vocabulary growth and reading development across the elementary school years. *Scientific Studies of Reading*, 15(1):8–25.

Ludo Verhoeven and Jan Van Leeuwe. 2008. Prediction of the development of reading comprehension: A longitudinal study. *Applied Cognitive Psychology: The Official Journal of the Society for Applied Research in Memory and Cognition*, 22(3):407–423.

Richard F West, Keith E Stanovich, and Harold R Mitchell. 1993. Reading in the real world and its correlates. *Reading Research Quarterly*, pages 35–50.

Oliver Wilhelm, Andrea Hildebrandt Hildebrandt, and Klaus Oberauer. 2013. What is working memory capacity, and how can we measure it? *Frontiers in psychology*, 4:433.

Summarization Evaluation meets Short-Answer Grading

Margot Mieskes
Hochschule Darmstadt
Germany
margot.mieskes@h-da.de

Ulrike Padó
Hochschule für Technik Stuttgart
Germany
ulrike.pado@hft-stuttgart.de

Abstract

Summarization Evaluation and Short-Answer Grading share the challenge of automatically evaluating content quality. Therefore, we explore the use of ROUGE, a well-known Summarization Evaluation method, for Short-Answer Grading. We find a reliable ROUGE parametrization that is robust across corpora and languages and produces scores that are significantly correlated with human short-answer grades. ROUGE adds no information to Short-Answer Grading NLP-based machine learning features in a by-corpus evaluation. However, on a question-by-question basis, we find that the ROUGE Recall score may outperform standard NLP features. We therefore suggest to use ROUGE within a framework for per-question feature selection or as a reliable and reproducible baseline for SAG.

1 Introduction

Teachers use short free-text questions both in second-language teaching (to evaluate reading comprehension and writing skills) and in content instruction (to probe content understanding and the ability to apply knowledge). Reducing the time needed for grading the answers greatly lightens teacher workloads and allows flexible self-study. Short-Answer Grading (SAG) is the corresponding NLP task of predicting grades for student answers containing up to three sentences.

The most difficult formulation of the SAG problem, which occurs frequently in real-world teaching, is the processing of completely unseen questions and their answers. The prevailing strategy in this situation is to compare student and reference answers and base the grade prediction on any similarities. While very shallow baselines like bag-of-word models are strong for SAG (Dzikovska et al., 2013), they fail to cover deeper levels of meaning. Therefore, features on different levels of language processing have been proposed to solve the central problem of comparing the meaning of two different texts (see Burrows et al. (2015)).[1]

Other NLP tasks facing a similar challenge are Machine Translation evaluation, Natural Language Generation evaluation and Summarization evaluation. Of the three, Summarization evaluation is most closely related to SAG: When determining the quality of an automatic summary, the standard evaluation method ROUGE (derived from Translation evaluation's BLEU) compares candidate summaries against manually created references (Lin, 2004), with the goal of comparing the meaning of the two texts with string-level evaluation tools. Graham (2015) points out that the parameter space of ROUGE is not trivial and that for individual tasks and/or data sets different parameter combinations might give the best results.

In this paper, we exploit the similarities of the tasks by applying ROUGE to SAG. We evaluate on four corpora from the content assessment domain, in English and German. We begin by determining an appropriate, robust set of parameters for ROUGE and by analyzing how well the metric is correlated with the gold grades in the different corpora.[2] We then go on to compare ROUGE with standard SAG features for machine learning. We find that ROUGE is a robust predictor on its own (and could therefore serve as a standardized baseline) and on the question level can outperform the

---

[1]Recently, neural network approaches have also been explored for educational scoring in general, e.g. Alikaniotis et al. (2016), and SAG in particular (Riordan et al., 2017).

[2]ROUGE results for the parameter sweeping and the ROUGE predictions for our corpora are available at https://bwsyncandshare. kit.edu/dl/fiL6mnSswKKhZttY687GtQgi/ MieskesPadoROUGE.zip.

Margot Mieskes and Ulrike Padó 2019. Summarization evaluation meets short-answer grading. *Proceedings of the 8th Workshop on Natural Language Processing for Computer Assisted Language Learning (NLP4CALL 2019)*. Linköping Electronic Conference Proceedings 164: 79–85.

standard SAG features (and is therefore useful for per-question feature selection approaches).

2 Related Work

Within SAG, we follow the research tradition that explores the use of informative features and helpful strategies from other areas of NLP, machine learning and educational research. Examples are the use of features from Information Retrieval, such as text similarity and textual inference (Zesch et al., 2013), the use of the machine learning strategy Active Learning (Horbach and Palmer, 2016) or empirically estimated question difficulty information (Padó, 2017).

ROUGE was presented by Lin (2004) and has since established itself as the de-facto standard evaluation metric in Summarization evaluation used in various summarization related shared tasks[3]. Other metrics have been presented in the past, but none have received a wide-spread usage similar to ROUGE. For an overview of various other methods and their comparison to ROUGE, but also manual evaluations see Louis and Nenkova (2013). ROUGE is based on counting the number of n-grams overlapping in one or several reference text(s) and a comparison text. While n-gram overlap has long been known to be a strong predictor in SAG (see, e.g., Dzikovska et al. (2013)), ROUGE offers a range of other parameters, including skip n-grams, which allow intervening words between the matching words and thus help to cover paraphrases.

ROUGE has been applied in the context of spoken (Loukina et al., 2014) and written (Madnani et al., 2013) learner summaries, thus providing a first bridge from Summarization evaluation to the educational domain. Gütl (2008) proposed the use of ROUGE for SAG in the e-Examiner system, but there is no formal evaluation. ROUGE is demonstrably suited to texts of similar length as short answers: In the DUC-2004 challenge, Task 1 resulted in texts which are at most 75 bytes long and Task 5 aimed at summaries of lengths up to 665 bytes – short answers in our largest data set (ASAP) range between 52 and 500 bytes.

3 Method and Data

We use four SAG corpora (see Table 1) in our experiments. The three English corpora (ASAP, SEB and Beetle) are large enough to have separate test

English Corpora	Dev #Q/#A	Test #Q/#A
ASAP (www.kaggle.com/c/asap-sas)	5/8182	5/2218
SEB (Dzikovska et al., 2013)	15/1070	15/733
Beetle (Dzikovska et al., 2013)	9/1236	9/819
German Corpus		
CSSAG (Padó and Kiefer, 2015)	–	31/1926

Table 1: Corpus sizes and characteristics (source, number of questions and answers in development (ASAP: training) and test sections)

sets for result verification. We use the development sets of SEB and Beetle and the training set of ASAP[4] for finding optimal parameter settings for ROUGE. We evaluate the final parameters on the unseen test sets and on the full data of CSSAG, the smallest corpus. This German corpus allows us to determine how well ROUGE performs across languages.

We evaluate the ROUGE predictions by correlating the gold human grades to ROUGE scores using Kendall's τ (Kendall, 1955). The standard Pearson's r is not applicable here, since our data are not normally distributed. We therefore choose a non-parametric correlation method. Specifically, Kendall's τ is less sensitive to ties than Spearman's ρ. Given the small number of grade levels in the human annotations, this property is key for a correlation-based approach. Note that τ as a non-parametric method is more conservative than Pearson's r and will produce smaller coefficient values than r would for the same data sets.

3.1 Experiment 1: Optimal ROUGE Parameters

We experimentally determine the set of ROUGE parameters that yields the best correlation of ROUGE scores against human SAG grades across corpora. As detailed in Graham (2015) there is a wide range of possible combinations. Therefore, our first step is a parameter sweeping experiment to determine the best settings for the following parameters[5]:

Stemming yes/no
Stopwords yes/no
ROUGE variant unigrams to 4-grams, longest common subsequence (LCS) and skip n-grams (S*)

---

[3] https://duc.nist.gov/

[4] We only use the five questions that have explicit reference answers.

[5] We did not experiment with the sampling size (-r), as the parameter space was large to begin with.

	ASAP	Beetle	SEB
Stemming	y	n	y
Stopwords	n	n	y
ROUGE	S*	S*	LCS
Eval Basis	s	s/t	s/t
Model	best	all	all
Measure	R	$F_{0.5}$	$F_{0.5}$
Conf Level	95	95/99	95/99
optimal τ	0.581	0.469	0.313
final τ	0.581	0.449	0.286

Table 2: Optimal ROUGE parametrizations with corresponding τs and τs for the final parametrization. Final parameter values in bold face.

Evaluation Basis sentences (s), tokens (t) or raw counts (r)
Model average or best
Measure Recall, $F_{0.5}$ or $F_{1.0}$
Confidence Interval 99% or 95%

Stemming and stopwords are options for text pre-processing, intended as rough measures to normalize the input and focus on content words.

The ROUGE measure itself can be calculated in different variants: Four are based on plain n-grams (uni- up to 4-grams), and there are the longest common subsequence (LCS) and skip bigrams model (S*, initially with a skip interval of 4), giving a total of 6 scores. We do not consider ROUGE-W* as it rarely produced stable results.[6]

The evaluation basis can be either ROUGE for all the tokens in the document or the average over sentence ROUGE scores; raw counts can also be output independent of ROUGE.

ROUGE usually evaluates against a number of samples – in a SAG context, this corresponds to having multiple reference answers. The evaluation can then be reported using the average results across all the reference samples for Precision, Recall and F-Score, or just for the best sample. We follow Summarization evaluation practice and experiment with Recall and F-Score, with different weightings of Precision and Recall. Finally, we varied the required confidence interval between 0.99 and 0.95.

ROUGE proved quite robust to many parameter instantiations. There were results for 75% (864) of parametrizations on the Beetle data, and for all parametrizations on SEB. In contrast, though, only 168 (14.5%) out of 1152 possible parameter combinations yielded results for ASAP. Beetle and ASAP

evaluations both failed for all runs which use raw counts as the basis of evaluation. This result is unproblematic in practice, since the raw scores are not a standard evaluation tool and are not in focus here. ASAP evaluations additionally failed for all runs that evaluated across all models, and yielded no results in the 0.99 confidence interval. The reason for the difficulties on ASAP may be that the model answers are quite long. The questions ask students to give multiple aspects or key points, and the model answers aim to list many possible correct aspects. However, any given student will answer with just the required number of aspects, so there is usually a relatively large difference between the student answers and the models they are compared to. Despite this drawback, we find throughout that the ROUGE output performs similarly for ASAP as for the other corpora, so it appears justified to use the ASAP data.

Table 2 shows the optimal parameters for the three corpora. While the ROUGE tool was brittle on ASAP, this corpus shows the largest correlation of ROUGE results and human ratings. Inversely, the correlation is lowest for SEB, the corpus without any failed ROUGE runs.

During parameter sweeping, the largest drops in τ compared to the optima are observed (in order) by changing the ROUGE variant, the F weighting and the combination of stemming and stop words (for all three corpora). Worst case, changing to ROUGE-4 on ASAP costs $\Delta\tau = 0.39$, and $\Delta\tau = 0.27$ on Beetle. This is in line with observations from the Summarization community, where the numerically highest scores are usually achieved using ROUGE-1 and the lowest using ROUGE-4. This pattern is ultimately due to sparse data caused by linguistic variation, which greatly reduces the chance of finding exactly matching 4-grams in two different documents compared to unigrams. The changes in F weighting and stemming/stop words cause much smaller drops in the range between $\Delta\tau = 0.1$ and 0.01, underscoring again the robustness of ROUGE performance to variations in parameter settings.

We found several more, stable patterns across parametrizations that helped inform our choice of final parametrization. For each pattern, we also discuss its plausibility in a SAG context.

To begin with the pre-processing steps, **stopwords** alone are detrimental for all three corpora. In combination with **stemming**, they work well for

---

SEB, but not at all for Beetle and not optimally for ASAP. This possibly points to a domain dependence of stopword lists. Stemming without stopwords is the best setting for ASAP and the second best by a small margin for Beetle and SEB. Since stemming is a step away from pure string comparison, this result is plausible for SAG.

ROUGE-S* using the standard skip of 4 tokens between the elements of a bigram works best for ASAP and Beetle, while LCS outperforms it slightly for SEB. In addition to the standard skip of 4 tokens, we also experimented with 2 and 6 tokens, but found the performance using a skip of size 4 to achieve the best numeric results. As mentioned above, ROUGE-4 is consistently the worst choice across corpora while ROUGE-S* proved to be quite robust. In a SAG context, this result is plausible, as ROUGE-S* flexibly allows paraphrases. In contrast, ROUGE-4 looks for a specific, fairly long sequence. With short answers of 2 to 3 sentences, the probability to find matching 4-grams drops considerably due to linguistic variation. ROUGE-1 fails to show optimal performance, but yields robust slightly lower results across the remaining parameters, in line with observations in Summarization evaluation.

There is a small preference for sentences as **evaluation unit**, while tokens perform just as well for SEB and Beetle. Raw scores, tested for the sake of completeness, lower the correlation for SEB and evaluation on raw scores breaks down for Beetle and ASAP. The standard SAG setting of using the **Best Model**, i.e., using the highest score produced by comparison to any reference is consistent with Beetle and SEB and optimal for ASAP.

While correlations of $F_{0.5}$-Scores with the human grades often are numerically slightly higher than correlations of **Recall** and human grades, the Recall predictions are much more robust across different combinations of parameters. This is plausible for the SAG task, since the recall of n-gram overlap between the student answer and reference answer shows how much of the reference answer content the student replicated. Precision would correspond to predicting a high human grade if the student only produced correct answer portions (but maybe missed important parts of the answer).

The chosen **confidence interval** did not make a difference to the results for SEB and Beetle, but there were no results in the 0.99 interval for ASAP (probably due to the form of the model answers).

Corpus	τ dev	τ test	Language
ASAP	0.581	0.356	
Beetle	0.449	0.306	EN
SEB	0.286	0.223	
CSSAG	–	0.385	DE

Table 3: Correlations between ROUGE predictions and manual grades for seen (dev) and unseen (test) corpus portions. All correlations significant at $p < 0.001$.

Given the optimal parametrizations and our general observations for the English data, we chose the parameters that work for the majority of corpora. The only departure from this rule is our use of Recall, which yields slightly lower figures, but seems overall more robust than F. We use stemming without stopwords, S* with gaps of up to four intervening words, and evaluate on the sentence level using the best model.[7] Incidentally, this is the optimal parametrization for ASAP, and causes only a small drop in τ for Beetle and SEB (see the bottom line in Table 2).

These parameters hardly differ from the most commonly used settings in Summarization evaluation (i.e. as used in DUC 2004). The only deviation from that standard is that we do not include unigrams in the skip-bigram (ROUGE-S*) calculation. This underlines the similarities between the summarization and SAG tasks. From a SAG perspective, the resulting parameters are also plausible given previous work, as discussed above.

3.2 Experiment 2: Robustness of Parameters

We next test the generalizability of these parameters for new data sets and a new language. We first try the test sets of the three English corpora and then the German corpus. For the German data, instead of the stemming step we externally performed lemmatization (using the TreeTagger, Schmid (1995)) to do more justice to German morphology.

Table 3 presents results for the optimal parameter setting determined in Exp.1. The top three rows of the table repeat the development set results for the final parametrization for the three English corpora and show performance on the unseen test

---

[7]The full parameter set for the ROUGE package is `-n 4 -m -s -2 4 -c 95 -r 1000 -p 0.5 -t 0`. Please note that we performed the lemmatization for the German data offline and removed this parameter when calling ROUGE for the German data.

sets. For all three data sets, performance drops, as must be expected. The most affected data set is ASAP. This was the most brittle corpus in parameter sweeping, so the optimal parameters possibly overfit the training data used for parameter setting. Least affected is SEB, which showed the highest drop between optimal and final parameters. All correlations remain highly significant (and recall that τ is a conservative measure).

For the German corpus, which was not used in parameter sweeping, the correlation is numerically the strongest of all. This allows us to conclude that the parameter set can be ported to another language with a similar outcome as porting to the unseen test portion of the development data. The method is clearly robust when using language-specific preprocessing tools.

In sum, we find that the ROUGE parameters we have determined on the training sets of three English SAG corpora are stable across corpora and languages. However, we find signs of brittleness and overfitting for our largest English corpus, ASAP, which are probably due to the nature of the available model answers. We therefore expect the identified parameters to be portable to new corpora, especially if model and students answers are comparable (as for SEB, Beetle and CSSAG).

3.3 Experiment 3: ROUGE and Standard SAG Features

Our final experiments evaluate the usefulness of the ROUGE predictions in combination with existing features for grade prediction by machine learning. We use the system from Padó (2016), which extracts features on the basis of a range of levels of linguistic analysis, such as n-grams, textual similarity, dependency parses, semantic representations and textual entailment.

We experiment with an SVM and a Random Forest (RF) learner for the correct-incorrect decision. All the corpora we work on provide several target labels representing partial credit. Prediction tasks with many target labels are harder than predicting a small number of labels. Our corpora have nine labels (CSSAG), five labels (ASAP) and two labels (SEB and Beetle, two-task annotation). In order to standardize the difficulty of the annotation task, we normalize the annotation of ASAP and CSSAG to a binary correct-incorrect annotation by labeling as correct all student answers that receive at least the middle label (50% of points).

We report F scores as the standard measure for classification tasks and in accordance with previous work for SEB, Beetle and CSSAG (Dzikovska et al., 2013; Padó, 2016). As mentioned in the Introduction, we consider the hardest instantiation of the label prediction task, the unseen question setting, where any questions in the test set are completely unseen (so no question-specific models can be trained). In order to achieve this, we use leave-one-question-out evaluation on the training portion of ASAP (the provided test data is for seen questions) and on the full (previously unused) CSSAG data. SEB and Beetle have test sets with unseen data.[8]

Table 4 shows evidence of the high unigram baseline for SAG at at least F=59.7 (RF on SEB; F=65.1 SVM) and up to F=86.7 (RF on ASAP). We also report the majority baseline (the performance of a hypothetical classifier that always predicts the more frequent class) as a learning algorithm-independent (low) baseline. The majority baseline is easy to beat for all classifiers and feature sets, but it highlights the strong label imbalance for ASAP, which is mirrored in its high numerical prediction results throughout.

Over all feature sets, the RF classifier deals better with the data than the SVM. The ROUGE scores alone perform robustly, but below the unigram baseline in most cases. They beat it numerically for RF on SEB and CSSAG. This verifies that ROUGE is predictive for the SAG task, and quite strongly in some configurations.

The deeper features in the NLP feature set generally numerically improve performance over the baseline (except for CSSAG and ASAP RF). Using ROUGE scores as features in addition to the NLP-based features yields no significant improvement and mixed trends. Results for CSSAG improve numerically. On the other hand, we see a small drop for both learners on the Beetle data and for ASAP and SEB, we observe a decrease for one learner, but an increase for the other. This indicates that ROUGE incorporates information also found in the standard NLP features. Since we work with ROUGE-S* skip n-grams, we assume that the shared information can be found in the uni-, bi- and trigrams in the standard NLP features.

We further investigate the impact of ROUGE by

---

[8]Note that our results are therefore not directly comparable to literature results for ASAP, but are comparable to the literature for SEB, Beetle and CSSAG in both evaluation measure and evaluation procedure.

	Majority	Unigram		ROUGE		NLP		NLP+R	
		RF	SVM	RF	SVM	RF	SVM	RF	SVM
ASAP	58.1	86.3	70.1	80.7	64.0	**86.8**	69.4	86.4	69.9
Beetle	42.6	72.8	71.3	60.7	55.1	**73.6**	73.0	71.9	72.6
SEB	43.7	59.7	65.1	61.4	58.1	66.7	65.2	**67.0**	64.7
CSSAG	45.3	66.2	**70.1**	67.7	64.0	67.6	69.4	68.3	69.9

Table 4: Grade prediction F-Scores for the majority and unigram baselines, ROUGE, all NLP features, and NLP+ROUGE. Random Forest (RF) and SVM classifiers. Best result per corpus in bold.

zooming in on performance on the question level for each corpus. We compute prediction F-scores for each question in the test sets (or in the leave-one-out setting) separately. We find that ROUGE alone performs the same or better than the NLP features for 52% of the 31 CSSAG questions (using RF). The standard NLP features always outperform ROUGE for the five ASAP questions, the nine questions from the Beetle test set and the fifteen questions from the SEB test set. However, for Beetle and SEB, we also analysed the questions in the (previously unused) training set by applying leave-one-question-out evaluation (recall that we always use this evaluation strategy for CSSAG and ASAP). ROUGE outperforms the standard NLP features for 16% of the 47 Beetle training questions and 44% of the 135 SEB questions. In sum, ROUGE is a good predictor for a sizeable subset of our data, but for that subset only.

This intriguing picture of a light-weight stand-in for our range of NLP features – but only in some cases – matches up well with findings from Padó (2016), who also found that n-gram (or n-gram and textual similarity) features suffice for reliable grade prediction for 18 out of the 30 CSSAG questions that were considered. Padó (2016) suggested question-specific feature selection to optimize overall system performance and processing effort. In our experiments on CSSAG, ROUGE also outperformed the n-gram features in 11 out of the 16 cases where it beat the NLP features. Taken together, these findings indicate that ROUGE should not be used as an addition to already established feature sets, but that it is a strong candidate for inclusion in a feature selection strategy that could further improve the overall classification result while at the same time simplifying the model. We expect the same to be true for SEB and Beetle.

A second take-away from our results is the possibility of using ROUGE as a well-defined, reproducible baseline for SAG. ROUGE-S* captures much of information present in a bag-of-words baseline while clearly defining implementational detail like the use of stemming and stop words. This increases transparency and reproducibility of results for the community.

4 Conclusions

We presented experiments on the transferability of the ROUGE metric, an established evaluation tool in the Automatic Summarization domain, to the related task of Short Answer Grading. Our first result is a ROUGE parametrization for the SAG task that is stable across corpora and languages and plausible both from the point of view of SAG evaluation and of best practices in the source domain of Summarization.

Our further experiments show that ROUGE robustly predicts human short-answer grades, although it does not add to the performance of existing NLP features. However, on the question level, it can outperform the NLP features and can therefore serve to replace them in a question-specific feature selection strategy to improve overall results at reduced processing effort. We also suggest to use ROUGE as a well-defined and reproducible baseline to be used for future experiments. As the package has been stable for several years and is widely used in the Summarization community, it allows for reproducible experiments – unlike individual baseline implementations which may use a range of undocumented parameters.

4.1 Future Work

There are a range of questions to address in the future. The first would be to extend these experiments to other evaluation metrics from summarization evaluation. In particular, the PYRAMID method, which compares the content, rather than the n-gram overlap, of two texts, might give additional insight by alllowing us to move away from the restrictions of string-level comparison. This could be further extended to include methods from the wider field of Natural Language Generation (NLG).

Another strand of investigation would be to determine the reasons for large variations within some parametrizations. For example, the ASAP data set was overall more brittle to parameter changes. We also found that stopwords helped for some corpora, but harmed performance on others. This could lead to the development of corpus-specific stopword lists.

Additionally, we plan a deeper analysis of which of the questions gave better results using ROUGE and on which questions it performed worse. This could support the development of more differentiated methods for automatic SAG.

References

Dimitrios Alikaniotis, Helen Yannakoudakis, and Marek Rei. 2016. Automatic text scoring using neural networks. In *Proceedings of ACL 2016*.

Steven Burrows, Iryna Gurevych, and Benno Stein. 2015. The Eras and Trends of Automatic Short Answer Grading. *International Journal of Artificial Intelligence in Education*, 25:60–117.

Myroslava Dzikovska, Rodney Nielsen, Chris Brew, Claudia Leacock, Danilo Giampiccolo, Luisa Bentivogli, Peter Clark, Ido Dagan, and Hoa Trang Dang. 2013. SemEval-2013 task 7: The joint student response analysis and 8th recognizing textual entailment challenge. In *Proceedings of SemEeval-2013*, Atlanta, Georgia.

Yvette Graham. 2015. Re-evaluating automatic summarization with BLEU and 192 shades of ROUGE. In *Proceedings of EMNLP 2015*.

Christian Gütl. 2008. Moving towards a fully automatic knowledge assessment tool. *International Journal of Emerging Technologies in Learning*.

Andrea Horbach and Alexis Palmer. 2016. Investigating active learning in short-answer scoring. In *Proceedings of BEA-11*, San Diego, California.

Maurice Kendall. 1955. *Rank Correlation Methods*. Hafner Publishing Co., New York.

Chin-Yew Lin. 2004. ROUGE: A package for automatic evaluation of summaries. In *Proceedings of ACL Text Summarization Branches Out Workshop*.

Annie Louis and Ani Nenkova. 2013. Automatically assessing machine summary content without a gold standard. *Computational Linguistics*, 39(2):267–300.

Anastassia Loukina, Klaus Zechner, and Lei Chen. 2014. Automatic evaluation of spoken summaries: the case of language assessment. In *Proceedings of BEA-9*, Baltimore, Maryland.

Nitin Madnani, Jill Burstein, John Sabatini, and Tenaha OReilly. 2013. Automated scoring of a summary-writing task designed to measure reading comprehension. In *Proceedings of BEA-8*, Atlanta, Georgia.

Ulrike Padó. 2016. Get semantic with me! The usefulness of different feature types for short-answer grading. In *Proceedings of COLING 2016*, Osaka, Japan.

Ulrike Padó. 2017. Question difficulty – How to estimate without norming, how to use for automated grading. In *Proceedings of BEA-12*, Copenhagen, Denmark.

Ulrike Padó and Cornelia Kiefer. 2015. Short answer grading: When sorting helps and when it doesn't. In *4th NLP4CALL Workshop at Nodalida*, Vilnius, Lithuania.

Brian Riordan, Andrea Horbach, Aoife Cahill, Torsten Zesch, and Chong Min Lee. 2017. Investigating neural architectures for short answer scoring. In *Proceedings of BEA-12*, Copenhagen, Denmark.

Helmut Schmid. 1995. Improvements in part-of-speech tagging with an application to German. In *Proceedings of the ACL SIGDAT-Workshop. Dublin, Ireland*.

Torsten Zesch, Omer Levy, Irina Gurevych, and Ido Dagan. 2013. UKP-BIU: Similarity and entailment metrics for student response analysis. In *Proceedings of SemEeval-2013*, Atlanta, Georgia.

Experiments on Non-native Speech Assessment and its Consistency

Ziwei Zhou
Iowa State University, USA
ziweizh@iastate.edu

Sowmya Vajjala
National Research Council, Canada
sowmya.vajjala@nrc-cnrc.gc.ca

Seyed Vahid Mirnezami
Iowa State University, USA
vahid@iastate.edu

Abstract

In this paper, we report some preliminary experiments on automated scoring of non-native English speech and the prompt specific nature of the constructed models. We use ICNALE, a publicly available corpus of non-native speech, as well as a variety of non-proprietary speech and natural language processing (NLP) tools. Our results show that while the best performing model achieves an accuracy of 73% for a 4-way classification task, this performance does not transfer to a cross-prompt evaluation scenario. Our feature selection experiments show that most predictive features are related to the vocabulary aspects of speaking proficiency.

1 Introduction

Advancements in NLP and speech processing have given rise to the research and development of automated speech scoring systems in the past 10-15 years. The goal of such systems is to provide efficient and consistent evaluation in oral proficiency tests. Whereas early systems scoring English proficiency predominantly made use of extracting low-level features, such as pronunciation (e.g. segmental errors, phone spectral match) and fluency (e.g. speech rate, number of pauses, lengths of silences), a sustained push to fully represent and evaluate test takers communicative competence has provided major momentum to the investigations in automated scoring for spontaneous or unconstrained speech rather than scripted or constrained speech. As a result, automated scoring systems expanded their inventories to include multiple dimensions of speaking proficiency such as prosody, vocabulary, grammar, content, and discourse, as well as exploiting complex models to makes sense of rich data in complex tasks from large-scale assessment contexts (Williamson et al., 2006).

However, the research and development of such systems has largely centralized around a few proprietary systems (e.g., SpeechRater (Xi et al., 2008; Chen et al., 2018)). Language assessment researchers expressed concerns about the validity of inferences made from such automated systems in high-stakes testing scenarios such as college admissions in the past (Chapelle and Chung, 2010). In this paper, we take first steps towards addressing these issues of proprietary work and validity by: a) reporting our experiments on a freely available corpus, b) looking the transferability of our approach by performing cross-prompt evaluations, c) studying the consistency of our results and d) understanding what features perform well for prediction.

Specifically, we explore the following research questions:

1. RQ1: Which classifier performs the best in terms of agreement with human scorers when compared using multiple performance measures?

2. RQ2: How consistent are the machine scores rendered by the best performing model?

3. RQ3: What features are influential in predicting human scores?

While the first and third questions were also studied in the past research (with proprietary datasets and software), the second question is some what under explored, to our knowledge.

The rest of this paper is organized as follows. Section 2 briefly surveys related work on the topic. Sections 3 and 4 describe our methods, experiments and results. Section 5 concludes the paper.

Ziwei Zhou, Sowmya Vajjala and Seyed Vahid Mirnezami 2019. Experiments on non-native speech assessment and its consistency. *Proceedings of the 8th Workshop on Natural Language Processing for Computer Assisted Language Learning (NLP4CALL 2019)*. Linköping Electronic Conference Proceedings 164: 86–92.

2 Related Work

SpeechRater^{TM}, developed by Educational Testing Service (ETS) can be considered as a leading strand of research into automated scoring of non-native speech (Xi et al., 2008; Chen et al., 2018). Since its initial deployment in 2006, a large amount of research has been conducted into the role of various features for this task (e.g., Evanini et al., 2013; Loukina et al., 2015; Tao et al., 2016). Other recent research (Johnson et al., 2016; Kang and Johnson, 2018b,a) explored the role of prosody features in automated proficiency scoring for unconstrained speech. However, much of the previous work in this direction has been on corpora that are not freely accessible, making replications or adaptions to new corpora difficult. In this paper, we follow existing approaches, but with a hitherto unexplored, publicly available corpus.

Since such test scores typically serve high-stake purposes, the need for ensuring the validity of machine scores arises. As reviewed by Yang et al. (2002), such validity enquiry can be approached by: (1) demonstrating the correspondence between human and machine scorers; (2) understanding the construct represented within the automated processes; and (3) examining the relationship between machine scores and criterion measures. In this paper, we take the first steps in this direction by addressing the first aspect.

3 Methods

3.1 Corpus

The data used in this study comes from the International Corpus of Network of Asian Learners (ICNALE-Spoken), which has a collection of speech data from learners in ten countries and areas in Asia China, Hong Kong, Indonesia, Japan, Korean, Pakistan, the Philippines, Sigapore, Taiwan, and Thailand, as well as from English native speakers (Ishikawa, 2013). The range of participants covers the three concentric circles Inner, Outer, and Expanding circles of English language use (Kachru, 1992).

This corpus consists of oral responses provided by college students to two opinion-based prompts (PTJ denoting part-time jobs and SMK denoting smoking behavior) over telephone recordings, lasting about 1 minute each. Each prompt was done in two trials and we used the first trial

(N=950 for each prompt). In order to protect the participants' identity, speech samples were morphed using a speech morphing system developed by ICNALE team (available for download). The program adjusted the pitch and formant of sound files without altering the sound file itself, thereby enabling corpus users to still conduct acoustic analyses on this data.

The participants English proficiency levels are indicated on the Common European Framework of Reference (CEFR) scale with four categories: A2_0 (N=100), B1_1 (N=211), B1_2 (N=469), and B2_0 (N=160). These scores are either directly converted from the participants existing proficiency scores from standard proficiency tests, such as TOEFL, IELTS, or TOEIC, or estimated from a vocabulary size test (Nation and Beglar, 2007) through multiple regression. We used the manual transcriptions provided with the corpus for extracting textual features related to language use.

3.2 Features

We extracted fluency features and audio signal features from the speech samples and lexical/syntactic features from text transcriptions.

Fluency Features: Fluency features are commonly used in oral proficiency modeling. A Praat script (De Jong and Wempe, 2009) was used (Boersma and Weenink, 2001) to analyze the speech samples for 7 automated measures of fluency: number of syllable nuclei, number of pauses, total response time, phonation time, speech rate, articulation rate, and average syllable duration[2]. A visual display from the scripts output texgtrid file is presented in Figure 1. As

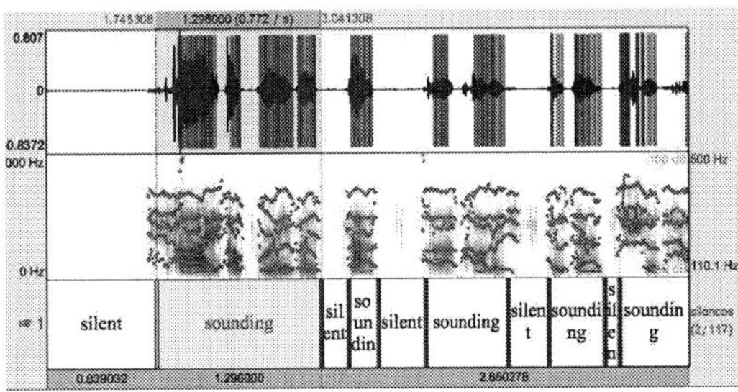

Figure 1: TextGrid Output From Praat Script That Calculates fluency Measures

shown in the figure, the continuous speech is au-

---

[2]The script was originally developed to automatically detect syllable nuclei in continuous stream of speech based on intensity (dB) and voicedness information.

tomatically segmented and the fluency measures can be calculated based on these segments. Other measures such as oral fluency can be simply calculated based on the output. Also, since the repairs were indicated in the original transcription by "-", the number of repairs in each spoken response were extracted. It should be pointed out that, since the transcriptions did not have any indication for fillers, fillers are not taken into account in the this study.

Audio Signal Features: To extract low-level signal features, which may be helpful in modeling the automated scoring models, PyAudio Analysis, which is an open-source Python library for audio feature extraction, classification, segmentation, and application, was used (Giannakopoulos, 2015). We extracted 34 signal level audio features in both time and frequency domains. These include: zero-crossing rate, energy, entropy of energy, spectral centroid, spectral spread, spectral entropy, spectral flux, spectral rolloff, Mel Frequency Cepstrum Coefficients (MFCCs-11), chroma vector (12), and chroma deviation. These kind of features (if not the specific ones we used) were used to build filter model to flag non-scorable responses (Higgins et al., 2011), but not in the scoring model in past research.

Lexical Features: Lexical Complexity Analyzer (Lu, 2012) was used to automatically extract 25 measures of lexical density, variation, and sophistication from the transcriptions.

Syntactic Features: The L2 Syntactic Complexity Analyzer was used to automatically extract 14 measures of syntactic complexity as proposed in the second language development literature (Lu, 2014). They were also used in past research on the topic (Chen and Zechner, 2011).

3.3 Model Building and Validation

We used Scikit-learn, (Pedregosa et al., 2011) to build and compare classification models using different classifiers with this feature set. Since the corpus was unbalanced across proficiency levels, Synthetic Minority Oversample Technique (SMOTE) (Chawla et al., 2002) was explored with the aim to help the prediction of minority class and avoid bias towards predicting the majority class. We explored two cases, both with and without oversampling:

- classification models trained and tested separately for each prompt, which we call intrinsic evaluation (with 10-fold cross validation)

- classification models trained on one prompt, but tested on the other, which we call extrinsic evaluation.

A variety of performance measures, including accuracy, precision, recall, F1-score, Cohens Kappa (CK), Quadratically Weighted Kappa (QWK), and Spearman Rho Correlation (SRC) statistics were reported. In addition, to further validate the consistency of the models, 95% confidence intervals were calculated both based on statistical theory and empirical bootstrap technique.

4 Results

Intrinsic Evaluation: We evaluated classification models using various classifiers: Naive Bayes, Logistic Regression, Random Forests (RF), SVMs, Gradient Boosting and Neural Networks. Hyperparameters were tuned for each of the candidate classifiers. For example, different hyperparameters including optimizers, loss function, number of layers, number of hidden units, and number of epochs were used to build different ANN models. Results for the model performance in terms of accuracies obtained through intrinsic evaluation from comparing multiple classifiers are shown in Table 1.

Table 1: Model Performances of All Classifiers in Training Set

Mod.	Orig. PTJ	SMOTE PTJ	Orig. SMK	SMOTE SMK
LR	0.48	0.62	0.48	0.6
RF	0.48	**0.74**	0.48	**0.73**
SVM	0.34	0.46	0.37	0.42
GB	0.49	0.71	0.48	0.72
ANN	0.43	0.61	0.47	0.54
DT	0.35	0.50	0.38	0.48
NB	0.42	0.45	0.41	0.46

RF model gave the best results in both intrinsic and extrinsic evaluation, and the model trained on over-sampled data showed the best result for both prompts during intrinsic evaluation, with an accuracy of 74% for both PTJ and 73% for SMK. The non-oversampled counterparts had an accuracy of 48% for both prompts. In general, oversampling increased the accuracy for all classifiers.

An analysis of the best model showed that RF performed better in predicting A2_0 level as well as B2_0 level, but did poorly for distinguishing between B1_1 and B2_2.

Accuracy is equivalent to the exact agreement between human and machine scores. Given that (Xi et al., 2006) reported exact agreement of only 51.8%, this result is promising, especially since both studies have four levels of speaking proficiency. However, considering the differences in the nature of data, construct definition, scores, features, and general approach, results are not directly comparable.

As accuracy only captures a specific aspect of the model performance, various other performance measures have been studied. Table 2 summarizes results with the conventionally used psychometric measures - CK, QWK and SRC. The highest Cohens Kappa reported in previous studies was 0.52 (Zechner et al., 2007), quadratically-weighted Kappa was 0.60 (Higgins et al., 2011) and SRC was 0.718 (Kang and Johnson, 2018b). This shows that our results are comparable to other research on this topic, albeit with different corpora and experimental setup. However, it has to be remembered that we are relying on manual transcriptions of speech and not using automatic speech recognition systems yet in these experiments. Considering that there is no publicly accessible code or data from other relevant research on this topic, exact replication may be challenging.

Table 2: Psychometric Measures for Model Performance

	PTJ	SMOTE PTJ	SMK	SMOTE SMK
CK	0.11	0.60	0.08	0.66
QWK	0.17	0.73	0.11	0.76
SRC	0.21	0.73	0.16	0.77

To estimate the stability of the model predictions, 95% confidence intervals are constructed for the 10-fold CV results using both statistical theory and bootstrapping using sampling-with-replacement technique. Specifically, the theoretical 95% CI was constructed by the following formula:

$$p = \frac{f + \frac{Z^2}{2N} \pm Z \sqrt{\frac{f}{2N} - \frac{f^2}{N} + \frac{Z^2}{4N^2}}}{1 + \frac{Z^2}{N}}$$

where p is the theoretical 95% CI, f is the mean accuracy of the 10-fold CV, Z is the is z-statistic

from the specified confidence level, and N is the sample size (Witten et al. (2016), p. 151). This assumes that the accuracies from 10-fold CV follow normal distribution with unknown parameters. This showed an interval of [71.65% –75.67%] for PTJ prompt and [70.99% – 75.03%] for SMK.

The empirical/ boostrapping 95% CI was constructed by repetitively fitting the same random forest classifier in 1000 iterations. This is shown in Figure 2 and Figure 3 for both the prompts respectively.

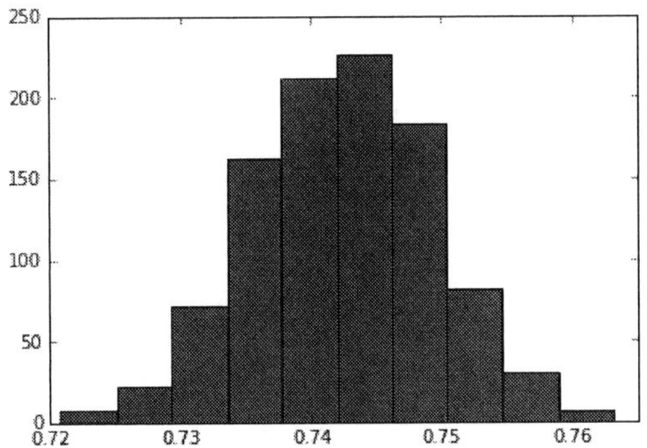

Figure 2: Confidence Interval for PTJ prompt model

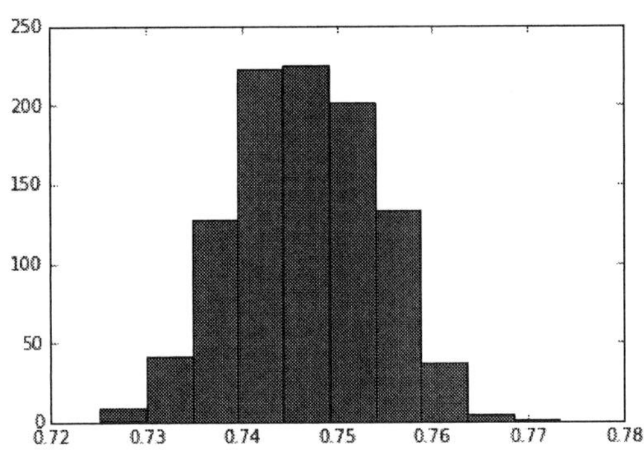

Figure 3: Confidence Interval for SMK Prompt model

This showed an interval of [72.8% -75.6%] for PTJ and [73.2% - 76%] for SMK. This adds extra evidence as to our degree of certainty about the consistency of the 10-fold CV accuracy through replications.

Extrinsic (Cross-Prompt) Evaluation: To further estimate the consistency of the models, we evaluated the best performing PTJ model on SMK data and vice versa. The accuracy dropped in cross-prompt evaluation when the training data was oversampled. For example, when the PTJ model was tested on SMK, the accuracy dropped from 74% 55.58%. When the SMK model was tested on PTJ, the accuracy dropped to 52.95%. Thus, the positive effect of oversampling in intrinsic evaluation is not seen in extrinsic evaluation. Interestingly, the non-oversampled models did not result in such stark degradation, with accuracies in both cases being closer to 55% and 53% respectively, which is actually better than their intrinsic evaluation performance. This leads to a conclusion that the non-oversampled model is somehow better agnostic to prompts.

The reason for this performance could be that the oversampling process with low frequency categories makes the dataset too specific. Whether this is an experimental artifact or is there something more to it needs to be evaluated in a future experiment.

Feature Diagnostics: In order to gain deeper understanding of the influential features that may figure prominently in the best-performing model (i.e., over sampled model), feature importance is computed for each prompt using the normalized total reduction of Gini impurity criterion brought by the feature. Results indicated that the random forest classifiers rather than relying on a subset of dominant features, relied on multiple features, although the influence of top few features is relatively larger for both models.

This result, in some sense, justifies the use of tree-based models for building automated scoring system in operational tests. From a fairness point of view, models that make use of all features rather than a subset of dominant features should be favored in that the latter may unduly advantage those test takers who learns to manipulate certain features such as complexity of vocabulary[3].

Zooming into the top ranking features that have the highest Gini decrease, we notice that influential features used in PTJ are: number of sophisticated tokens, number of unique words, number of repairs in speech fluency, standard deviation of the 2nd and 13th MFCCs, number of dependent clauses, corrected type-token ratio, and

number of syllables. Influential features for SMK are number of different words, correct type-token-ratio, square root of type-token-ratio, different word types, number of word tokens, spectral flux, and number of repairs in speech fluency. Thus, the majority of the important features seem to be related to the diversity or variability of vocabulary use and repairs in speech fluency. Such Gini-based feature selection result was consistent with other feature evaluation measures such as correlation and information gain.

When we compare the best models with the non-oversampled models, however, the top most important features differ significantly. For PTJ, the top 10 features include 5 audio signal features and 5 vocabulary based features. The top 10 features for SMK include 5 vocabulary based features, 2 syntactic features (Complex nominals per T-unit and mean length of T-unit) and 3 audio signal features. Considering that the oversampled model did not transfer its performance in a cross prompt evaluation, it needs to be studied in future whether these features play a role in having better results across prompts.

5 Conclusion and Discussion

We reported some of our initial experiments with automated scoring of non-native speech using a new corpus and a set of audio, speech, and text features. In terms of our research questions, for RQ1, our results indicate that the best-performing model with accuracy of about 73% for both prompts is achieved by using oversampling and random forests. For RQ2, our results showed that the accuracies drop substantially for the oversampled data sets, but the accuracies for the non-oversampled versions remain consistent. For RQ3, various feature selection schemes consistently pointed to the dominance of vocabulary related features for this classification task.

Limitations and Outlook: Firstly, we relied on the manual transcriptions of speech instead of an ASR output. While this is in itself is not a limitation, it becomes one when we attempt to test this model on new speech samples. Additionally, we calculated repair feature based on the specific notation used in the manual transcriptions of this corpus. These issues make applying these models directly on unseen texts or making a direct comparison with other existing speech scoring approaches on a common test set difficult. Further,

---

[3] When features based on feature importance are ranked in descending order, the plot showed a smooth curvature, rather than abrupt gaps. Detailed figures and tables with feature scores are provided in the supplementary material available at: `https://github.com/nishkalavallabhi/ZhouEtAl2019-SupMat`

ICNALE speech samples were morphed to de-identify speaker voice. We did not verify the accuracy of the praat script used to estimate fluency features with such morphed speech. Considering that these are the first results on a publicly available dataset for this task (to our knowledge), future work includes incorporating these aspects into our approach.

Finally, as was pointed out earlier in Section 3, the class labels used in this study may be problematic in that are either directly converted from the participants existing proficiency scores from other tests, which need not have reflected in the current responses. While we don't have a solution for this yet, we believe these experiments would still result in further research in the direction of exploring more generalizable approaches, using non-proprietary resources.

References

Paul Boersma and David Weenink. 2001. Praat, a system for doing phonetics by computer. *Glot International*, 5(9/10):341–345.

Carol A Chapelle and Yoo-Ree Chung. 2010. The promise of nlp and speech processing technologies in language assessment. *Language Testing*, 27(3):301–315.

Nitesh V. Chawla, Kevin W. Bowyer, Lawrence O. Hall, and W. Philip Kegelmeyer. 2002. Smote: Synthetic minority over-sampling technique. *Journal of Artificial Intelligence Research*, 16:321–357.

Lei Chen, Klaus Zechner, Su-Youn Yoon, Keelan Evanini, Xinhao Wang, Anastassia Loukina, Jidong Tao, Lawrence Davis, Chong Min Lee, Min Ma, Robert Mundkowsky, Chi Lu, Chee Wee Leong, and Binod Gyawali. 2018. https://doi.org/10.1002/ets2.12198 Automated scoring of nonnative speech using thespeechratersm v. 5.0 engine. *ETS Research Report Series*, 2018(1):1–31.

Miao Chen and Klaus Zechner. 2011. Computing and evaluating syntactic complexity features for automated scoring of spontaneous non-native speech. In *Proceedings of the 49th Annual Meeting of the Association for Computational Linguistics: Human Language Technologies*, pages 722–731.

N. H. De Jong and T. Wempe. 2009. Praat script to detect syllable nuclei and measure speech rate automatically. *Behavior Research Methods*, 41:385–390.

Keelan Evanini, Shasha Xie, and Klaus Zechner. 2013. Prompt-based content scoring for automated spoken language assessment. In *Proceedings of the eighth workshop on innovative use of NLP for building educational applications*, pages 157–162.

T. Giannakopoulos. 2015. Pyaudioanalysis: An open-source python library for audio signal analysis. *PloS One*, 10:1–17.

Derrick Higgins, Xiaoming Xi, Klaus Zechner, and David Williamson. 2011. A three-stage approach to the automated scoring of spontaneous spoken responses. *Computer Speech & Language*, 25(2):282–306.

S. Ishikawa. 2013. The ICNALE and sophisticated contrastive interlanguage analysis of asian learners of english. *Learner Corpus Studies in Asia and the World*, 1(1):91–118.

David O. Johnson, Okim Kang, and Romy Ghanem. 2016. https://doi.org/10.1007/s10772-016-9366-0 Improved automatic english proficiency rating of unconstrained speech with multiple corpora. *Int. J. Speech Technol.*, 19(4):755–768.

B. Kachru. 1992. *he other tongue: English across cultures*. University of Illinois Press.

Okim Kang and David Johnson. 2018a. The roles of suprasegmental features in predicting english oral proficiency with an automated system. *Language Assessment Quarterly*, 15(2):150–168.

Okim Kang and David O Johnson. 2018b. Automated english proficiency scoring of unconstrained speech using prosodic features. In *Proceedings of the International Conference on Speech Prosody*, volume 2018, pages 617–620.

Anastassia Loukina, Klaus Zechner, Lei Chen, and Michael Heilman. 2015. https://doi.org/10.3115/v1/W15-0602 Feature selection for automated speech scoring. In *Proceedings of the Tenth Workshop on Innovative Use of NLP for Building Educational Applications*, pages 12–19, Denver, Colorado. Association for Computational Linguistics.

Xiaofei Lu. 2012. The relationship of lexical richness to the quality of esl learners' oral narratives. *The Modern Language Journal*, 96:190–208.

Xiaofei Lu. 2014. Computational methods for corpus annotation and analysis. *International Journal of Corpus Linguistics*, 21:133–138.

I.S.P. Nation and D. Beglar. 2007. A vocabulary size test. *The Language Teacher*, 31(7):9–13.

F. Pedregosa, G. Varoquaux, A. Gramfort, V. Michel, B. Thirion, O. Grisel, M. Blondel, P. Prettenhofer, R. Weiss, V. Dubourg, J. Vanderplas, A. Passos, D. Cournapeau, M. Brucher, M. Perrot, and E. Duchesnay. 2011. Scikit-learn: Machine learning in Python. *Journal of Machine Learning Research*, 12:2825–2830.

Jidong Tao, Lei Chen, and Chong Min Lee. 2016. Dnn online with ivectors acoustic modeling and doc2vec distributed representations for improving automated speech scoring. *Interspeech 2016*, pages 3117–3121.

David M Williamson, Robert J Mislevy, and Isaac I Bejar. 2006. *Automated scoring of complex tasks in computer-based testing*. Psychology Press.

Ian H Witten, Eibe Frank, Mark A Hall, and Christopher J Pal. 2016. *Data Mining: Practical machine learning tools and techniques*. Morgan Kaufmann.

Xiaoming Xi, Derrick Higgins, Klaus Zechner, and David M Williamson. 2008. Automated scoring of spontaneous speech using speechratersm v1. 0. *ETS Research Report Series*, 2008(2):i–102.

Xiaoming Xi, Klaus Zechner, and Isaac Bejar. 2006. Extracting meaningful speech features to support diagnostic feedback: an ecd approach to automated scoring. *Proc. Annu. Meet. Natl. Counc. Meas. Educ.(NCME)*.

Yongwei Yang, Chad W Buckendahl, Piotr J Juszkiewicz, and Dennison S Bhola. 2002. A review of strategies for validating computer-automated scoring. *Applied Measurement in Education*, 15(4):391–412.

Klaus Zechner, Isaac I. Bejar, and Ramin Hemat. 2007. https://doi.org/10.1002/j.2333-8504.2007.tb02044.x Toward an understanding of the role of speech recognition in nonnative speech assessment. *ETS Research Report Series*, 2007(1):1–76.

The Impact of Spelling Correction and Task Context on Short Answer Assessment for Intelligent Tutoring Systems

Ramon Ziai   Florian Nuxoll
Kordula De Kuthy   Björn Rudzewitz   Detmar Meurers

Collaborative Research Center 833
Department of Linguistics, ICALL Research Group*
LEAD Graduate School & Research Network
University of Tübingen

Abstract

This paper explores Short Answer Assessment (SAA) for the purpose of giving automatic meaning-oriented feedback in the context of a language tutoring system. In order to investigate the performance of standard SAA approaches on student responses arising in real-life foreign language teaching, we experimented with two different factors: 1) the incorporation of spelling normalization in the form of a task-dependent noisy channel model spell checker (Brill and Moore, 2000) and 2) training schemes, where we explored task- and item-based splits in addition to standard tenfold cross-validation.

For evaluation purposes, we compiled a data set of 3,829 student answers across different comprehension task types collected in a German school setting with the English tutoring system FeedBook (Rudzewitz et al., 2017; Ziai et al., 2018) and had an expert score the answers with respect to appropriateness (correct vs. incorrect). Overall, results place the normalization-enhanced SAA system ahead of the standard version and a strong baseline derived from standard text similarity measures. Additionally, we analyze task-specific SAA performance and outline where further research could make progress.

1 Introduction

Short Answer Assessment (SAA) is the task of determining whether an answer to a question is correct or not with respect to meaning. The task is also often called Automatic Short Answer Grading (ASAG) in cases where the outcome to determine is on an ordered scale (e.g., a numeric score). After a surge of attention (cf., e.g., Burrows et al., 2015) including shared tasks at SemEval (Dzikovska et al., 2013) and Kaggle[1], the field has quietened down somewhat, with a couple of recent exceptions (Riordan et al., 2017; Gomaa and Fahmy, 2019).

However, SAA cannot be considered a solved problem. In particular, it is still unclear how well standard SAA approaches work in real-life educational contexts, for example when integrating language tutoring systems into a regular school setting. In such systems, the goal is to give immediate feedback on the language produced by the learner, e.g., to help students complete homework exercises in the system step by step. For meaning-oriented exercises, such as reading and listening comprehension, this is especially challenging, since the system needs to evaluate the meaning provided by the student response and possibly give helpful feedback on how to improve it in the direction of an acceptable answer. SAA can help with the evaluation part: if an answer is deemed correct, the feedback is positive, if not, further diagnosis can be carried out. The purpose of SAA in this context is thus to help the tutoring system decide whether the feedback to be given needs to be positive or negative.

In this paper, we therefore report on SAA work in progress on authentic data from a language tutoring system for 7th grade English currently in use in German schools. We employ an alignment-based SAA system (CoMiC, Meurers et al., 2011a) shown to work well for several data sets where target answers are available (Meurers et al., 2011b; Ott et al., 2013), and use it to train a classifier mimicking a trained language teacher's

[1] https://www.kaggle.com/c/asap-sas

Ramon Ziai, Florian Nuxoll, Kordula De Kuthy, Björn Rudzewitz and Detmar Meurers 2019. The impact of spelling correction and task context on short answer assessment for intelligent tutoring systems. *Proceedings of the 8th Workshop on Natural Language Processing for Computer Assisted Language Learning (NLP4CALL 2019)*. Linköping Electronic Conference Proceedings 164: 93–99.

judgments on whether a student response is acceptable or not.

We investigate two main factors for SAA performance: 1) the impact of automatic spelling normalization on SAA using a noisy channel approach (Brill and Moore, 2000), and 2) the influence of using different training/test splits, namely 'unseen answers', 'unseen items' (questions), and 'unseen tasks', following Dzikovska et al. (2013).

Overall, results show that using spelling normalization yields superior performance for the SAA system we use, and that the performance gap widens when only using out-of-domain training data ('unseen tasks'). We also conduct a by-task analysis of spelling and non-spelling variants of the SAA system, revealing that normalization effects are not uniform across tasks.

The paper is organized as follows: Section 2 introduces the data source we use for our experiments before section 3 outlines the spelling correction approach. Section 4 then delves into the setup and results of our experiments before section 5 concludes the paper.

2   Data

Our data comes from the FeedBook (Rudzewitz et al., 2017, 2018; Ziai et al., 2018), an English tutoring system for 7th grade used in German secondary schools as part of a full-year randomized controlled field study (Meurers et al., 2019). The system includes interactive feedback on form for all grammar topics on the curriculum, but also a first version of meaning feedback for meaning-oriented tasks, such as reading and listening comprehension activities.

For our purposes in this paper, we extracted all student responses that were entered in reading or listening tasks where the task objective is meaning-oriented, i.e., comprehension. We excluded duplicate answers. After filtering out answers to tasks that were erroneously classified as meaning-oriented or that require knowledge external to the task material (for example, asking about aspects of the individual student's life), we obtained 3,829 answers entered into 123 answer fields of 25 tasks.

Table 1 lists the tasks in the data set together with the required student input (full sentence(s) vs. gap-filling), comprehension type (reading vs. listening), number of answers, and mean answer token length. The distribution of answers

Task	input	type	# answers	∅ tokens
2B1	gap-filling	reading	1,511	7.04
3A3a	sentence(s)	reading	463	9.77
1CYP2b	sentence(s)	listening	411	7.83
1ET5	sentence(s)	reading	360	4.68
2CYP3	sentence(s)	reading	255	7.71
1B7b	gap-filling	listening	220	1.79
2C5b	sentence(s)	reading	177	9.24
1AP37	sentence(s)	reading	126	8.90
1AP38	sentence(s)	reading	85	14.15
2ET3	gap-filling	reading	61	2.59
3AP19a	gap-filling	listening	35	1.54
3AP20a	sentence(s)	listening	23	4.13
3AP16a	sentence(s)	listening	17	4.47
2AP34	sentence(s)	listening	15	5.00
3AP32	gap-filling	reading	15	2.27
4AP16	gap-filling	listening	13	8.15
3CYP2b	sentence(s)	listening	9	3.89
2AP33	gap-filling	listening	8	1.25
4AP15b	sentence(s)	listening	8	9.50
4C2	sentence(s)	reading	6	7.83
4B6	gap-filling	listening	5	2.00
3AP33	sentence(s)	reading	2	14.50
4AP17	sentence(s)	listening	2	14.00
4AP31	sentence(s)	listening	1	7.00
6A4	gap-filling	reading	1	1.00
overall			3,829	7.11

Table 1: Data set properties by task

is rather uneven across tasks, with almost 40% of the answers coming from one task. This may be a result of this task being favored by teachers, but reflects real-life usage of the system. On the whole, answers consist of 7.11 tokens on average, with gap-filling tasks typically triggering shorter responses than full sentence tasks.

Figure 1 shows an example gap-filling task for listening comprehension. For the purposes of this paper, we use 'item' to refer to a field that a student can type an answer into, and 'task' refers to the whole exercise that is made up of items and the surrounding context.

In order to obtain a gold standard for our classification approaches to train on, an experienced English teacher rated every response with respect to whether it is an acceptable answer or not. The majority class is 'correct' with a percentage of 62.05% among the 3,829 responses.

3   Task-dependent Spelling Correction

The spelling correction approach we employ is based on the noisy channel model described by Brill and Moore (2000) as implemented by Adri-

Figure 1: Example listening task

ane Boyd[2]. The approach requires a list of misspellings (non-word/correction pairs) to derive its model from, as well as a dictionary of valid words to draw its suggestions from. Given a non-word, i.e., one that is not found in its dictionary, it returns an n-best list of valid candidate words.

We trained the approach on a list of approximately 10,000 misspellings made by German learners of English, which we extracted from the EFCamDat corpus (Geertzen et al., 2013). The dictionary we used is compiled from the vocabulary list of English school books used in German schools up to 7th grade, approximating the vocabulary that German 7th graders learning English in a foreign language learning setting were exposed to and may use.[3]

In order to make the spelling correction approach somewhat context-aware, we used the weighting of dictionary entries offered by the Brill and Moore approach, giving a weight of 1 to standard entries, and increasing the weight of forms found in the specific task's reading or listening text by their term frequency in that text. As a result of this weighting, task-specific spelling corrections are more likely to happen, given a sufficiently close learner production.

4 Experiments

In this section, we describe the experiments we carried out, and the results obtained.

4.1 Setup

For Short Answer Assessment (SAA), we employed a variant of the CoMiC system (Meurers et al., 2011a). CoMiC is a so-called alignment-based system. It aligns different linguistic units (tokens, chunks, dependencies) of the learner and the target answers to one another and then extracts numeric features based on the number and type of alignments found. The features are then used to train a classifier for new unseen answer pairs.

For the experiments in this paper, we used a Support Vector Machine (SVM) with a polynomial kernel as the classification approach, based on the *kernlab* package (Karatzoglou et al., 2004) in *R* (R Core Team, 2015) via the *caret* machine learning toolkit (Kuhn, 2008). We used default hy-

---

[2]https://github.com/adrianeboyd/
BrillMooreSpellChecker

[3]Naturally, English movies, video games such as Minecraft, and English Let's Play videos are quite popular in the targeted age group and will impact their vocabulary knowledge in a way not captured here.

perparameters for the SVM approach.

Complementing to CoMiC approach, we created a baseline system using nine standard string similarity measures from the *stringdist* package (van der Loo, 2014) in *R*, calculated between student and target response. These similarity scores were used in the same classification setup we used for the CoMiC features.

To incorporate the spelling correction approach described in section 3, we ran it on all student responses as a preprocessing step to obtain a second version of CoMiC enhanced with spelling correction. Apart from this preprocessing, the two CoMiC versions are exactly the same.

Each of the systems just described was given the classification task of determining whether a given response is correct or not, given a prompt and the one or more target answers from the task specification. We used the following test scenarios, roughly following Dzikovska et al. (2013):

- 'unseen answers': tenfold cross-validation across all answers, randomly sampled.

- 'unseen items': for each item, all answers for that item (gap/field) are held out; training is done on all other answers.

- 'unseen tasks': for each task, all answers for that task are held out; training is done on all other answers.

Whereas 'unseen answers' is the most desirable scenario from a computational perspective (training answers for all items are available), 'unseen tasks' is much closer to a real-life situation where educators or material designers add new exercises to the tutoring system for which no pre-scored answers exist. This setting is thus of special importance to a real-life approach.

4.2 Results

We first report and discuss overall results, before diving into a task-specific analysis.

4.2.1 Overall Results

The overall results are shown in Table 2. In addition to the systems described in the previous section, we list the majority baseline ('Majority'). 'CoMiC' is the standard CoMiC system, whereas '+SC' is the variant enhanced by spelling correction preprocessing. We report both accuracy and Cohen's κ (Cohen, 1960).

SAA System	Unseen					
	answers		items		tasks	
	%	κ	%	κ	%	κ
Majority	62.05%, $\kappa = 0.00$					
stringsim	78.35	0.52	76.97	0.48	75.61	0.45
CoMiC	81.25	0.59	81.20	0.59	80.80	0.58
+SC	**82.63**	**0.62**	**82.63**	**0.61**	**82.45**	**0.61**

Table 2: Overall accuracy (%) and Cohen's κ

All models clearly outperform the majority baseline. The string similarity model is surprisingly strong, showing that many real-life cases can actually be scored with such surface-based methods if one has access to reference answers. However, the majority baseline and the string similarity model are clearly outperformed by CoMiC. This is particularly evident when looking at the κ-values, which include chance correction based on the distribution of labels. Note that CoMiC generalizes much better to 'unseen items' and 'unseen tasks' than the string similarity model, indicating that the higher level of linguistic abstraction bears fruit especially in these settings.

CoMiC is in turn systematically outperformed by its spelling-enhanced counterpart. Interestingly, the performance gap is about the same for 'unseen items' and 'unseen answers', but greater for 'unseen tasks'. This suggests that the effect of spelling correction is more pronounced for out-of-domain training scenarios, which may be due to the fact that the training basis for the spelling correction approach is disjunct from that of the SAA system, and thus does not suffer from generalization problems on this data set.

Since these are the first results on this data set, we cannot directly compare them to any previous ones. Looking at recent related work on similar data, we can see that, e.g., the results of Ziai and Meurers (2018) on reading comprehension data in German are in the same ballpark, though slightly higher. We suspect this is the case because that data was more uniform, both with respect to task diversity and the resulting nature of the answers.

4.2.2 Results by Task

In order to find out more about the effects of adding spelling correction to the CoMiC model, we analyzed the 'unseen tasks' results of 'CoMiC' and 'CoMiC+SC' on a per-task level. These results are listed in Table 3. The tasks are listed in the same order as in Table 1, namely by descend-

Task	CoMiC		CoMiC+SC	
	%	κ	%	κ
2B1	80.15	0.53	**82.46**	**0.57**
3A3a	79.70	0.53	**82.51**	**0.58**
1CYP2b	**88.32**	**0.71**	88.08	0.71
1ET5	93.33	0.86	**93.61**	**0.87**
2CYP3	72.94	0.45	**75.29**	**0.49**
1B7b	64.09	0.29	**70.45**	**0.42**
2C5b	84.75	0.69	**85.88**	**0.72**
1AP37	**73.81**	**0.44**	70.63	0.38
1AP38	87.06	0.74	87.06	0.74
2ET3	**62.30**	**0.25**	54.10	0.10
3AP19a	88.57	0.60	**91.43**	**0.68**
3AP20a	91.30	0.75	91.30	0.75
3AP16a	82.35	-0.09	82.35	-0.09
2AP34	86.67	0.00	86.67	0.00
3AP32	73.33	0.00	73.33	0.00
4AP16	84.62	0.70	84.62	0.70
3CYP2b	55.56	0.10	55.56	0.10
2AP33	62.50	0.33	62.50	0.33
4AP15b	87.50	0.75	**100.00**	**1.00**
4C2	100.00	1.00	100.00	1.00
4B6	80.00	0.55	80.00	0.55
3AP33	100.00	n/a	100.00	n/a
4AP17	50.00	0.00	50.00	0.00
4AP31	100.00	n/a	100.00	n/a
6A4	100.00	n/a	100.00	n/a

Table 3: Unseen tasks accuracy (%) and κ for CoMiC with and without spelling correction

ing number of answers. For every task, superior results of either model in comparison to the other are marked in **bold**.

The results show that for the task with by far the most answers, '2B1', spelling correction had a very noticeable positive impact (+2.45%). For other tasks, the effect seems to be less pronounced, though still present, e.g., '1ET5'. For some tasks, the effect is actually negative (e.g., '1AP37' and '2ET3'), suggesting that spelling correction introduced additional noise for these tasks. One hypothesis for this phenomenon would be that for these tasks, spelling correction over-corrected wrong answers or non-answers into more acceptable versions, which then got scored better than they should have been. After inspecting concrete normalization cases, we indeed found examples such as the following one for '1AP37':

(1) Prompt: 'Robin ran away because of trouble with his father.'

A_{orig}: 'Robin ran away because of trouble with his stepfather.'

A_{corr}: 'Robin ran away because of trouble with his stepmother.'

Here, the task is to correct the statement in the prompt with the help of a reading text (not shown here). 'stepfather' apparently neither occurred in the general dictionary nor anywhere in the reading text and was thus corrected to 'stepmother', which is wrong in this context and is not aligned to 'stepfather' by CoMiC.

We also suspected that the task properties we showed in Table 1, such as the task type (reading vs. listening), the input (gap-filling vs. sentence(s)), or the mean length of answers would interact in some manner with the addition of spelling correction. For example, very short answers, occurring systematically in gap-filling exercises such as '2ET3', could proportionally be altered more by automatic spelling correction, thus potentially introducing more noise for the SAA classifier. However, this suspicion does not seem to be supported by the results in Tables 1 and 3. For example, both '2B1' and '2ET3' are gap-filling tasks, but while there is a performance gain for the former, there is a drop for the latter.

In search for reasons for the positive impact of spelling correction, we manually inspected some of the student responses given for task '2B1', which is shown in Figure 2, since due to the higher number of answers, the improved result for this task is the most stable. We found that a number of the spelling problems in responses to this task were related to the Welsh proper names introduced by the reading text, such as 'Gruffudd' or 'Llandysul'. These are very hard to spell for 7th grade English learners, but were successfully corrected by our spelling correction approach. Based on this information, we hypothesize that the effect of spelling correction is connected to the lexical material involved in the task rather than its more formal properties. In order to investigate this hypothesis, a systematic analysis of lexical complexity and/or complex word identification (cf., e.g., Yimam et al. 2018) within SAA could be a promising avenue to follow.

5   Conclusion

We presented work in progress on Short Answer Assessment (SAA) on data from the FeedBook, an English language tutoring system we employed in a real-life school setting in Germany. The purpose of SAA in this context is to help the tutoring system decide whether the feedback to be given needs to be positive or negative.

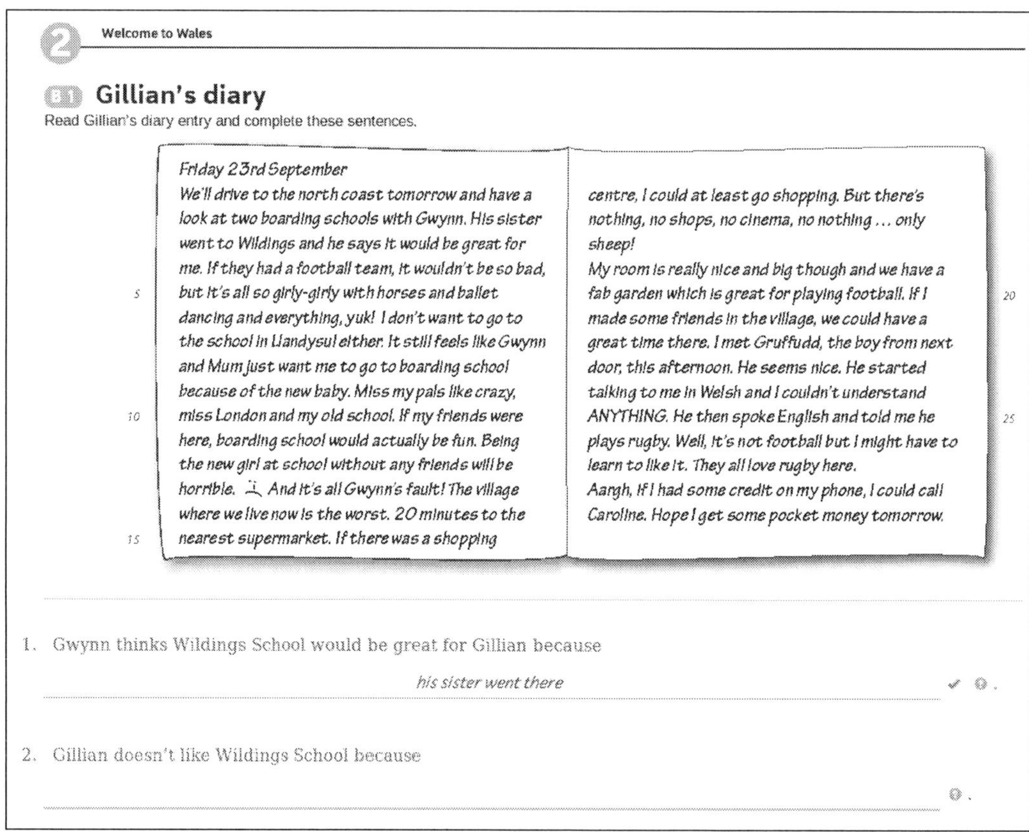

Figure 2: Reading task '2B1' (abbreviated)

To investigate the influence of spelling correction on SAA, we added a noisy channel spelling correction component to a standard SAA approach and found that it generally increases classification performance for the data we collected. In addition, we found that spelling correction helps the SAA system generalize to out-of-domain data.

A task-by-task analysis revealed that the effect of spelling correction is not uniform across tasks. Manual inspection of relevant student responses indicated that this may be related to lexical characteristics of the language employed in the task context. To investigate this hypothesis, it would be interesting to systematically analyze different aspects of lexical complexity, and integrating complex word identification (Yimam et al., 2018) within SAA could be a promising avenue to follow.

Acknowledgments

We would like to thank Louisa Lambrecht for training and tuning the spell checking approach. We also thank the two anonymous reviewers for their helpful comments. Furthermore, we are grateful to the Westermann Gruppe who collaborated with us on the FeedBook project and enabled work such as the one described in this paper, and finally to the Deutsche Forschungsgemeinschaft for funding the project in the first place.

References

Eric Brill and Robert C. Moore. 2000. An improved error model for noisy channel spelling correction. In *Proceedings of the 38th Annual Meeting of the Association for Computational Linguistics*, pages 286–293, Hong Kong. ACL.

Steven Burrows, Iryna Gurevych, and Benno Stein. 2015. The eras and trends of automatic short answer grading. *International Journal of Artificial Intelligence in Education*, 25(1):60–117.

Jacob Cohen. 1960. A coefficient of agreement for nominal scales. *Educational and Psychological Measurement*, 20(1):37–46.

Myroslava Dzikovska, Rodney Nielsen, Chris Brew, Claudia Leacock, Danilo Giampiccolo, Luisa Bentivogli, Peter Clark, Ido Dagan, and Hoa Trang

Dang. 2013. Semeval-2013 task 7: The joint student response analysis and 8th recognizing textual entailment challenge. In *Proceedings of the Seventh International Workshop on Semantic Evaluation (SemEval 2013)*, pages 263–274, Atlanta, Georgia, USA. Association for Computational Linguistics.

Jeroen Geertzen, Theodora Alexopoulou, and Anna Korhonen. 2013. Automatic linguistic annotation of large scale L2 databases: The EF-Cambridge open language database (EFCAMDAT). In *Proceedings of the 31st Second Language Research Forum (SLRF)*. Cascadilla Press.

Wael Hassan Gomaa and Aly Aly Fahmy. 2019. Ans2vec: A scoring system for short answers. In *Proceedings of the International Conference on Advanced Machine Learning Technologies and Applications (AMLTA2019)*, pages 586–595, Cham. Springer International Publishing.

Alexandros Karatzoglou, Alex Smola, Kurt Hornik, and Achim Zeileis. 2004. kernlab – an S4 package for kernel methods in R. *Journal of Statistical Software*, 11(9):1–20.

Max Kuhn. 2008. Building predictive models in R using the caret package. *Journal of Statistical Software*, 28(5):1–26.

Detmar Meurers, Kordula De Kuthy, Florian Nuxoll, Björn Rudzewitz, and Ramon Ziai. 2019. Scaling up intervention studies to investigate real-life foreign language learning in school. *Annual Review of Applied Linguistics*, 39:161–188.

Detmar Meurers, Ramon Ziai, Niels Ott, and Stacey Bailey. 2011a. Integrating parallel analysis modules to evaluate the meaning of answers to reading comprehension questions. *IJCEELL. Special Issue on Automatic Free-text Evaluation*, 21(4):355–369.

Detmar Meurers, Ramon Ziai, Niels Ott, and Janina Kopp. 2011b. Evaluating answers to reading comprehension questions in context: Results for German and the role of information structure. In *Proceedings of the TextInfer 2011 Workshop on Textual Entailment*, pages 1–9, Edinburgh.

Niels Ott, Ramon Ziai, Michael Hahn, and Detmar Meurers. 2013. CoMeT: Integrating different levels of linguistic modeling for meaning assessment. In *Proceedings of the 7th International Workshop on Semantic Evaluation (SemEval)*, pages 608–616, Atlanta, GA. ACL.

R Core Team. 2015. *R: A Language and Environment for Statistical Computing*. R Foundation for Statistical Computing, Vienna, Austria.

Brian Riordan, Andrea Horbach, Aoife Cahill, Torsten Zesch, and Chong Min Lee. 2017. Investigating neural architectures for short answer scoring. In *Proceedings of the 12th Workshop on Innovative Use of NLP for Building Educational Applications*, pages 159–168, Copenhagen, Denmark. ACL.

Björn Rudzewitz, Ramon Ziai, Kordula De Kuthy, and Detmar Meurers. 2017. Developing a web-based workbook for English supporting the interaction of students and teachers. In *Proceedings of the Joint 6th Workshop on NLP for Computer Assisted Language Learning and 2nd Workshop on NLP for Research on Language Acquisition*.

Björn Rudzewitz, Ramon Ziai, Kordula De Kuthy, Verena Möller, Florian Nuxoll, and Detmar Meurers. 2018. Generating feedback for English foreign language exercises. In *Proceedings of the 13th Workshop on Innovative Use of NLP for Building Educational Applications (BEA)*, pages 127–136. ACL.

M.P.J. van der Loo. 2014. The stringdist package for approximate string matching. *The R Journal*, 6:111–122.

Seid Muhie Yimam, Chris Biemann, Shervin Malmasi, Gustavo Paetzold, Lucia Specia, Sanja Štajner, Anaïs Tack, and Marcos Zampieri. 2018. A report on the complex word identification shared task 2018. In *Proceedings of the Thirteenth Workshop on Innovative Use of NLP for Building Educational Applications*, pages 66–78, New Orleans, Louisiana. ACL.

Ramon Ziai and Detmar Meurers. 2018. Automatic focus annotation: Bringing formal pragmatics alive in analyzing the Information Structure of authentic data. In *Proceedings of the 16th Annual Conference of the North American Chapter of the Association for Computational Linguistics: Human Language Technologies (NAACL-HLT)*, pages 117–128, New Orleans, LA. ACL.

Ramon Ziai, Björn Rudzewitz, Kordula De Kuthy, Florian Nuxoll, and Detmar Meurers. 2018. Feedback strategies for form and meaning in a real-life language tutoring system. In *Proceedings of the 7th Workshop on Natural Language Processing for Computer-Assisted Language Learning (NLP4CALL)*, pages 91–98. ACL.